T0289992

To Our Parents:

Drs. Glenwood and Naomi D. Ross
G.R.II

Edward and Venerandah Mbaijana
P.K.

*The authors would like to acknowledge Dr. Grace Onodipe of Georgia Gwinnett College for the major graphical contribution that she made to this project.
We would also like to acknowledge the many constructive criticisms and corrections to the first edition provided by students and teachers of The Global Economy. A special thanks goes out to Dr. Muhammad Husain of Oxford College, Dr. Fatma Romeh of the Center for Disease Control, Dr. Robert Moore of Georgia State University (GSU) and Tom Gairdino, an eagle eyed undergraduate at GSU

Introduction
to the GLOBAL
ECONOMY

Second Edition

Paul Kagundu

Glenwood Ross II

Kendall Hunt
publishing company

Cover image © Shutterstock, Inc.

Kendall Hunt
publishing company

www.kendallhunt.com
Send all inquiries to:
4050 Westmark Drive
Dubuque, IA 52004-1840

Copyright © 2013, 2016 by Kendall Hunt Publishing Company

ISBN 978-1-5249-0409-8

Printed in the United States of America

Contents

Preface

Introduction to the Global Economy is first and foremost an economics textbook. It assumes that the reader has had little or no formal exposure to the economics discipline. It is designed as a core curriculum text. The purpose of *Introduction to the Global Economy* is to:

1. provide students with a basic understanding of key economic terms and concepts,
2. expose students to globalization and the forces that contribute to it,
3. examine the growing importance of international trade and finance in the world economy, and
4. explore economic challenges of globalization.

Ultimately we would like the readers of this text to gain a fuller appreciation of the world around them and the role that economics plays in their daily lives. We hope that this book serves as a gateway to further explorations in the economics discipline.

Introduction to the Global Economy is divided into four parts. Part 1: *Tools of the Trade* introduces the reader to basic terms, fundamental principles, and models of economics, including supply and demand, Gross Domestic Product, inflation, and the production possibilities frontier. Part 2: *Globalization* provides a basic description of globalization, its measures, as well as its pros and cons. In addition, major agents or drivers of globalization will be discussed. These include prominent international organizations such as the International Monetary Fund, the World Bank, and the World Trade Organization. In addition, Part 2 will briefly examine the role of multinational corporations in the global economy. Part 3 includes chapters on global trade in goods and services, trade regulations, and preferential trade agreements. Part 4 introduces global finance. The chapters in Part 4 focus on the balance of payments and the foreign exchange market.

PART 1

TOOLS OF THE TRADE

1

Introduction: Key Concepts and Principles in Economics

ntroduction to the Global Economy is first and foremost an economic text. As such, it is imperative that we know what economics is about. In this chapter, we will explore some of the basic principles and concepts that guide and define this discipline. In addition, we will discuss why it is important to study the global economy.

LEARNING GOALS

➤ Define economics.
➤ Understand the crucial role that scarcity plays in economics.
➤ Explain marginalism and opportunity cost.
➤ Explain the significance of incentives in economics.
➤ Distinguish between microeconomics and macroeconomics.
➤ Distinguish between positive and normative economics.
➤ Recognize the importance of studying economics.
➤ Recognize the importance of studying the *global economy*.

ECONOMICS DEFINED

Economics is concerned with how people, both individually and collectively, make choices. Just like other disciplines that deal with human behavior, economics is a social science. Disciplines such as sociology (the study of society), psychology (the study of the mind), and political science (the study of the state) are also social sciences. The term *economics* comes from the Ancient Greek *oikonomia,* which means "management of a household." In 1932, the British economist Lionel Robbins coined a definition for economics that is still widely accepted today. Robbins's definition states that "economics is the science which studies human behavior as a relationship between ends and scarce means which have alternative uses." This definition introduces the concept of *scarcity*. It is because resources are scarce that we have to make choices. A resource is anything that can be used to produce something. **Resources** include *land, labor,* and *capital*. To an economist *land* includes Earth and the minerals, fish, water, and forests found on it. *Labor* is the people that provide the mental or physical effort, while *capital* is the goods—like machinery and equipment—needed to make finished products or the education and training that people acquire. Capital in the form of goods is referred to as *physical capital*, while capital in form of education and training is denoted as *human capital*.

MARGINALISM AND OPPORTUNITY COST

Two important concepts that will set you well on your way to thinking like an economist are *marginalism* and *opportunity cost*. Both of these concepts help to analyze and explain the choices that are made, providing important insights into the decision-making process. Let's take a look at these one at a time. Economists like to say that all decisions are made at the margin. **Marginalism** or "*thinking at the margin*" means that one must analyze the additional or incremental costs and benefits arising from a choice or decision. We refer to incremental costs and benefits as **marginal cost** (MC) and **marginal benefit** (MB), respectively. The **economic decision rule** states that if the marginal benefit is greater than the marginal cost (i.e., MB > MC), then one should pursue that activity; however, if the marginal cost is greater than the marginal benefit (i.e., MC > MB), then one should not pursue that activity. In the rare case that MC = MB, one would be indifferent in regard to pursuing the activity.

Image © Cartoonresource, 2013. Used under license from Shutterstock, Inc.

Let's say that Delta flies a 100-seat passenger airplane between Atlanta and Los Angeles and that it costs Delta $40,000 to operate this plane. In this case, the average cost of each seat on the plane turns out to be $400 (i.e., $40,000 / 100). If the plane is about to take off with a few empty seats, should Delta offer a standby ticket for say $200? A good way to think about this question is to ask what the incremental benefits are and what the incremental costs to the airline are. Of course, the incremental benefit to Delta would be the extra $200 it receives for the standby ticket. But what would be the additional costs? Altogether, the extra cost of the additional fuel it would take to carry one more passenger along with the bag of peanuts and a can of soda that the passenger consumes on the flight would probably be negligible. So the marginal benefit exceeds the marginal cost and Delta, according to the economic decision rule, should offer the standby ticket for $200. By doing so, Delta will increase overall profits.

Opportunity cost captures the idea of tradeoffs. For example, if you decide to spend Saturday night studying *The Global Economy*, the opportunity cost might be the benefit from a movie with a friend or an evening at a favorite night club. In other words, opportunity cost is computed in terms of what else you are giving up. *Opportunity cost is defined as the value of the next best alternative that we forgo, or give up, when we make a decision.* This implies that you don't get something for nothing and that everything has a cost. For example, the cost of your attending college fulltime includes the cost of tuition, the cost of books, the cost of room and board, transportation expenses, and many other miscellaneous costs. Let's say that all of these costs add up to $20,000 per year. Clearly, these out-of-pocket expenditures could have been spent on something else. For instance, you could have purchased two round-trip tickets around the world on Delta Airlines, a used Lexus, or a high-end safari in Krueger National Park in South Africa. Any one of these options might be your next best alternative to attending college; however, by attending college you are prevented from pursuing any of these options. However, this only tells part of the opportunity cost story because attending college fulltime precludes you from working. However, that kid who graduated from high school with you decided not to go to college and took an entry level job at McDonald's and is earning $15,000 a year. That $15,000 also represents what you could have earned in a year if you had not gone to college full time. Another way of looking at this is that after four years of study, that kid who is working at McDonald's is $60,000 ahead of you. This is a hidden expense and represents money that you have indeed forgone. It represents the opportunity cost of your time. So your total opportunity cost of attending college fulltime is comprised of what you could have done with your out-of-pocket expenditures of $20,000 per year and the hidden expenditures of $15,000 per year. Sometimes we refer to out-of-pocket expenditures as **explicit costs** and hidden expenditures as **implicit costs**.

Keep in mind that for most students the choice of either going to college after high school or going to work still favors going to college. Expected future incomes of college graduates far surpass those of high school graduates even after considering the high opportunity cost[1]. However, this is not the case for all students. Consider LeBron James for example. His opportunity cost of attending college would have been astronomical considering that at the age of 19 his first NBA contract with the Cleveland Cavaliers was for roughly $13 million for three years and his first contract with Nike was for $93 million for seven years. This highlights an important point that opportunity cost will vary by individual.

---

[1] Various sources suggest that lifetime earnings of college graduates are in the range of $500 million to $1.5 million greater than that of high school graduates.

It is also important to keep in mind that opportunity costs do not have to be measured in dollar terms. For example, I'm a married man with two children. Let's say that through some sort of miracle I was able to arrange a date for myself with Halle Berry. Once exposed, the opportunity cost would probably mean the loss of my wife and the loss of respect of my children. From my perspective, this is a high price to pay, and it explains why I will never date Halle Berry.[2] Here we are talking about psychic costs and not necessarily dollar costs and, I must say, a bad case of delusion. However, we can think of a more plausible example. For instance, let's say that Billie has the choice of going to a party on Saturday night or staying at home and studying for her upcoming economics test. She must decide which activity to pursue. She cannot do both because her time is limited. If she goes to the party, she risks doing poorly on the test, and if she stays home and studies for the test she will forego the benefits received from going to the party. Her choice will reveal what she values more.

THE ROLE OF INCENTIVES

While *marginalism* and *opportunity cost* are used to explain the decision-making process, they can both be influenced by **incentives.** *Incentives are rewards and penalties that motivate behavior.* Economists believe that since people usually exploit opportunities to make themselves better off they will respond to incentives. For example, if the salaries of school teachers start to rise, more students will major in education, and when parking enforcement starts to aggressively ticket and boot cars around the university campus, fewer students will park illegally. In the above example, raising salaries can be looked upon as rewards and stiffer parking enforcement can be looked upon as penalties. Economists are generally skeptical of attempts to change people's behavior without changing their incentives. For instance, when I first started teaching, I would suggest my students in introductory economics classes how important it was for them to come by and see me during office hours. Most of the students were freshmen and sophomores, and I tried to convey that this was a good habit to get into with all of their professors. After all, by the time they got to be seniors and needed letters of recommendation, they would know a faculty member who could vouch for them. So what was the upshot of my suggestion? Well, very few students actually visited my office. I subsequently enacted a policy that stated that if a student would come by my office during the course of the semester with a substantive class issue, I would give him or her a 2-percentage-point bonus on the course grade. More than half of my students now take me up on the offer. Incentives matter.[3]

---

[2] Someone else (not me) might conclude that the benefit received from going out with Halle Berry exceeds the cost, so they would go on the date.

[3] Improper incentives were a major problem for the centrally planned economy of the old Soviet Union. Reportedly, there was a serious shortage of household cooking utensils (i.e., pots, pans) at one point in time. In response to this shortage the Soviet Union reportedly declared that bonuses would be given to factories that exceeded the previous year's tonnage by a certain percent. The result was that all of the factories surpassed targeted levels and all received bonuses, and yet the shortage was not impacted one iota. Why? The incentives were wrong. The factories ended up making large heavy pots and other cooking utensils that were useless for the typical household. In a capitalist environment prices would have provided the proper incentive. High prices for the goods that were in shortage would have provided a signal to factories to produce more.

THE SCOPE OF ECONOMICS

There are two major divisions of economics: microeconomics and macroeconomics. The major difference between these two divisions is in their respective points of view. **Microeconomics** focuses on individual decision-making agents such as individuals, households and firms, while **macroeconomics** focuses on the aggregates or economy-wide issues. Microeconomics is the older of the two divisions. Economists generally date the start of microeconomics to the 1776 publication of the book *An Inquiry into the Nature and Causes of the Wealth of Nations* by the Scottish Philosopher Adam Smith. This book is typically referred to by the shorter title *The Wealth of Nations*. Microeconomics is the branch of economics that deals with the decision-making process of the individual, the household, the firm, and the industry. For the individual and the household, consumption decisions are paramount. Microeconomics examines how individuals and households determine what and how much to buy and factors that influence these decisions. The ultimate goal of an individual consumer or household is to maximize satisfaction or happiness given his or her income. For the firm and the industry, production decisions are dominant. Here, microeconomics investigates how firms and industries determine what to produce and how much to charge.[4] The ultimate goal of the firm and/or industry is assumed to be profit maximization. Therefore, the firm seeks the best allocation of its resources in order to make the most profits. Microeconomics is also concerned with issues such as income, wealth inequality, and poverty. Keep in mind that *micro* means small or detailed in the Greek language. So microeconomics looks at the individual parts of the economy. Figuratively speaking, the study of microeconomics is like examining individual trees in a forest.

Macroeconomics, on the other hand, looks at the economy in its entirety. It deals with sums or aggregates. Figuratively speaking, the study of macroeconomics is like examining the entire forest. For instance, macroeconomics is concerned with (1) aggregate prices and not just the price of one commodity, (2) aggregate labor supply and not just the labor supplied by one individual or household, and (3) aggregate national production and not just the output of one firm or industry. By examining aggregate prices, labor supply, and national production macroeconomics provides insights into inflation, unemployment, and economic growth, both short term and long term. Macroeconomics is a much younger division of economics. Most economists date the start of macroeconomics with the 1936 publication of the book *The General Theory of Employment, Interest and Money* by John Maynard Keynes, a renowned British economist. This book was written during the time of the Great Depression. The Great Depression, a period of declining GDP and high unemployment, started in 1929 and ended around 1939.

Economics is a really broad and diverse discipline. If you decide to major in economics, you will be exposed to a number of different fields. Economic electives include courses like economic history—which examines the growth in economic developments and ideas

---

[4] It's important to keep in mind that individuals and households do make production decisions and that firms and industries also make consumption decisions. For instance, individuals and households must decide how much labor to supply to the market, while firms and industries must determine how much labor to purchase.

over time; international economics—which looks at cross-border trade and financial flows; labor economics—which examines workforce participation, wage rate determination, and unions; public finance—which studies government expenditures and revenues; and urban economics—which adds a spatial dimension to the study of economics. These are just a few of the many sub-fields in economics.

POSITIVE AND NORMATIVE ECONOMICS

Another divide that we see in economics is in regard to positive and normative economics. Unlike microeconomics and macroeconomics, which represent differences in points of view (i.e., the trees vs. the forest), positive and normative economics represent differences in analytical approaches. Analysis that tries to answer questions about the way the world works, which have definite right and/or wrong answers, is known as **positive economics,** while analysis that involves how the world *should* work is known as **normative economics**. Positive economics seeks to understand behavior and the operation of systems without making judgments. It describes what is and how it works. For instance, if I say that the Georgia Sales Tax is regressive, this is a positive statement, and we can test it empirically. We can indeed test to see if lower income people are paying a higher percentage of their earnings in sales taxes than do higher income people. On the other hand, normative economics is judgmental. It analyzes outcomes of economic behavior, evaluates them as good or bad, and may prescribe a course of action. For example, if I say that the Georgia Income Tax should be progressive, that is judgmental. It is my opinion that people with higher incomes should pay a higher percentage of their earning in income taxes. Any time you see the words *should* or *ought,* that is a clue that you are dealing with a normative statement. It is important to keep in mind that positive economics attempts to describe and understand economic behavior while normative economics evaluates economic behavior. Many of the disagreements that one comes across in economics are of a normative nature.

PITFALLS AND HAZARDS

As you go through the study of economics there are a couple of pitfalls you should be aware of. The first pitfall is the **post hoc fallacy**. *Post hoc* is a shortened version of the Latin phrase *Post hoc, ergo propter hoc,* which literally means "after this, therefore because of this." The post hoc fallacy is a pitfall that deals with correlation and causation. It cautions that just because two events happen to be correlated does not mean that one has caused the other to occur. In other words, there may not be a cause and effect. For example, every morning the rooster crows and then the sun comes up. This happens day after day, month after month, and year after year. Although these events are highly correlated, you would never claim that the rooster is causing the sun to rise, would you? A few years back a study came out that revealed that people who drank red wine had substantially fewer heart attacks. The conclusion was that you should drink red wine to lessen your chances of getting a heart attack. People started drinking more red wine (including yours truly). A subsequent study revealed that people who drank red wine led healthier lifestyles. Therefore, it may not be the red wine that made people healthier, but rather red wine drinkers are also associated with other health-improving habits such as regular exercise. In economics we have plenty of examples of the post hoc fallacy. For example, we notice that people with high educational attainment have high incomes and that people with high incomes typically have high educational attainment. In other words, income and education are highly correlated. However, we don't know the causal effect. Does high education lead to high incomes or do people with higher incomes consume more education? We don't know for sure.

The second pitfall that you need to be on guard against is the **fallacy of composition**. This pitfall is related to aggregation. Oftentimes, when we go from the individual level of analysis to group-level analysis, there might be a breakdown in the logic. In other words, what is true for the individual may not be true for the group. For example, at a sold-out football game, you might decide that it would be in your self-interest to stand up in order to see well. So you stand up. However, if everyone acted in his or her own self-interest, no one would see better, and you would be no better off than if everyone was seated. So what is good and rational for the individual could prove to be detrimental for the group.

Examples of the fallacy of composition in economics abound. For instance, if an individual wheat farmer has a bumper crop, he is better off; however, if all wheat farmers have bumper crops at the same time, that might not be a good thing for any of the farmers. Why? If all farmers have bumper crops, this could lead to oversupply and could depress farm prices and lower farmers' income. One of the best examples of the fallacy of composition is John Maynard Keynes' "paradox of thrift." The paradox of thrift illustrates how the ramifications of individuals acting in their own self-interest might lead to harmful national outcomes, which in turn hurts the individual. For instance, let's say we experience a period of economic slowdown and one is uncertain about the stability of his job. Well, a rational action for the individual might be to save more and spend less. In other words, the individual becomes thrifty. However, if everyone responded to this uncertainty in the same manner, the economy might actually worsen since thriftiness in aggregate could lead to lower economic activity. This in turn could lead to fewer jobs and less savings on the aggregate level. In this case, more individual thriftiness leads to less thriftiness in aggregate. Thus, the paradox!

WHY STUDY ECONOMICS?

There are a number of reasons for studying economics; however, one of the best is that economics will provide you with a new way of thinking. By studying economics, you will gain an understanding of the significance of "thinking at the margin," of considering opportunity costs in your decision-making process, and of the role incentives play in our daily lives. Armed with such tools, you will be better equipped to analyze problems and issues of the day. By studying economics, you will also gain insights into how people make choices and how they interact with each other as consumers and producers. In addition, economics will help you to understand how and why economies grow, and it will provide insights into the effectiveness of policies that are designed to promote overall economic growth and development.

Image ©Cristi Matei, 2013. Used under license from Shutterstock, Inc.

By studying economics you will, no doubt, become a more informed member of society and a clearer thinker. For example, to the layperson the seemingly disparate topics of welfare, the mortgage interest deduction, and farm subsidies would have nothing in common. However, a student of economics would easily point out that each of these represent some form of government transfer payment.[5] So in a sense, economics will help you to organize the clutter of facts in a more systematic way. It will help you to see patterns and to better analyze seemingly ambiguous situations. To those of you who will go further in the study of economics, it could very well enable you to make a valuable contribution to society.

WHY STUDY THE GLOBAL ECONOMY?

This is a simple question to answer. Regardless of whether you know it, we are already active participants in the global economy, and it is important for each of us to understand how the global economy works. A large part of the "global economy" consists of exploring **globalization**—the "increasing *interconnectedness* of people and societies and the growing *interdependence* of economies, governments, and environments." Through vast improvements in communication and transportation technology, the world has become a much smaller place and, as a result, we can more easily impact others and others can more easily impact us. Take a look at the label on the back of your shirt or blouse. Chances are it was made in a place far away from where you are now. The banana that you had on your cereal this morning probably came from Central America. The platinum that is contained in each automobiles catalytic converter probably comes from South Africa. The smartphone you are using was probably assembled in China. Globalization is not just the growing trade

---

[5] Each of these can be looked upon as a type of welfare. Of course, welfare is what we typically think of when we think of government subsidies for the poor. However, the mortgage interest deduction represents government subsidies to the middle-class, while farm subsidies represent government transfer payments to the rich. The vast majority of farm subsidies go to the largest and wealthiest farm operations in the country.

in commodities that are bringing us closer together, it is also the growing interdependence among our economies. For example, an economic crisis in Europe has a direct impact on the United States and vice versa. Similarly, fluctuations in the value of the U.S. dollar have global implications, as does the price of oil. Globalization is also being enhanced by growing international travel, mass communication, and immigration. These developments have directly contributed to the *internationalization* of diseases, cultural norms, and values. We see evidence of this in the global dispersion of diseases like HIV/AIDS, in the widespread embrace of ethnic cuisines, the broad dissemination of western fashion style, and even in the "Arab Spring" movement, where popular dissatisfaction with the status quo and civil uprising in Tunisia had a rapid contagion effect on many other countries in North Africa and the Middle East.

By studying the global economy, you will also explore some important economic linkages that exist among countries and groups of nations. We will focus much of our attention on trade and international monetary flows, two areas of growing importance in the global marketplace of the 21st century. Moreover, we will investigate the effects and "agents" of globalization and assess the role of the United States in the world economy.

SUMMARY

- Economics is concerned with how people, both individually and collectively, make choices given that resources are limited. It can be defined as "the science which studies human behavior as a relationship between ends and scarce means which have alternative uses."
- Resources include *land, labor,* and *capital.* To an economist land includes Earth and the minerals, fish, water, and forests found on it. Labor is the people that provide the mental or physical effort. While capital is the goods—like machinery and equipment—needed to make finished products or the education and training that people acquire. Capital in

the form of goods is referred to as *physical capital*, while capital in form of education and training is denoted as *human capital*.

- Economists like to say that all decisions are made at the margin. *Marginalism* or "*thinking at the margin*" means that one must analyze the additional or incremental costs and benefits arising from a choice or decision. We refer to incremental costs and benefits as *marginal cost (MC)* and *marginal benefit (MB)*, respectively.
- The *economic decision rule* states that if the marginal benefit is greater than the marginal cost (i.e., MB > MC) then one should pursue that activity; however, if the marginal cost is greater than the marginal benefit (i.e., MC > MB), then one should not pursue that activity. In the rare case that MC = MB, one would be indifferent in regard to pursuing the activity.
- *Opportunity cost* captures the idea of tradeoffs. It is defined as the value of the next-best alternative that we forgo, or give up, when we make a decision. This implies that you do not get something for nothing and that everything has a cost.
- *Incentives* are rewards and penalties that motivate behavior. Economists believe that since people usually exploit opportunities to make themselves better off they will respond to incentives.
- *Microeconomics* is the branch of economics that deals with the decision-making process of the individual, the household, the firm, and the industry. For the individual and the household consumption decisions are paramount. Microeconomics examines how individuals and households determine what and how much to buy. For the firm and the industry production decisions are dominant. Here, microeconomics investigates how firms and industries determine what to produce and how much to charge.
- *Macroeconomics* examines the economy in its entirety. It deals with total sums or aggregates. Macroeconomics is concern with (1) aggregate prices and not just the price of one commodity, (2) aggregate labor supply and not just the labor supplied by one individual or household, and (3) aggregate national production and not just the output of one firm or industry. By examining aggregate prices, labor supply, and national production macroeconomics provide insights into inflation, unemployment, and economic growth, both short term and long term.
- Analysis that tries to answer questions about the way the world works, which have definite right and wrong answers, is known as *positive economics*. While analysis that involves saying how the world *should* work is known as *normative economics*.
- The *post hoc fallacy* is a pitfall that deals with correlation and causation. It cautions that just because two events happen to be correlated doesn't mean that one has caused the other to occur. In other words, there may not be a cause and effect. The *fallacy of composition* is related to problems associated with aggregation. Oftentimes when we go from the individual level of analysis to the group, there is a breakdown in the logic. In other words, what is true for the individual may not be true for the group.
- *Globalization* is defined as the "increasing *interconnectedness* of people and societies and the growing *interdependence* of economies, governments, and environments."

KEY TERMS

Economics	Incentives
Resources	Microeconomics
Marginalism	Macroeconomics
Marginal cost	Positive economics
Marginal benefit	Normative economics
Economic decision rule	Post hoc fallacy
Opportunity cost	Fallacy of composition
Explicit cost	Globalization
Implicit cost	

PROBLEMS

1. If the going rate of interest on savings accounts is 5% per year, what is the opportunity cost of putting $100 under your mattress for a year?

2. Knowing that you have an important economics exam coming up next week, what is your opportunity cost of going to a party on Saturday night?

3. What are the opportunity costs of you attending college? Be sure to differentiate between explicit and implicit costs.

4. Lately, there has been recent discussion about the elimination of the mortgage interest deduction for homeowners. In essence, this would increase the cost of home ownership for the consumer. What might be the result if this deduction is eliminated? How is this related to *incentives*?

5. In 1696, the United Kingdom imposed a tax on windows. Two shillings per year were charged if a building had less than 10 windows, four shillings were charged if the building had 10 to 20 windows, and eight shillings were charged if the building had more than 20 windows. What do you think the impact of this tax was on building owner? What did this incentivize them to do?

6. Indicate which of the following are microeconomic or macroeconomic concerns.

   a. There was a 10% rise in the price of apples.
   b. There was a 10% rise in inflation.
   c. The unemployment rate in June fell by 2%.
   d. Ford Motor Company laid off 2,000 workers in May.
   e. The economy grew by $1 trillion in 2012.
   f. Microsoft's profits grew by $2 billion in 2012.
   g. The impact of higher per unit taxes on the sale of cigarettes.
   h. The impact of higher income taxes on domestic consumption.

7. Given the following table, which depicts quantities of a product produced and the additional revenues/benefits and additional costs associated with each level of output, how much should be produced based on the economic decision rule? Why wouldn't you just produce two units of this product? Why not six?

Quantity	Marginal Benefit	Marginal Cost
1	6	2
2	6	4
3	6	6
4	6	8
5	6	10
6	6	12

8. Indicate which of the following statements are positive or normative.

a. The income tax should be progressive—that is, people who make more money should pay a higher portion of their income in taxes.

b. Sales taxes on food are regressive—that is, the poor pay a higher share of their income on sales taxes than do the rich.

c. Professional basketball players are paid more than economics professors.

d. Economics professors should be paid more than professional basketball players.

e. More ice cream is sold when the weather is hot.

f. When the weather is hot, everyone should go for a swim.

g. Everyone ought to own a gun.

h. Owning a gun lead to fewer deaths.

2

Supply and Demand

W hy do hotels in South Florida charge higher prices in winter than they do in summer? Why are roses more expensive in early February than other times of year? Why does Lebron James earn more than the best college professor? The answer to each of these questions can be explained through the use of supply and demand analysis. Supply and demand is one of the most useful tools that we have in economics. Supply and demand helps us to understand how markets work, and markets help us to understand how the economy works. So by studying supply and demand, one can gain valuable insights into the workings of the economy.

LEARNING GOALS

➤ Understand the basic workings of markets.
➤ Be able to
  ▪ Differentiate between a change in demand and a change in quantity demanded.
  ▪ Differentiate between a change in supply and a change in quantity supplied.
  ▪ Discuss supply-side and demand-side shift factors.
  ▪ Make predictions using supply and demand.
➤ Understand consumer and producer surplus.
➤ Describe global equilibrium.

MARKETS

In order to understand supply and demand we must first understand **markets**. Markets consist of a group of buyers and sellers of a particular good or service. Markets can take many forms and may be organized (as in the case of agricultural commodities) or less organized (as in the case of ice cream). A competitive market is a market in which there are so many buyers and so many sellers that each has no influence over market price. Because buyers and sellers must accept the market price as given, they are often called "price takers." For the time being we will assume that markets are perfectly competitive.

Keep in mind that not all goods are sold in a perfectly competitive market. A market with only one seller is called a *monopoly*. Some markets fall between perfect competition and monopoly. Because some degree of competition is present in most markets, many of the lessons that we learn by studying supply and demand under perfect competition apply in more complicated markets.

DEMAND

When introducing supply and demand we typically start off, by convention, on the demand side of the market. Demand can be looked upon as the buyers or consumers in the market. More formally, demand represents the quantities of a good that buyers or consumers are able and willing to buy at various prices. Consumers respond to price changes in a predictable way. When prices increase, the quantity demanded decreases, and when prices fall, the quantity demanded increases. This behavior occurs so regularly that we refer to it as the **law of demand**. The law of demand states that, *all other things constant, there is an inverse relationship between the price of a good and the quantity demanded of the good.* In other words, there is a negative (or inverse) relationship between the price (P) of a good and quantity demanded (Q_D).

$$\textit{If } P \uparrow Q_D \downarrow \textit{ and if } P \downarrow Q_D \uparrow$$

Q_D is simply the amount of a good that buyers are willing and able to purchase at a given price. The graphical representation of the Law of Demand is the **demand curve** (see Figure 2.1).

Individual Demand versus Market Demand

Keep in mind that the typical demand curve that you see is actually the market demand curve. In actuality, the market demand curve is comprised of the individual demand curves for each consumer in the market. You derive the market demand curve by horizontally summing

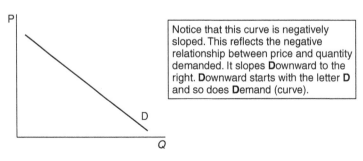

Figure 2.1   The Demand Curve

individual demand curves. Since the demand curve is drawn with quantities on the horizontal axis and with prices on the vertical axis, one can think of horizontal summation as adding up the quantities at each price. For instance, let's say we're talking about demand for apples and that there are three consumers that comprise the entire market—Diane, John, and Bill. When the price of apples is $1 per pound, Diane and Bill purchase five apples each, and John buys ten apples. When the price is $2 per pound, Diane buys four apples, John buys eight apples, and Bill buys three apples. At a price of $3 per pound, apple purchases for Diane, John and Bill are three, six and one, respectively. When the price rises to $4 per pound, Bill drops out of the market altogether, while Diane buys two apples and John buys four apples[1]. At $5 a pound Diane's purchase of apples drops to one and John's drop to two. Table 2.1 summarizes the apple purchases at the various prices by the three consumers in the market.

The above table is known as a *demand schedule*. A demand schedule shows the quantities of a product that an individual or household would be willing to buy at different prices. We derive the market demand curve for apples by adding the quantity of apples demanded by the various consumers in the market at each price. For example, when the price of apples is $1 per pound market demand is 20 apples. We added the quantities demanded by Diane, John, and Bill when the price of apples is $1 per pound (i.e., 5 + 10 + 5 = 20). When the price is $5 per pound, market demand is three apples (i.e., 1+2+0 = 3) (see Table 2.2).

Table 2.3 presents the market demand schedule, which is simply columns 1 and 5 of Table 2.2. To the right of the market demand schedule is the market demand curve (see Figure 2.2). When the price changes, we get a movement along the demand curve, and we get a **change in quantity demanded** (Q_D). So when prices increase from $1 to $2 per pound, quantity demanded falls from 20 to 15 apples, and when the price falls from $5 to $4 per pound, quantity demanded increases from three to six apples (see Figures 2.3 and 2.4). Therefore, a change in quantity demanded is due to a change in the price of the good and nothing else.

Table 2.1   Individual Demand Schedules

P	Diane Q_{DD}	John Q_{DJ}	Bill Q_{DB}
1	5	10	5
2	4	8	3
3	3	6	1
4	2	4	—
5	1	2	—

---

[1] What might explain Bill's dropping out of the market at a price of $4?

Table 2.2   From Individual to Market Demand

P	Diane Q_{DD}	John Q_{DJ}	Bill Q_{DB}	Market Demand $(Q_D = Q_{DD} + Q_{DJ} + Q_{DB})$
1	5	10	5	20
2	4	8	3	15
3	3	6	1	10
4	2	4	—	6
5	1	2	—	3

Table 2.3   Market Demand Q_D

P	Market Demand Q_D
1	20
2	15
3	10
4	6
5	3

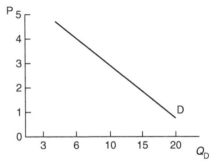

Figure 2.2   Market Demand Curve

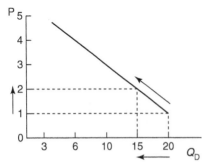

Figure 2.3   Decrease in Quantity Demanded

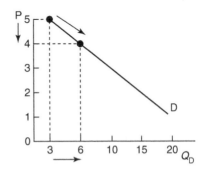

Figure 2.4   Increase in Quantity Demanded

It should be noted that when we allow prices to change, we are holding constant all other factors that could influence the demand curve. We use the Latin phrase *ceteris paribus*, which translates as *all other things being equal*, to indicate that nothing else is changing other than price in this case. As a result, we are able to isolate the influence of price changes on quantities demanded. By holding everything else constant the law of demand is revealed when we allow prices to change.

Demand-Side Shift Factors

When we allow factors other than price to change, we no longer get a movement along the demand curve; instead we get a shifting of the entire demand curve outward or inward. This outward or inward movement of the demand curve is referred to as a **change in demand**. A rightward shift of the demand curve represents an increase in demand and a leftward shift of the demand curve is referred to as a decrease in demand (see Figure 2.5).

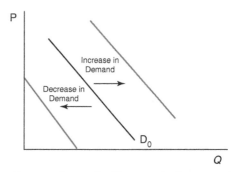

Figure 2.5   **A Change in Demand**

There are five **demand-side shift factors** that we focus on. They include

1. Change in income
2. Change in the prices of related goods or services
3. Change in consumer preferences
4. Change in the number of consumers
5. Expectations

Let's take a look at these one by one.

Income. At the individual level there is no doubt that one's income determines how much one is willing and able to buy of a commodity. Other things constant, a change in one's income will determine if more or less of a commodity will be demanded. We can extend this to the market level as well. What happens to demand when incomes go up, *ceteris paribus*?[2] Well, it depends. It depends on the product or service that we're dealing with. If demand increases (i.e., demand curve moves to the right) when buyers' incomes go up, we say that that product or service is a *normal good*. Similarly, the demand for a normal good decreases (i.e., demand curve moves to the left) when buyers' incomes go down. By definition, normal goods are goods that exhibit a positive or direct relationship between income and demand. In other words, income and demand move in the same direction. When income increases, so does demand, and when income decreases, demand decreases as well. Demand for most goods normally behaves in this manner in regard to income changes. Demand for new automobiles, new clothes, and new furniture would typically increase with an increase in income and decrease with drops in income. The same would be true for a service like airline flights.

There are some goods, however, that exhibit a negative or inverse relationship between income and demand. These goods are called *inferior goods*. When incomes go up, demand for inferior goods goes down (i.e., demand curve moves to the left), and when incomes go down, demand for inferior goods goes up (i.e., demand curve moves to the right). Demand for used automobiles, used clothes, and used furniture would decrease with an increase in income and increase with drops in income. In addition to many types of used products, goods like noodles, beer, and bologna are often considered inferior goods. Bus service could be another example of an inferior good.

Prices of Related Goods or Services. What happens to the demand for one good when the price of another good changes? The answer to this question is also "it depends." It depends on how the goods or services in question are related. If the goods or services are *complements* (i.e., goods or services that are used together), then there is a negative or inverse relationship between the price of one and demand for the other. For instance, we know that air travel and jet fuel are complements. Airlines need jet fuel in order to fly. If airfares fall, *ceteris paribus*, we would expect the demand for jet fuel to increase (i.e., demand curve moves to the right). Why? Because if the price of flying falls, the quantity demanded of air flights increases, which increases the demand for jet fuel. Therefore, in the market for jet fuel, the demand curve would shift to the right (signifying an increase in demand). Can you think of other examples of complements?

On the other hand, goods or services that are used in place of one another are called *substitutes*. Goods or services that are related in this manner exhibit a positive or direct relationship between the price of one and the demand for the other. So if the price of a substitute good or service drops, *ceteris paribus*, we would expect the demand for the other substitute good or service to drop as well. For example, we know that air travel and long distance bus service are substitute goods. If the price of air travel drops, we would expect to see a decrease in demand (i.e., demand curve shifts to the left) for bus service. This occurs because the drop in airfares will lead to an increase in the quantity demanded of

---

[2] Here we're using *ceteris paribus* to indicate that nothing else other than income is being allowed to change and to impact demand.

air flights and, since air and bus travel are substitute goods, there will be less demand for bus services.

Note that in both the complementary and substitute goods examples, we assumed a decrease in airfares. However, the impact of declining airfares on demand for the other good or service varied depending on the relationship the good in question had with air travel. In the case of the complementary good, there was an inverse relationship and with the substitute good there was a positive relationship.

$$\text{Complements:} \quad \downarrow \text{airfares} \Rightarrow \uparrow \text{demand for jet fuel}$$

$$\text{Substitutes:} \quad \downarrow \text{airfares} \Rightarrow \downarrow \text{demand for bus service}$$

It's important to keep in mind that most goods are not related to one another. For instance, what would be the impact of declining airfares on the demand for apples? None, because air flights and apples are not related!

Consumer Preferences (Tastes). Change in consumer tastes and preferences have a direct impact on demand for a good or service. When preferences for a good or service increase, we should expect that an increase in demand for the good or service results. On the other hand, if preferences decline, we should expect to observe a decrease in demand. Often, companies advertise in order to shift preferences in favor of their product. This is expected to increase the demand for the company's product (shift the demand curve to the right). Advertising is just one of a multitude of factors that can influence tastes and preferences. For instance, the weather, medical pronouncements, and celebrity endorsements heavily influence consumer preferences and demand for products and services. On a rainy day, what happens to the demand for umbrellas? When a medical journal reports that a glass of red wine a day leads to fewer heart attacks, what happens to demand for red wine? Or when Oprah Winfrey names a book to her book club list, what happens to sales of that book, and when she declares that she will no longer eat burgers, what happens to the demand for red meat?[3]

Number of Consumers. An increase in the number of consumers in a market will cause demand for a good or service to increase, and a decrease in the number of consumers will cause demand for that good or service to decrease. In other words, there is a positive relationship between the number of consumers and demand. The change in the number of consumers can have a profound influence on market demand and on market outcomes. For instance, a number of economists predict that the growing retirement of the Baby

---

[3] In 1996, Oprah Winfrey aired a show on mad cow disease in which it was revealed that cows are ground up and fed back to other cows. In response to that revelation she declared that "It has just stopped me cold from eating another burger!" In 1998, a group of Texas cattlemen sued Oprah, claiming that the show had driven down cattle prices by misleading and frightening consumers.

Boom generation over the next decade or so will place a damper on the stock market.[4] Why? Because the Baby Boom generation, which represented a dramatic increase in the size of the U.S. population (i.e., number of consumers), will no longer be purchasing stocks. Instead, they will be dis-saving and drawing down their 401k and other stock-based portfolios. In other words, there will be a decline in the number of consumers in the stock market. Conversely, as these Boomers continue to age, there will be increasing demand for healthcare services.

Expectations. Expectations about the future can impact your demand for goods and services today. For example, if you know that you will be getting a pay raise next month, you may be willing to buy more clothes today. However, if you think that you might lose your job in the near future, you may cut back on your purchases today. On the other hand, you may have expectations about future prices. For example, if you expect the price of apples to go up next week, you may be inclined to buy more apples today. However if you expect the price of gasoline to drop significantly next week, you might want to hold off making purchases this week if you can.

SUPPLY

Now, let's turn our attention to the supply side of the market. Supply can be looked upon as the producers' or sellers' side of the market. *Supply* represents the quantity of a good or service that producers or sellers are able and willing to put on the market for sale at various prices. Quantity supplied refers to the amount of a good or service that producers or sellers are able and willing to put on the market for sale at a given price. Therefore, supply represents a relationship between price and quantity supplied. As in the case of consumers, producers also respond to price changes in a predictable way. When price increases, the quantity supplied increases, and when price falls, the quantity supplied decreases. In other words, other things constant, there is a *positive* or *direct* relationship between the price (P) and quantity supplied (Q_s). This behavior is known as the **Law of Supply**.

$$\textit{If } P \uparrow Q_s \uparrow \textit{ and if } P \downarrow Q_s \downarrow$$

Q_s denotes the amount of a good that sellers are willing and able to supply to the market. The graphical representation of the Law of Supply is the **supply curve** (see Figure 2.6).

Just as in the case of demand, the typical supply curve that you see is actually the market supply curve. In reality, the market supply curve is comprised of the individual supply curves for each producer in the market. You obtain the market supply curve by horizontally summarizing individual supply curves. Let's say there are three producers of apples in the market—Orchard 1, Orchard 2, and Orchard 3. When the price of apples is $1 per pound, Orchard 1 supplies two apples, Orchard 2 supplies one apple, and Orchard 3 doesn't supply any apples to the market. When the price is $2 per pound, Orchard 1 supplies four apples, Orchard 2 supplies two apples, and again, Orchard 3 doesn't supply any apples to the market. When the price increases to $3, Orchard 1 supplies six apples, Orchard 2 supplies three

---

[4] The dramatic increase in the number of births in the wake of World War II (1946–1964) is called the Baby Boom. In the United States approximately 79 million babies were born during the Baby Boom.

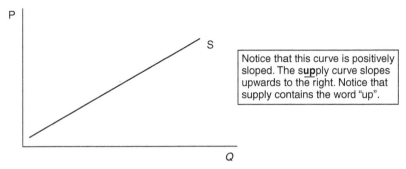

P

S

Notice that this curve is positively
sloped. The s**up**ply curve slopes
upwards to the right. Notice that
supply contains the word "up".

Q

Figure 2.6   **The Supply Curve**

Table 2.4   **The Supply Schedule**

P	Orchard 1 Q_{S1}	Orchard 2 Q_{S2}	Orchard 3 Q_{S3}
1	2	1	—
2	4	2	—
3	6	3	1
4	8	4	3
5	10	5	5

apples, and Orchard 3 now supplies one apple to the market.[5] At a price of $4 per pound, Orchard 1 supplies eight apples to the market, while Orchards 2 and 3 supply four and three apples, respectively. Finally, at $5 per pound, Orchard 1 supplies ten apples, Orchard 2 supplies five apples, and Orchard 3 supplies five apples to the market.

Table 2.4 represents the supply schedule. A supply schedule shows the quantity of a product that an individual firm or producer would be willing to supply to the market at different prices. We derive the market supply curve by horizontally adding the quantity of apples supplied by the various firms in the market at the various prices. For example, when the price of apples is $1 per pound, market supply is three apples. We added horizontally the quantities supplied by Orchard 1, Orchard 2, and Orchard 3 when the price of apples is $1 per pound (i.e., 2 + 1 + 0). When the price is $5 per pound, market supply is 20 apples (i.e., 10 + 5 + 5) (see Table 2.5).

So the market supply schedule is as shown in Table 2.6 below. This is simply columns (1) and (5) in Table 2.5.

To the right of the market supply schedule is the market supply curve (see Figure 2.7). Just as in the case of the demand curve, when the price of the good changes, we move along

---

[5] What might explain Orchard 3's not entering the market until the price of apples reached $3 per pound?

Table 2.5   From Individual Supply Schedule to Market Supply Schedule

P	Orchard 1 Q_{S1}	Orchard 2 Q_{S2}	Orchard 3 Q_{S3}	Market Supply $(Q_S = Q_{S1} + Q_{S2} + Q_{S3})$
1	2	1	—	3
2	4	2	—	6
3	6	3	1	10
4	8	4	3	15
5	10	5	5	20

Table 2.6   The Market Supply Schedule

P	Market Supply Q_S
1	3
2	6
3	10
4	15
5	20

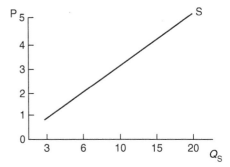

Figure 2.7   Market Supply Curve

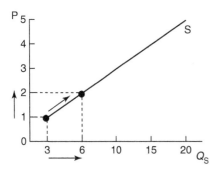

Figure 2.8   Increase in Quantity Supplied

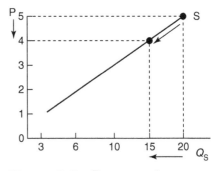

Figure 2.9   Decrease in Quantity Supplied

the supply curve. This movement along the supply curve is associated with a **change in quantity supplied** (Q_S). So when prices increase from \$1 to \$2 per pound, quantity supplied increases from three to six apples; when prices fall from \$5 to \$4 per pound, quantity supplied decreases from 20 to 15 apples (see Figures 2.8 and 2.9).

Again, in order to isolate the influence of price changes on quantities supplied, we are holding all other factors that could impact supply constant. By imposing the *ceteris paribus* condition here, we are able to reveal the *Law of Supply* at work.

Supply-Side Shift Factors

When we allow factors other than price of the good to change, we no longer get a movement along the supply curve. Instead, we get a shifting of the supply curve outward or inward (see Figure 2.10). This outward or inward movement of the supply curve is referred to as a **change in supply**. Recall that the supply curve represents the entire relationship between the price of the good and the amounts sellers are able and willing to put on the market. Therefore, a change in supply is represented by a shifting of the supply curve as opposed to moving along the supply curve. A rightward shift of the supply curve represents an increase in supply and a leftward shift of the supply curve represents a decrease in supply.

There are six **supply-side shift factors** that we focus on. They include

1. Changes in the cost of inputs
2. Advances in technology
3. Taxes and producer subsidies
4. Changes in the prices of related goods or services
5. Change in the number of producers
6. Expectations

Let's take a look at these one by one.

Changes in the Cost of Inputs. Costs are no doubt a major determinant of how much producers are willing to supply to the market. If costs go up, less is supplied to the market (i.e., supply curve shifts inward or to the left), and if costs go down, more is supplied to the market (i.e., supply curve shifts outwards or to the right). The *cost of inputs* refers to the price of resources used to produce the good or service. If the price of the resources used to produce a product or service goes up, then the cost to produce the good or service goes up and producers will supply less to the market and the supply curve would shift to the left. On

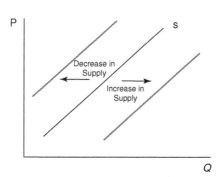

Figure 2.10   **Shifts in Supply**

Keep in mind that when the supply curve shifts to the **left**, that represents a **decrease in supply**. Many students mistakenly assume that since a curve to the left of the original supply curve lies above the original supply curve, it must represent an increase in supply. This is mistaken. Don't be confused.

the other hand, if the price of the resources used to produce a product or service goes down, then the cost to produce the good or service goes down and producers will supply more to the market and the supply curve would shift to the right. For example, what happens to the supply of automobiles if the price of labor increases? Since labor is a major input in the production of automobiles, the cost of producing an automobile would increase and fewer would be supplied to the market. In contrast, if the price of computer chips goes down, what happens to the supply of computers? Computer chips are used in the production of computers, and if the price of computer chips falls, then the cost of producing computers will fall and more computers will be supplied to the market.

Advances in Technology. Advances in technology typically result in increases in productivity. As a result, firms can produce more with the same amount of resources or they can produce the same output with fewer resources. Either way, production costs are lowered. Producers are thus willing to supply more at every available price and the supply curve will shift to the right.

Taxes and Production Subsidies. Taxes and subsidies directly impact production costs. If there is a tax on production, then the cost of production increases and supply decreases (the supply curve shifts inwards or to the left). If a subsidy is provided on production, the supply curve shifts outward or to the right since costs are reduced.

Changes in the Prices of Related Goods or Services. Just like on the demand side of the market, changes in the prices of related goods or services also cause a shift factor on the supply side. Here we are talking about two things, (1) *substitutes in production* and (2) *complements in production*. It is important to remember that a single producer often produces a mix of goods rather than a single product from the same resources.

For example, an oil refinery can produce a number of different products from a barrel of crude oil, including gasoline and heating oil.[6] If the price of gasoline increases, the refineries will produce more gasoline and supply less heating oil to the market, shifting the supply curve for heating oil to the left. In other words, the producer will *substitute* production of gasoline for production of heating oil. On the other hand, if the price of gasoline decreases, the producer will *substitute* production of heating oil for production of gasoline and the supply curve for heating oil will shift to the right. Gasoline and heating oil are *substitutes in production*. In other words, they are products of the same production process, and if more of one is being produced, it is taking away resources devoted to the other and, as a result, less of the other can be produced. Substitutes in production exhibit an inverse or negative relationship between the price of one product and supply of another.

In some cases products are always produced together. When you get one, you always get the other. These kinds of products are called *complements in production*. Complements in production exhibit a positive relationship between the price of one good and supply of the other. For instance natural gas is often produced as a by-product from oil wells. In other words,

---

[6] Other products derived from crude oil include diesel oil, propane, kerosene, paraffin, asphalt, plastics, polyester, nylon, lubricants, and much more.

natural gas and crude oil are complements in production. If the price of crude oil goes up, the supply of natural gas will increase. Conversely, if the price of crude oil goes down, the supply of natural gas will decrease. Why? Because producers of crude oil will supply less crude oil to the market when prices fall (Remember the *law of supply*) and since crude oil and natural gas are typically produced together, the supply of natural gas will fall.

Number of Producers, Analogous to consumers on the demand side of the market, an increase in the number of producers leads to an increase in supply, and a decrease in the number of producers will lead to a decrease in supply. Other things constant, there is a positive relationship between the number of producers and supply. A change in the number of producers can significantly impact market supply and market outcomes.

Expectations. Producer expectations about future prices can also impact supply. If a firm expects the price of ice cream to go up in the future, it may put some of its current production into deep freeze storage and supply less to the market today.

SUPPLY AND DEMAND TOGETHER: THE MARKET

Now, let's put **supply and demand together.** We know that the supply curve slopes upward to the right and that it represents quantities supplied at the various prices of the good or service. We also know that the demand curve slopes downward to the right and that it represents quantities demanded at the various prices of the good or service. The intersection of the supply and demand curves represents *market equilibrium.* **Market equilibrium** determines the equilibrium market price and equilibrium quantities. By definition, the intersection of supply and demand results in quantity demanded being equal to quantity supplied (i.e., $Q_D = Q_S$). In other words, at this point of intersection, the quantity that consumers are willing and able to buy exactly matches the amount that sellers are willing and able to sell. Using the market demand and supply schedules that we derived earlier in the chapter (see Table 2.7), we can plot the market demand and supply curves (See Figure 2.11). In the schedule below, the equilibrium price is $3 and the equilibrium quantity is 10 units. This corresponds to the point where the demand curve intersects the supply curve on the graph. When the market is

Table 2.7   Demand and Supply

P	Market Demand	Market Supply
1	20 →	3
2	15	6
3	10	10
4	6	15
5	3	20

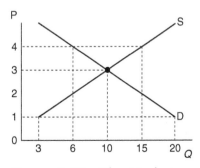

Figure 2.11   The Market Equilibrium

in equilibrium, there is no desire on the part of producers to enter or leave the market, and there is also no desire on the part of consumers to enter or leave the market.

But what happens when the actual price is above the equilibrium price? At a price of $4, for example, producers would be willing to supply more to the market than they would at a price of $3(recall the *law of supply*). Conversely, consumers would be willing to purchase less at $4 than they would at a price of $3 (recall the *law of demand*). In the example above, producers would be willing to supply 15 units at a price of $4, and consumers would be willing to purchase just 6 units. The market is now out of balance. In this case we would say that the market is in *surplus* or excess quantity supplied (i.e., $Q_D < Q_S$). In fact, there would be a surplus of 9 units (15 units − 6 units). On the other hand, if the price is below $3, say $1, the market would be in *shortage* or excess quantity demanded because at a price of $1, quantity demanded would be 20 units and quantity supplied would be 3 units (i.e., $Q_D > Q_S$). In fact, at a price of $1 the market would be in shortage by 17units of the good (20 units − 3 units).

> Keep in mind that when the actual price is above the equilibrium price, the market will always be in surplus, and when the actual price is below the equilibrium price, the market will always be in shortage

When the market price is equal to the equilibrium price of $3, the market is in balance. At a price of $3 quantity demanded is 10 units and quantity supplied is 10 units (i.e., $Q_D = Q_S$). The market is in equilibrium and this represents a stable result. In other words, the market "clears" and in this specific case the "market-clearing" price is $3. At the market clearing price there is no desire on the part of producers or consumers to enter or leave the market. This is quite different from the case of market shortage or market surplus. In the case of market shortage (i.e., actual price is below the equilibrium price), producers realize that prices can be raised and that they can still sell all of their output. As long as the actual price is below the equilibrium price, quantity demanded will exceed quantity supplied and producers will continue to raise prices and increase output up until the equilibrium price level is reached. In the case of a market surplus, actual prices are above the market-clearing price and quantity supplied is greater than quantity demanded. When the market is in surplus, producers are not selling all of their output. In response to this situation, they will decrease their output and lower prices. As price is lowered, quantity demanded increases, quantity supplied decreases, and the surplus is reduced. The surplus would be eliminated altogether once the price falls to the equilibrium price level.

CONSUMER AND PRODUCER SURPLUSES

Once a market price is determined for a particular product, benefits accrue to certain producers and consumers of that product. For example, in the above example some producers are willing to supply the market at a price below the equilibrium price of $3. These producers might be the low-cost firms in the industry. Let's say that one firm would have been willing

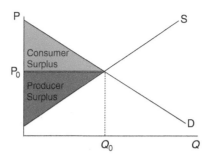

Figure 2.12   **Producer Surplus and Consumer Surplus**

to supply the market at a price of $2 per unit; however, because the market price is $3, this firm receives a $1 per unit premium. All other firms in this market that would have been willing to supply the market at a price below the equilibrium would receive a premium. This premium is known as the *producer surplus*. The **producer surplus** is calculated as the difference between the minimum price the producer is willing to accept for a good or service and the market price (the price the seller actually receives). Graphically, producer surplus is depicted as the area above the supply curve and below the market price (the red-shaded area in Figure 2.12). On the other hand, there are some consumers who would be willing to purchase a good or service at a price greater than the market price. These might be high income consumers. Since these consumers only have to pay the market price, they will gain a consumer surplus. **Consumer surplus** is equal to the difference between the maximum price a buyer is able and willing to pay for a product and the market price (the price the buyer actually pays). Graphically, a buyer's *maximum willingness* to pay is represented by the buyer's demand curve. Therefore, the amount of consumer surplus is graphically represented by the area of the triangle under the demand curve and above the market price (the blue-shaded area in Figure 2.12).

MAKING PREDICTIONS USING SUPPLY AND DEMAND

The power of the simple supply and demand is evident in its usefulness in making market predictions. When we allow the supply and demand curves to shift, we can make predictions about market prices and quantities. Let's see what happens when we start off in equilibrium and we allow demand to change while keeping supply constant. Figure 2.13a illustrates a situation in which demand increases. Demand could have increased due to a change in any of the demand-side shift factors discussed earlier in this chapter. For example, if the product in question is a normal good and incomes went up, this would lead to the increase in demand demonstrated in Figure 2.13a. The shifting of the demand curve leads to a new equilibrium price and quantity. Here the results indicate that when demand increases and supply stays the same, we predict that the price would go up and equilibrium quantity would increase as well. Figure 2.13b shows demand decreasing. We would make the opposite prediction in the case of a decrease in the price of a substitute product. In Figure 2.13b, the drop in the price of a substitute product leads a decrease in demand for the product in question. The new equilibrium suggests that both the equilibrium price and equilibrium quantity will be reduced.

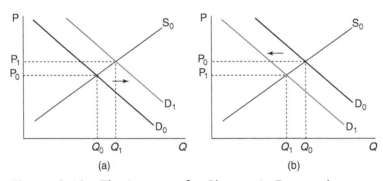

Figure 2.13 The Impact of a Change in Demand

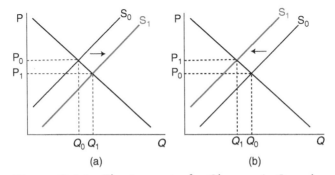

Figure 2.14 The Impact of a Change in Supply

Keep in mind that whenever we have a change in equilibrium, quantity demanded and quantity supplied always move together. In other words, if one increases (decreases), the other also increases (decreases).

Now, let's allow supply to change while keeping demand constant. In Figure 2.14(a) below, we have a situation in which supply increases. Supply could have increased due to changes in any of the supply-side shift factors discussed earlier in this chapter. For instance, the number of producers could have increased or there could have been advancement in technology used in the production of the good in question. In either case, there would be a rightward movement of the supply curve. Given the new equilibrium, we would predict a lower equilibrium price and a larger equilibrium quantity. On the other hand, a leftward movement of the supply curve (i.e., a decrease in supply) could be caused by a tax on production or by expectations that prices will increase in the near future. If we experience a decrease in supply while demand stays the same, we would predict that the market price would go up while equilibrium quantity would drop (see Figure 2.14b).

SIMULTANEOUS SHIFTS IN SUPPLY AND DEMAND: MOVING TOGETHER

Now, let's examine what happens when we allow demand and supply curves to move at the same time. What predictions can we make if, for instance, supply and demand change together? In other words, what happens when demand and supply both increase and when they both decrease? When demand and supply both increase, we end up with a situation like the one depicted in Figure 2.15a. Here we get an increase in equilibrium quantity, but it is uncertain what the affect would be on equilibrium price. With demand unchanged, an increase in supply (supply curve shift to the right) unambiguously increases equilibrium

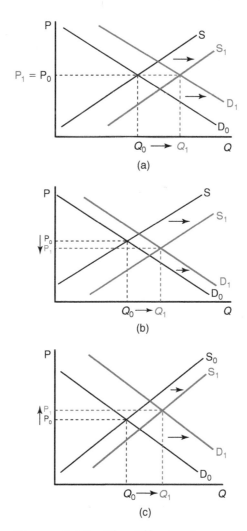

Figure 2.15   The Effects of a Simultaneous Increase in Demand and Supply

quantity. However, other things equal, the increase in supply is predicted to decrease the equilibrium price. On the other hand, an increase in demand while holding supply constant is predicted to increase equilibrium price as well as equilibrium quantity. Therefore, a simultaneous increase in demand and supply unambiguously increases equilibrium quantity. However, an increase in supply decreases the equilibrium price, while an increase in demand increases the equilibrium price. Since the effect on the price goes in opposing directions, the ultimate effect of a simultaneous increase in demand and supply depends on the relative magnitudes of the shifts in demand and supply. With the initial shifting of the demand and supply curves (i.e., the supply curve shifts from S to S_1, while the demand curve shifts from D to D_1), it appears that prices haven't changed (see Figure 2.15a). However, if demand had exhibited a smaller increase relative to the increase in supply (Figure 2.15b), we would end up with a lower equilibrium price. On the other hand, if demand had exhibited a larger increase relative to the increase in supply (Figure 2.15c) we would end up with a higher equilibrium price than we had originally.[7] This illustrates the ambiguous price effect of a simultaneous increase in demand and supply.

In the case where demand and supply both decrease, we can predict with certainty that equilibrium quantity will decrease. However, the effect on the equilibrium price is indeterminate. In Figure 2.16a, with the initial shifting of the demand and supply curves (i.e., the supply curve shifts from S to S_1, while the demand curve shifts from D to D_1), it appears that prices were unchanged. However, as discussed above, the price effect of a simultaneous decrease in demand and supply would depend on the relative magnitudes of the changes in demand and supply. In Figure 2.16b, if supply had exhibited a smaller decrease relative to the decrease in demand, we would end up with a lower equilibrium price; if supply had exhibited a larger decrease relative to the decrease in demand (Figure 2.16c), we would end up with a higher equilibrium prices than we had originally.[8]

SIMULTANEOUS SHIFTS IN SUPPLY AND DEMAND: MOVING IN OPPOSITE DIRECTIONS

In the preceding subsection, we looked at two cases of simultaneous shifts in supply and demand where they both increase or where they both decrease. However, this does not have to be the case in the real world. Supply and demand could shift at the same time but in opposite directions. Let's see what happens when demand increases and supply decreases (Figure 2.17a). If we start off in equilibrium at the intersection of the demand curve labeled "D" and the supply curve labeled "S" and allow the demand curve to shift to the right (an increase in demand) and the supply curve to shift to the left (a decrease in supply), we get a new equilibrium at the intersection of the demand curve labeled "D_1" and supply curve labeled "S_1." At this new equilibrium, the price has increased while the equilibrium quantity

---

[7] If we had allowed for multiple increases in the supply curve instead of the demand curve, the results would still be the same. Try it.

[8] If we had allowed for varying shifts in the demand curve instead of the supply curve, as in the above example, the results would still be the same. Try it.

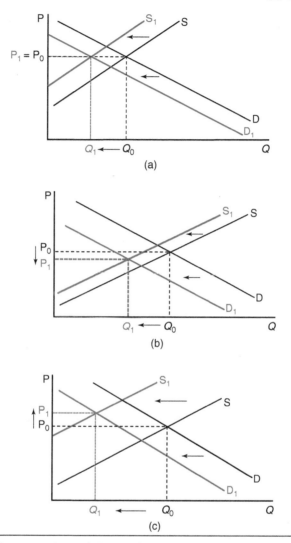

Conclusion: When supply and demand move together (in the same direction), you can make solid predictions about equilibrium quantity, but the effect on the equilibrium price is indeterminate (or ambiguous).

Figure 2.16   The Effects of a Simultaneous Decrease in Demand and Supply

has remained unchanged. Notice that both an increase in demand and a decrease in supply would lead to an increase in the market price. The two effects reinforce each other to increase the market equilibrium price. Therefore, the price effect of a simultaneous increase in demand and decrease in supply is unambiguous. However, we cannot say the same for equilibrium quantity. An increase in demand leads to a higher equilibrium quantity, other things constant. On the other hand, a decrease in supply leads to a lower equilibrium quantity. The net effect of a simultaneous increase in demand and a decrease on supply on the

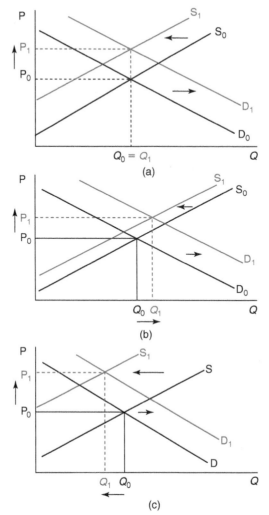

Figure 2.17   A Simultaneous
Increase in Demand and
Decrease in Supply

equilibrium quantity depends on the relative magnitudes of the changes in demand and supply. For example, if we experienced a smaller decrease in supply relative to the increase in demand (Figure 2.17b), we would still see an increase in the price, but now the equilibrium quantity would also increase. On the other hand, if we allowed for a larger decrease in supply relative to the increase in demand (Figure 2.17c) the price would again increase, but this time the equilibrium quantity would decrease.

Now let's see what happens when we have a simultaneous decrease in demand and an increase in supply (Figure 2.18a). Starting off in equilibrium at the intersection of the demand curve labeled "D" and supply curve labeled "S," we allow the demand curve to shift to the left (a decrease in demand) and the supply curve to shift to the right (an increase in supply). These shifts yield a new equilibrium at the intersection of the demand curve labeled "D_1" and the supply curve labeled "S_1." At this new equilibrium the equilibrium price is lower while equilibrium quantity has remained unchanged.

However, if we allowed for a smaller decrease in demand relative to the increase in supply (Figure 2.18b), we would still see a fall in the price, but now the equilibrium quantity would increase. On the other hand, if we had allowed for a larger decrease in demand relative to the increase in supply (Figure 2.18c) the price would again fall, but this time equilibrium quantity decreases.

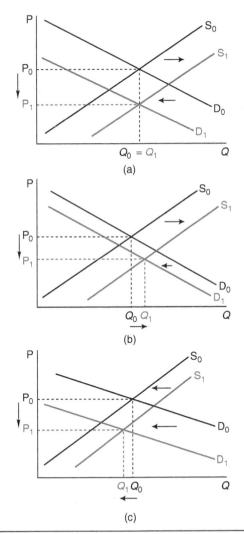

(a)

(b)

(c)

Conclusion: When supply and demand simultaneously change in opposite directions, you can make solid predictions about the effect on equilibrium price, but the effect on equilibrium quantity is indeterminate (ambiguous).

Figure 2.18   A Simultaneous Decrease in Demand and Increase in Supply

THE GLOBAL EQUILIBRIUM

The supply and demand model that we described in this chapter focused on the closed economy. A *closed economy* is one that does not interact with economies of other countries. However, in today's world, most nations have at least some degree of openness. An *open economy* is one that allows for international trade. Fortunately for us, the supply and demand model can be extended to the open economy. In an open economy the **global equilibrium** price is the one that equates excess quantity supplied in exporting countries (quantity of exports supplied) with excess quantity demanded in importing countries (quantity of imports demand). For example, in Figure 2.19 we have the supply and demand conditions in two hypothetical countries that produce and consume rice. The hypothetical economies are *Ricemore* and *Riceless*. Prior to trade, the domestic price in Ricemore is $450 per ton, and the domestic price in Riceless is $650 per ton. In an open economy the $450 per ton price would leave the domestic market in Ricemore in equilibrium. Therefore, at a global price of $450, trade in rice between Ricemore and Riceless cannot take place. Why? At a price of $450 per ton, Ricemore does not have any excess quantity supplied of rice to ship to Riceless. Therefore, despite the fact that Riceless has a huge shortage of rice equal to 70,000 tons (quantity demanded of 100,000 tons minus quantity supplied of 30,000 tons), no trade will take place between the two economies. As a result, global prices would have to rise in order to eliminate the shortage. On the other hand, a price of $650 per ton would leave the domestic market in Riceless in equilibrium while Ricemore would have a surplus of 60,000 tons (quantity supplied of 90,000 tons and quantity demanded of 30,000 tons). As a result, the global price of rice would have to fall. At a price of $550 a ton Ricemore has a 30,000 ton surplus of rice and Riceless has a 30,000 ton shortage of rice and, hence, the global market is in equilibrium and $550 represents the global equilibrium price.

It is important to keep in mind that if the global equilibrium price for a product is above the domestic in a given country, the country becomes an exporter of the good or service. On the other hand, if the global equilibrium price is below the domestic price, the country becomes an importer of the good in question.

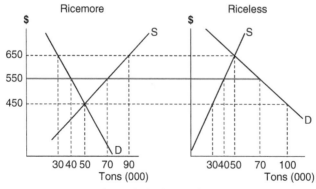

Figure 2.19   **The Global Equilibrium**

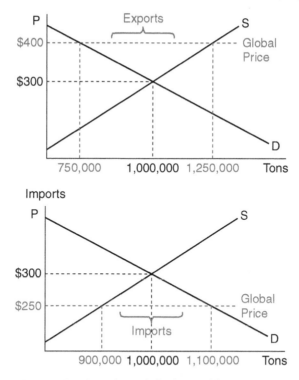

Figure 2.20   **The Global Equilibrium**

For example, suppose that in country A the domestic price of wheat was $300 per ton and that 1 million tons was supplied and demanded at this price (see Figure 2.20). If country A decides to open its economy to the world and it finds that the global equilibrium price for wheat is $400 per ton, disequilibrium in the domestic market will result. Since the global price of $400 per ton is above the domestic equilibrium price, domestic consumers will demand less than before, let's say 750,000 tons, and domestic producers will supply more than before, let's say 1,250,000 tons.[9] The 500,000 ton excess in domestic supply can now be sold or exported abroad. Notice that the surplus (excess quantity supplied) in the closed economy is now exports in the open economy.

On the other hand, if country A, upon opening up its economy, finds that the global equilibrium price for wheat is $250 per ton, imports will result. Why? Because this drop in price will lead to a larger quantity demanded, let's say 1,100,000 tons, and less quantity supplied, let's say 900,000 tons. In the global setting the 200,000 ton shortage [1,100,000 − 900,000] in the domestic market will be satisfied through imports. The graphs above illustrate this dynamic.

---

[9] Remember the law of demand and the law of supply. If price increases, quantity demanded falls and quantity supplied increases.

SUMMARY

- *Markets* consist of a group of buyers and sellers of a particular good or service. A competitive market is a market in which there are so many buyers and sellers that each has no influence over the market price. A market with only one seller is called a monopoly. Some markets fall between perfect competition and monopoly.

- The *law of demand* states that there is an inverse relationship between the price of a good and the quantity demanded of the good. The graphical representation of the law of demand is the *demand curve*. When we allow the price of a commodity to change, we get a movement along the demand curve for that particular commodity. This movement is known as a *change in quantity demanded*.

- When we allow factors other than the price of a particular commodity to change, we get a shifting of the demand curve outward or inward. A shifting of the entire demand curve is known as a *change in demand*. The five *demand-side shift factors* that we focused on are buyers' income, prices of related goods or services, consumer preferences, number of consumers, and expectations.

- The *law of supply* states that there is a positive relationship between the price of a good and the quantity supplied of the good. The graphical representation of the law of supply is the *supply curve*. When we allow the price of a commodity to change, we get a movement along the supply curve for that particular commodity. This movement is known as a *change in quantity supplied*.

- When we allow factors other than the price of a particular commodity to change, we get a shifting of the supply curve outward or inward. A shifting of the entire supply curve is known as a *change in supply*. The six *supply-side shift factors* that we focus on are cost of inputs, advances in technology, taxes and production subsidies, prices of related goods or services, number of producers, and expectations.

- The intersection of the supply and demand curves represents the *market equilibrium*. At the market equilibrium price, quantity demanded is equal to quantity supplied. A price above the equilibrium price would lead to an excess quantity supplied (surplus). A price below the market equilibrium price would lead to an excess quantity demanded (shortage).

- *Consumer surplus* results from the fact that some consumers in the market for a particular commodity or service would be willing to pay more than the market price; however, since they only have to pay the market price, they receive a premium or surplus in the sense that they pay less than the maximum price they were willing to pay. On the other hand, *producer surplus* results from the fact that some producers would be willing to supply a good or service to the market at a price below the market price; however, since they will receive the market price, they will in essence earn a premium or surplus over and above the minimum price they would have been willing to receive for the good or service.

- When we hold supply constant and allow demand to increase, we can predict an increase in equilibrium price and an increase in equilibrium quantity. If demand decreases while holding supply constant, we can predict a fall in both equilibrium price and equilibrium quantity. If, on the other hand, we hold demand steady and allow supply to change, we would predict that the equilibrium price would drop and that equilibrium quantity would increase if supply increases. If supply decreases while holding demand constant, we would predict that the equilibrium price would increase and that equilibrium quantity would fall. When there is a change in equilibrium quantity demanded and quantity supplied move together.

■ When supply and demand change in the same direction, you can make solid predictions about the effect on equilibrium quantity, but the effect on the price is indeterminate. When supply and demand change in opposite directions, the effect on equilibrium price is unambiguous, but the effect on equilibrium quantity is indeterminate.

■ An open economy is one in which international trade takes place. If the *global equilibrium* price for a product is above the domestic market price in a particular country, the country becomes an exporter of the good. On the other hand, if the global equilibrium price is below the country's domestic equilibrium price, the country becomes an importer of the good.

KEY TERMS

Markets	Change in quantity supplied
Law of demand	Change in supply
Demand curve	Supply-side shift factors
Change in quantity demanded	Supply and demand together
Change in demand	Market equilibrium
Demand-side shift factors	Consumer surplus
Law of supply	Producer surplus
Supply curve	Global equilibrium

PROBLEMS

1. In the market for desktop computers, several events occur, one at a time. State whether the event causes a change in demand of desktop computers, a change in the quantity demanded of desktop computers, or no change at all. In other words, what is the impact of the event on the demand curve? Does the demand curve shift, or is there a movement along the demand curve? (assume desktop computers are normal goods)

   a. The price of desktop computers increase.
   b. We experience an economic recession and incomes fall.
   c. The number of computer manufacturers doubles.
   d. The price of iPads is cut in half.
   e. The price of desktop computers falls.

2. Illustrate graphically the effects of each of the above events by either a movement along the demand curve or a shift in the demand curve for desktop computers.

3. In the market for desktop computers, several events occur, one at a time. State whether the event causes a change in supply of desktop computers, a change in the quantity supplied of desktop computers, or no change at all. In other words what is the impact of the event on the supply curve? Does the supply curve shift or is there a movement along the supply curve?

a. The price of desktop computers increase.
b. We experience an economic recession and incomes fall.
c. The number of computer manufacturers doubles.
d. The price of computer chips rises dramatically.
e. The price of desktop computers falls.

4. Illustrate graphically the effects of each of the above events by either a movement along the supply curve or a shift in the supply curve for desktop computers.

5. In an attempt to fight obesity, former Mayor Bloomberg of New York City proposed banning the sale of jumbo-sized, sugar-filled drinks. Illustrate the intended impact of this on the demand curve for sodas.

6. What other actions could lead to less consumption of sugar-filled sodas?

7. Using supply and demand analysis, illustrate the following graphically and predict what will happen to prices (P), demand (D), quantity demanded (Q_d), supply (S), and quantity supplied (Q_s).

a. The price of computer chips just increased by 30%. What happens to P, D, (Q_d), S, and (Q_s) in the desktop computer market, ceteris paribus?
b. The price of a Lexus has dropped 25%. What happens to P, D, (Q_d), S, and (Q_s) in the Mercedes Benz market, ceteris paribus?
c. Incomes go up by 50%. What happens to P, D, (Q_d), S, and (Q_s) in the market for new clothes, ceteris paribus? [Hint: New clothes are normal goods.]
d. Incomes go down by 50%. What happens to P, D, (Q_d), S, and (Q_s) in the market for used clothes, ceteris paribus? [Hint: Used clothes are inferior goods.]
e. New technology has increased productivity in steel production. What happens to P, D, Q_d, S, and (Q_s) in the steel market after this technology was introduced, ceteris paribus?
f. The number of Baby Boomers who are retiring is increasing rapidly. What is likely to happen to P, D, (Q_d), S, and (Q_s) in the market for financial assets as more and more Baby Boomers retire, ceteris paribus?

8. If the price of automobiles is expected to double next month, what would be the impact of this development on prices, quantity demanded, and quantity supplied of cars this month?

9. The following table represents the willingness to pay of five buyers.

Buyer	Willingness to Pay
Billie	$100
Glen	$60
Trey	$40
Whitney	$20
Paul	$10

If the market price of the product is $36, then total consumer surplus is how much?

10. The following table represents the cost of five possible sellers.

Buyer	Willingness to Pay
Paul	$3,000
Ann	$2,400
Krista	$2,000
Klara	$1,500
Glen	$1,000

If the market price of the product is $2,000, then total producer surplus is how much?

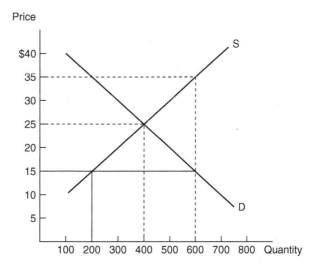

11. Based on the above graph, would the market be in surplus, shortage, or equilibrium if the price was $35? If this is an open economy, would the country be an exporter or importer of the good at a global price of $35? How much would the country import or export?

12. Based on the above graph, if the global price is $15, how much is quantity supplied at the global price? How much is quantity demanded at the global price? How will the excess quantity demanded be met?

APPENDIX TO CHAPTER 2

Supply and Demand Using Algebra

In Chapter 2, we solved the Supply and Demand problem using graphs. Oftentimes demand and supply are expressed in equation form and equilibrium price and quantity can be solved algebraically. Let's go through an example. The following set of equations represents the supply and demand for widgets:

1. $Q_= 12 - 1P$
2. $Q_= -3 + 2P$

   Before we solve for the equilibrium price and quantity, how do we know which equation represents the supply curve for widgets and which represents the demand curve for widgets? One easy way of figuring this out is to plug in a few sequential numbers for P (i.e., prices) in both equations and see what happens to Q (i.e., quantities). If quantities increase when prices increase then that represents a positive relationship. In other words, we are dealing with the supply curve. Remember that the *Law of Supply* states that there is a positive relationship between prices and quantities supplied. If, on the other hand, quantities decrease when prices increase then that is a negative or inverse relationship. This is indicative of the demand curve. The *Law of Demand* states that there is an inverse relationship between prices and quantities demanded.

   So let's plug in a few sequential numbers for P and see what happens to Q in equation 1.

Table A2.1

P	$Q_=12 - 1P$
0	12
1	11
2	10
3	9

   As you can see, when prices increase the quantities are decreasing so equation (1) represents the demand curve for widgets. We can now infer through the process of elimination that equation (2) must be the supply curve for widgets. Let's check to make sure by plugging in sequential numbers for P.

Table A2.2

P	$Q_=-3+2P$
0	-3
1	-1
2	1
3	3

In this case quantities increase when there is an increase in prices. Equation (2) does indeed represent the supply curve for widgets.[1]

So we now have the following demand and supply equations for which we would like to solve for equilibrium price and quantity.

1. $Q_D = 12 - 1P$
2. $Q_S = -3 + 2P$

One tedious way of approaching this problem is to keep plugging in numbers. For example:

Table A2.3

P	Demand Curve $Q_=12-1P$	Supply Curve $Q_=-3+2P$
0	12	−3
1	11	−1
2	10	1
3	9	3
4	8	5
5	7	7
6	6	9
7	5	11
8	4	13
9	3	15
10	2	17
11	1	19
12	0	21

[1] Another way that we can figure out which equation represents the demand curve and which represents the supply curve is by determining their respective slopes. A negative slope would indicate the demand curve, while a positive slope would indicate the supply curve.

We know that the market is in equilibrium when quantity demanded is equal to quantity supplied. This happens in our example when the price for widgets is five. A graphical depiction of the above demand and supply curves for widgets, together with equilibrium price and quantity, are as follows:

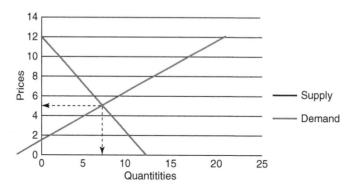

The problem with just plugging in numbers for prices in order to see where quantity demanded is equal to quantity supplied is that it could take a very long time to figure out a solution. For example, if the equilibrium price turned out to be 256 it might take an inordinate amount of time to get to this point just by plugging in numbers (and that's if the number happens to be a whole number). A much easier and accurate way of solving for equilibrium price and quantity is to use algebra.

Solving the Supply and Demand Problem Using Algebra

Let's go back to our supply and demand equations for widgets:

$$Q_D = 12 - 1P$$
$$Q_S = -3 + 2P$$

We know that in equilibrium, quantity demanded is equal to quantity supplied. Knowing this we can set the right hand side terms of each equation equal to each other and we can solve for the equilibrium price.

Step 1: Solving for the Equilibrium Price:

$$Q_D = Q_S$$
$$12 - 1P = -3 + 2P$$
$$12 - 3P = -3$$
$$-3P = -15$$
$$P = \$5$$

So the equilibrium price for widgets is $5.

Once we have the equilibrium price we can solve for equilibrium quantities by substituting the equilibrium price (i.e., $5 in this case) back into either the demand equation or the supply equation.

Step 2: Solving for the Equilibrium Quantity:

Let's plug the equilibrium price into the demand equation.

$$Q_D = 12 - 1P \rightarrow \qquad\qquad Q_D = 12 - 1(5) \rightarrow Q_D = 12 - 5 = 7$$

So our equilibrium quantity is 7 units of widgets.

Step 3: Checking Your Answer:

You can check your answer by simply plugging the equilibrium price into the supply equation. If we get the same answer that we got when we substituted the equilibrium price into the demand equation we would know that our answers are correct. Let's give it a try.

$$Q_S = -3 + 2P \rightarrow Q_S = -3 + 2\,(5) \rightarrow Q_S = -3 + 10 = 7$$

The equilibrium quantity is indeed 7 units of widgets and we have checked our answers. If the results for the demand and supply equations had been different that would have prompted us to redo the problem and to check our math.[2]

Shortages and Surpluses Using Algebra

We can also use algebra to inform us about shortages and surpluses. For example, given our supply and demand equations for widgets and the fact that the equilibrium price was $5, what would the state of the market be in if we observed a market price of $3 for widgets? Well, we know that any price below the equilibrium price would always result in the market being in shortage (i.e., $Q_D > Q_S$). To determine how much the shortage is, we can just plug in $3 for P in both the demand and supply equations.

Quantity demanded: P = $3:	*Quantity supplied: P = $3:*
$Q_D = 12 - 1P$	$Q_S = -3 + 2P$
$Q_D = 12 - 1(3)$	$Q_S = -3 + 2(3)$
$Q_D = 9$	$Q_S = 3$

So when the price is $3, quantity demanded is 9 units of widgets and quantity supplied is 3 units of widgets. Quantity demanded exceeds quantity supplied. This result verifies that the market is indeed in shortage when the price is $3. However, we now also know exactly

---

[2] In this case, we started off by plugging in the equilibrium price into the demand equation and we verified our result by plugging in the equilibrium price into the supply equation. We could have started with the supply equation and verified our answer with the demand equation. The order doesn't matter.

how much the shortage is. The shortage is 6 units of widgets, the difference between quantity demanded at a price of $3 and quantity supplied at a price of $3 (i.e., $9 - 3 = 6$).[3]

If on the other hand, we observed a market price for widgets of $8 we would know that the market is in surplus because this price is above the equilibrium price of $5 for widgets. We can determine with preciseness how much the surplus is by plugging in $8 for P in both the demand and supply equations.

Quantity demanded: $P = \$8$:	$Q_D = 12 - 1P$ $Q_D = 12 - 1(8)$ $Q_D = 4$
Quantity supplied: $P = \$8$:	$Q_S = -3 + 2P$ $Q_S = -3 + 2(8)$ $Q_S = 13$

When the price is $8 quantity demanded is 4 units and quantity supplied is 13 units. In this case quantity supplied is greater than quantity demanded (i.e., $Q_S > Q_D$) and this confirms that the market is in surplus. The surplus is 9 units of widgets (i.e., $13 - 4 = 9$).[4]

PROBLEMS

1. Given the following two equations;

$$\text{i. } Q\_ = 155 - 20P$$
$$\text{ii. } Q\_ = -25 + 25P$$

   a. Which of the above equations represents the supply curve? Why?
   b. Which of the above equations represents the demand curve? Why?
   c. Calculate equilibrium price and quantities.

2. Given the following two equations;

$$\text{i. } Q\_ = -25 + 25P$$
$$\text{ii. } Q\_ = 200 - 20P$$

   a. Which of the above equations represents the supply curve? Why?
   b. Which of the above equations represents the demand curve? Why?
   c. Calculate equilibrium price and quantities.

[3] These numbers check with those in Table A2.3.
[4] These numbers check with those in Table A2.3.

3. Let's say that the demand equation for peaches is $Q_D = 60 - 2P$ and that the supply equation for peaches is $Q_S = 20 + 3P$.

    a. What is the equilibrium price?

    b. What are equilibrium quantities?

    c. If the price in the above market is $10 would the market be in equilibrium, surplus, or shortage? If it is in surplus or shortage, how much would the surplus or shortage be?

    d. If the price in the above market is $5 would the market be in equilibrium, surplus, or shortage? If it is in surplus or shortage, how much would the surplus or shortage be?

3

Gross Domestic Product (GDP): A Measure of Economic Output

W hen you hear that "the United States has the world's largest economy," what do you think this means? Conversely, when you are told that India and China have economies that rank among the fastest growing, how do we come to this conclusion? In order to answer these questions, we need some way of measuring the size of an economy. In this chapter, we explore Gross Domestic Product, which is commonly referred to as just GDP. It is the standard tool that we use to measure economic output and economic growth. We also briefly discuss how GDP statistics are used to measure the rate of economic growth. We explore the role of changes in prices of goods and services in measuring a country's GDP.

LEARNING GOALS

➤ Define and understand Gross Domestic Product.
➤ Recognize the limitations of GDP.
➤ Be able to measure GDP using the expenditure approach.
➤ Understand the difference between
  ▪ GDP and per capita GDP.
  ▪ Real GDP and nominal GDP.
➤ Calculate the GDP deflator.
➤ Measure economic growth.

GROSS DOMESTIC PRODUCT

Gross Domestic Product (GDP) is a measure of a country's output of goods and services. More specifically, **Gross Domestic Product (GDP)** is defined as the *market value* of all *final goods and services produced within a country in a given time period.* Let's take a closer look at the components of this definition one at a time.

Market value: Let's assume that our hypothetical economy produces just two goods—apples and oranges. If we know that our economy produced 10 apples and 20 oranges in the course of a year, what is the total size of our economy? In actuality, the total size of our economy is 10 apples and 20 oranges. That's what we produced in a year. However, to state the size of the economy in this manner is quite awkward even for a two-good economy. Imagine what it would be like for a 10-good economy or, for that matter, an economy like that of the United States, which produces millions of different goods and services each year. In order to add up apples and oranges we must first multiply the quantity of apples and oranges by their respective market prices in order to obtain their market values. If apples sell for $1 apiece and oranges sell for $0.50 apiece, then the market value of apples is $10 (i.e., 10 × $1) and the market value of oranges is also $10 (i.e., 20 × $0.50). We can now add the market values for apples and oranges together and we can conclude that we have a $20 economy. Table 3.1 tabulates the information in this example.

Final goods and services: A final good is an item that is bought by its final or end user. What ultimately is counted in GDP really does depend on the end use. Consider the following question: When KFC buys chicken from a farmer and you buy cooked chicken from KFC, how should these transactions be recorded in the country's GDP calculation? You are the end user or consumer of the chicken because you bought a meal at a KFC restaurant. Therefore, only the value of your purchase from KFC should be included in GDP because you are the end user. KFC's chicken purchases are further processed (cooked) and resold to you, the end user. KFC's chicken purchases are known as **intermediate goods**. An intermediate good is one that is used in the production of a final good. Intermediate goods are inputs in the production of final goods. The value of intermediate goods are not included in GDP. Only the value of the final good is included in GDP.

Continuing with the KFC example above, how would your answer change if instead of you purchasing a chicken meal from KFC you bought uncooked chicken from a supermarket? It

Table 3.1   **GDP of a Two-Good Hypothetical Economy**

Goods Produced	Quantities Produced (Q)	Prices (P)	Market Value (P × Q)
Apples	10	$1.00	$10.00
Oranges	20	$0.50	$10.00
Total Economy			**$20.00**

wouldn't change. You are still the end user. Why should we care to count only final goods and services? Imagine if KFC purchases of chicken were included in GDP. In this case, we would be double counting the value of the chicken and total GDP would be overstated. Chicken purchased by KFC is considered an intermediate good because KFC is not the end user. The chicken you buy from KFC in the form of a meal is the same chicken KFC bought from the poultry farmer. Including the value of the chicken both as a KFC purchase and as a meal would be counting the value of the chicken twice. This is what is meant by double counting. The following example helps to illuminate this point.

Let's say the fried chicken industry is composed of three basic stages: the chicken egg producers, the chicken raisers and processors (e.g., Perdue Chicken Farms), and the final processor and retailer (i.e., KFC). Since chicken egg producers are the first stage of production, we assume that they are starting from scratch. They have to provide housing, feed, and drink to their chickens to encourage them to lay eggs. The cost of doing this is included in the sale price of their product. In this case, it is 10 cents per egg. This sale price becomes the cost of goods to Perdue Chicken Farms, which hatch, raise, and process the chickens. The cost of the additional work provided by Perdue Chicken Farms is included in the sale price. In our example, Perdue Chicken Farms sells the semi-processed chickens for $2.00 each. This $2.00 per chicken becomes the cost of goods to KFC. KFC further processes the chicken and sells it to the public for the equivalent of $5.00 per chicken.

How much should the transaction in Table 3.2 add to GDP? If you answered $7.10, the sum of all the sales, think again. You would be double counting the cost of goods that are included in the sale price. The correct answer is $5.00, which is the sale price to the final user.

An alternative approach to arriving at the correct GDP (avoiding double-counting) is to add up the *value added* at each stage of production. **Value added** is given by the sale price minus the cost of intermediate goods. In the first stage (i.e., Chicken Egg Producers) 10 cents ($0.10 − $0.0) was added.[1] In the second stage, Perdue Chicken Farms added $1.90 ($2.00 − $0.10). KFC added value of $3.00 ($5.00 − $2.00) in the third stage. Summing up the value added at various production stages yields $5.00. Therefore, all these transactions together

Table 3.2 Calculating GDP Using the Sale Price to the End User

Stage	Cost of Goods	Sale Price
I. Chicken Egg	0	$0.10
II. Purdue Chicken Farms	$0.10	$2.00
III. KFC	$2.00	$5.00
Totals	$2.10	$7.10

[1] Recall that we assumed the chicken egg producers start from scratch—zero cost of intermediate goods.

Table 3.3   **The Value-Added Approach**

Stage	Cost of Goods	Sale	Value Added
I. Chicken Egg	0	$0.10	$0.10
II. Purdue Chicken Farms	$0.10	$2.00	$1.90
III. KFC	$2.00	$5.00	$3.00
Totals	$2.10	$7.10	$5.00

add $5.00 to GDP. Notice that we arrive at the same figure when we subtract the total cost of intermediate goods ($2.10) from total sales ($7.10) (see Table 3.3).

Goods produced within a country: The "Domestic (D)" in "Gross Domestic Product" is there for a reason. It is there to underscore the fact that only final goods and services that are produced *within a country* count as part of that country's GDP. So the output of the Japanese-owned Toyota Plant in Kentucky is part of the U.S. GDP, while the output of the American-owned General Motors Plant in South Africa is not part of U.S. GDP. Conversely, the output of the Japanese-owned Toyota Plant in Kentucky would not be included in Japan's GDP, but the output of the American-owned General Motors Plant in South Africa would be included in South Africa's GDP.

GDP versus GNP: For a long time the United States used a measure of national output called Gross National Product (GNP). Gross National Product measures the value of final goods and services produced by nationals (citizens) of a country and their resources. In the case of the output of the Toyota Plant in Kentucky, that would not be a part of U.S. GNP. However, the output of General Motors Plant in South Africa would be a part of U.S. GNP.[2]

---

[2] Technically, the entire output of GM in South Africa would NOT be included in U.S. GNP. Essentially, GNP measures the production of a country's resources (broadly defined to include its people). However, when GM produces in South Africa, it uses South Africa's resources (land, labor, etc.) as well as American resources (capital, design engineers, etc.). Only the contribution of American resources to GM production in South Africa should be added to U.S. GNP.

This requires separating GM production in South Africa into two distinct parts—contribution by U.S. resources and contribution by South Africa's resources.

A practical way to do this is to consider incomes earned by owners of American resources in South Africa. This would include GM profits from its operations in South Africa and salaries of GM American employees based in South Africa. This is why GNP is sometimes referred to as Gross National Income (GNI).

So to move from GDP to GNP, one needs to add earnings of a country's resources abroad and subtract payments to domestic-based foreign resources. In other words, adding the country's Net Factor Income (NFI) to GDP yields GNP.

Goods produced within a given time period: It's important to keep in mind that GDP measures the value of national output over a given time period. The period most often used is a year. Since GDP is measured over a period of time, it is a *flow* variable. On the other hand, national wealth—a measure of the total sum value of a nation's monetary assets minus liabilities at one point in time—is a *stock* concept. So GDP is to your income (e.g., salary per year) as national wealth is to your net worth.

So there you have it. GDP is the *market value* of *all final goods and services* produced *within a country* within *a given time period.* It seems simple enough. However, there are some cautions one needs to be aware of in dealing with GDP.

- First, GDP is concerned only with new or current production. Old output is not counted in current year's GDP because it was already counted back at the time it was produced. In other words, GDP ignores all transactions in which money or goods change hands but in which no new goods and/or services are produced. For example, if you go out today and buy a 2005 Ford Explorer from your cousin for $20,000, should this transaction impact this year's GDP? It should not impact it at all. Nothing has been produced this year. What changes if you buy this car from a used car dealership? In this case, the value-added by the dealership should be included in current year GDP. The value-added in this case is the difference between the amount paid by the dealership to the previous owner and the price you pay to the dealership for the car. The value added captures the value of the dealership's service as an intermediary between you (the new owner) and the previous owner of the car. Recall that GDP measures the market value of both goods (tangibles) and services (intangibles).
- Sales of stocks and bonds are not counted in a country's GDP. Although we commonly refer to stocks and bonds as investment or financial assets, their values are not included in GDP. Why? Because they are merely a transfer of funds. When an individual buys shares in a company, she is merely buying partial ownership of the company. No production of a good or service has taken place and therefore, nothing is added to GDP. Similarly, a purchase of a corporate bonds simply means that you are lending money to the corporation that issued (or sold) the bond. No new production has taken place, and therefore, no addition to the country's GDP is made. However, if one bought or sold stocks through a stock broker, the commission paid to the broker contributed to the country's GDP to reflect the services provided by the broker.
- Since GDP is only concerned with the market value of goods and services, goods and services not sold in the formal marketplace are not included in GDP. As a result, the value of services such as cutting your own grass, doing your own tax returns, or the work of house spouses do not get counted in GDP. This can make international GDP comparisons problematic. This is particularly true if one is comparing GDP of developed nations with that of developing nations. For example, in the United States, shelter, clothing, and food are typically bought in markets. However, in many developing nations, shelter, clothing, and food are self-produced by a large segment of the population. As a consequence, GDP generally understates national production in lesser developed countries.
- Not all market activity is included in GDP. For instance, the revenues from criminal enterprises, unreported tips, and unreported yard sale revenues are all a part of the underground economy and, as such, are not included in GDP.

■ GDP may not be a very good measure of economic well-being of individuals in a country. GDP omits factors in the quality of life including leisure, crime, and the quality of the environment. For instance, leisure, no doubt adds to an individual's quality of life. However, little is added to GDP regarding many leisure activities such as reading a book, watching TV, or playing with a sibling. If crime levels went down, society would be better off, but a decrease in crime is not an increase in output and is not reflected in GDP. In some instances, additions to GDP can actually reflect decreases in the quality of life for the individual. For example, when we produce more, the level of pollution often increases. This decreases our quality of life. Also, when we have to spend more on personal security, this may indicate that the fear of crime is on the rise. Although GDP increases, this particular kind of spending signifies that our quality of life has diminished.[3]

■ GDP says nothing about income distribution. It is conceivable to experience GDP growth, while at the same time experiencing a more unequal distribution of income and wealth.

Regardless of these shortcomings, GDP is a useful measure of economic activity and well-being. Just ask yourself this question, "Would you rather live in the United States of 200 years ago, when rivers were less polluted and crime rates were probably lower, or in the United States of today?" A higher GDP does help us achieve a good life. Nations with larger GDP generally have better education and healthcare, and the citizens of such countries generally have greater life satisfaction.

Understanding GDP

State whether current GDP increases, decreases, or stays the same when:

1. An individual sells her 2001-built house on her own.
2. An individual sells his 2001-built house through a broker.
3. Government increases Social Security Payments.
4. Stock prices rise by 20%.
5. The United States legalizes marijuana.

Answers:

1. Nothing happens to GDP, nothing has been produced.
2. Only the brokerage fee will be added to current GDP.
3. Nothing happens to GDP, nothing has been produced. This is just a government transfer.
4. Nothing happens to GDP, nothing has been produced.
5. GDP increases. The marijuana business is now a part of the formal economy.

---

[3] Forty years ago, there was very little need for home security systems, car alarms, or even airport metal detectors. Security is now a billion-dollar-a-year industry.

Measuring GDP

So how do we measure GDP? One method is the expenditure approach.[4] The expenditure approach involves adding up the values of all final goods. It can be expressed by the formula:

$$GDP = C + I + G + (X - M) \tag{3.1}$$

where **C** is personal consumption or consumer spending, **I** is business investment (business spending), **G** is government spending, and **X − M** is exports minus import (i.e., net export spending). Consumer spending (**C**) is by far the largest component of U.S. GDP, accounting for roughly 70% of national output. In 2015, GDP in the United States amounted to $17.9 trillion with consumer spending accounting for about $12.3 trillion of this total (see Table 3.4). If you look closely at the table, you will notice that there was a drop in GDP in 2009. What caused this drop? If you answered "the recession," you are correct! A **recession**

Table 3.4   **Components of GDP (in Billion $)**

Stage	2008	2009	2010	2011	2012	2013	2014	2015
Gross Domestic Product (GDP) of which	14,719	14,419	14,964	15,518	16,156	16,663	17,348	17,943
Personal consumption expenditures (C)	10,014	9,847	10,202	10,689	11,051	11,392	11,866	12,269
Investment (I)	2,425	1,878	2,101	2,240	2,512	2,665	2,860	3,021
Government expenditures (G)	3,003	3,089	3,174	3,169	3,159	3,114	3,152	3,183
Net exports of goods and services (X − M) of which	−723	−395	−513	−580	−566	−508	−530	−530
Exports	1,842	1,588	1,852	2,106	2,198	2,263	2,342	2,253
Imports	2,565	1,983	2,365	2,686	2,764	2,772	2,872	2,783

Source: Bureau of Economic Analysis, U.S. Department of Commerce

---

[4] The other is called the income approach. The income approach to measuring GDP is approximately equal to the expenditure approach. Money spent on domestically produced goods and services generate an equal amount of income to households in the form of wages, interest payments, rent, and profit.

represents a slowdown in economic activity, and that is exactly what we experienced in 2009. Upon closer inspection, you will also notice that the slowdown was most severe in investment spending. Investment spending by businesses in the United States dropped by over $500 billion between 2008 and 2009, or by nearly 25%. Although investment has recovered it took more than three years to do so.

The bracketed term, net exports $(X - M)$, in equation (3.1) has consistently been negative. In other words, we have been running a trade deficit (i.e., imports greater than exports). It's important to keep in mind that since GDP is ultimately concerned with how much we produce, not consume, it's appropriate that we subtract imports since a part of consumption (C) and investment (I) is spent on foreign goods. If we did not do so, we would be overstating GDP.

INTERNATIONAL COMPARISON OF GDP

How does the U.S. economy stack up against the rest of the world? According to the World Bank's *World Development Indicators*, the United States is by far the largest economy in the world, accounting for more than a fifth of world output. Its $17.4 trillion GDP in 2014 was larger than that of the next two largest economies combined (i.e., China's $10.4 trillion GDP and Japan's $4.6 trillion GDP).[5]

In fact, the U.S. economy, as measured by GDP, is only 6% smaller than that for the entire 28-country *European Union* (i.e., 2014 GDP of $18.5 trillion) (see Table 3.5). In general, we can conclude that world GDP is highly skewed. Together, the top 10 countries account for roughly 65% of world output. In other words, the top 10 countries account for 1.8 times as much GDP than the rest of the world combined.

GDP PER CAPITA

Economists often use GDP per capita as a measure of economic development and as an indicator of the economic well being of people in different nations[6]. **GDP per capita** is simply the GDP of a nation divided by that nation's population. In other words, it is the average GDP per person. Although this is not a perfect measure of economic well-being, it does provide us with an idea of what life is like for the "hypothetical" average person in

---

[5] Notice that this 2014 GDP figure for the United States as reported by the World Bank is slightly different than that computed by the Bureau of Economic Analysis (see Table 3.4).

[6] In recent years a more comprehensive measure of economic development has been developed by the United Nations. It is known as the *Human Development Index* or simply as HDI. (See Textbox on *"The Human Development Index: An Alternative Measure of Economic Development and Economic Well-Being"*)

Table 3.5   **International Comparisons, 2014 GDP**

Rank	Country	GDP (in Billion $)	Percentage Share of World
1	United States	$17,419	22.4%
2	China	10,354	13.3
3	Japan	4,601	5.9
4	Germany	3,868	5.0
5	United Kingdom	2,988	3.8
6	France	2,829	3.6
7	Brazil	2,346	3.0
8	Italy	2,141	2.8
9	India	2,048	2.6
10	Russian Federation	1,860	2.4
	Share of Top 10	50,458	64.8
	Rest of World Share	27,387	35.2
	World	77,845	100.0
	European Union	18,514	23.8

Source: World Development Indicators 2014, the *World Bank*–Current Dollars

a particular nation.[7] As can be seen in Table 3.6, GDP per capita varies widely around the world. In 2014, the country with the highest per capita GDP, Luxemburg, had a GDP per capita 264 times the GDP per capita of the Democratic Republic of the Congo (DRC), one of the world's poorest countries. Put differently, while the average person in the DRC survives on $1.20 a day, the typical citizen of Luxembourg lives on roughly $320 per day. In fact, Luxembourg had more than twice the per capita GDP of the United States and 15 times the per capita GDP of China, the two largest economies in terms of overall GDP.

---

[7] For instance, GDP per capita says nothing about income distribution, and so using this measure as an indicator of economic well-being could be misleading in some instances. As an example, if Bill Gates, Oprah Winfrey, and Warren Buffett walked into our classroom, on average we would all be billionaires. Clearly, there is a big difference between our economic well-being and that of the three billionaires.

Table 3.6   **2014 Per Capita GDP for Selected Countries**

Country	Per Capita GDP
Luxembourg	$116,613
Norway	97,300
Qatar	96,732
Australia	61,980
Sweden	58,899
United States	54,629
Canada	50,231
Germany	47,774
United Kingdom	46,297
Japan	36,194
Korea, Rep.	27,970
Equatorial Guinea	18,918
Russian Federation	12,736
Brazil	11,727
Mexico	10,326
China	7,590
South Africa	6,484
Nigeria	3,203
India	1,582
Congo, Dem. Rep.	442

Source: World Development Indicators 2011, the *World Bank–*
Current Dollars

THE HUMAN DEVELOPMENT INDEX

An Alternative Measure of Economic Well-Being

The *Human Development Index* or *HDI* is a widely accepted measure of economic well-being. It is deemed a better indicator of economic development than is GDP per capita (i.e., per capita income) because it is a more comprehensive gauge. *HDI* is a composite index developed by the *United Nations*, which takes into account measures of a country's population life expectancy and educational attainment levels, in addition to per capita income. The *HDI score* ranges from zero to one. The closer the *HDI score* is to one the higher is the level of development. For example, Norway ranks number one out of 188 countries in terms of development with a *HDI score* of .944 (see table below). In 2014, life expectancy in Norway at birth was 81.6 years, the mean years of schooling was 12.8 years, and per capita income was $64,992. In contrast, life expectancy in Niger—the least developed country with a *HDI score* of .348—is 61.4 years, the means years of schooling is just 1.5 years, and per capita income is a paltry $908.

Human Development Index & Rank (Out of 188)

	Top 10			Selected Others	
Rank	Country	HDI	Rank	Country	HDI
1	Norway	.944	14	United Kingdom	.907
2	Australia	.935	22	France	.888
3	Switzerland	.930	50	Russia	.798
4	Denmark	.923	74	Mexico	.756
5	Netherlands	.922	75	Brazil	.755
6	Germany	.916	90	China	.727
7	Ireland	.916	106	Botswana	.698
8	United States	.915	116	South Africa	.666
9	Canada	.913	130	India	.609
10	New Zealand	.912	188	Niger	.348

Source: United Nations 2015 Human Development Report

REAL VERSUS NOMINAL GDP

Earlier in this chapter, we mentioned the use of market values in order to aggregate the millions of disparate products and services that an economy produces. In other words, the products of each final good produced and its respective market price are added up to yield GDP. This process of deriving GDP can pose some challenges when we attempt to compare national economic output across time. For example, if GDP grew from $10 trillion in 2005 to $11 trillion in 2006, what might account for this increase in GDP? There are three plausible explanations for the rise in total spending/output between 2005 and 2006. First, output of goods and services could have actually grown. Second, goods and services could be selling at higher prices. Third, a combination of higher prices and higher output could be responsible for the change. What we are really interested in, however, is how economic output has changed from year to year, not prices. So how do we go about figuring this out? The following example should provide some insights.

Example

Let's say we have a simple two-good hypothetical economy that produces hotdogs and hamburgers. In Table 3.7, we have listed the respective prices and quantities of hotdogs and hamburgers produced from 2009 to 2011.

In order to calculate GDP for each year, we multiply the prices by the quantities to derive the market values and then we add up the market values for hotdogs and hamburgers to yield GDP for each year. For instance, GDP for 2009 is calculated in the following manner. We multiply the price of a hotdog in 2009 ($1) by the quantity of hotdogs produced that year (100) to get a market value for hamburgers in 2009 of $100. We then multiply the price of a hamburger in 2009 ($2) by the quantity of hamburgers produced that year (50) to get a market value for hamburgers in 2009 of $100. Adding the two market values together yields a GDP of $200 in 2009. The corresponding GDP figures for 2010 and 2011 are $600 and $1,200, respectively. (see Table 3.8)

When GDP is calculated using *current year prices,* it is called **nominal GDP**. GDP for 2009, 2010, and 2011 in the above example was calculated using the prevailing current prices in the respective years. It is clear that part of the growth in nominal GDP over these years can be attributed to rising prices, while another part of the growth is due to increases in real output. Keep in mind that it is the growth in real output that we are really interested in. So what do we do to arrive at the growth in real production? We need to control for price changes. One way that economists control for price changes is to pick the prevailing set of prices in a particular year. The chosen set of prices is applied in the valuation of output of all the years in question. In other words, we are using **constant prices**. GDP derived in this manner is called **real GDP**. The year for which the set of prices are chosen is called the **base year** and the prices from this year are called **base year prices**.

Table 3.7   Production and Prices in a Hypothetical Two-Goods Economy

Year	Price of Hotdogs	Quantity of Hotdogs	Price of Hamburgers	Quantity of Hamburgers
2009	$1	100	$2	50
2010	$2	150	$3	100
2011	$3	200	$4	150

Table 3.8   Nominal GDP for a Hypothetical Two-Good Economy

Year	Market Value of Hotdogs	Market Value of Hamburgers	GDP
2009	$100	$100	$200
2010	$300	$300	$600
2011	$600	$600	$1,200

Continuing with our example in Table 3.7, let's use 2009 as the base year. In 2009 the price of a hotdog was $1 and the price of a hamburger was $2. We use these prices to replace those for 2010 and 2011 (see Table 3.9a). Using these prices to calculate new markets values we are able to derive real GDP figures of $200, $350, and $500 for 2009, 2010, and 2011, respectively (see Table 3.9b). We notice that only in the case of 2009 is real GDP equal to its nominal GDP (see Table 3.9c). Since 2009 is the base year, the new calculations for its market values and real GDP is not any different from before. This is an important discovery. *Nominal GDP is always equal to real GDP for the base year.*

Let's take a closer look at the comparison between the calculations for nominal and real GDP for the period 2009–2011. This is presented in Table 3.9c. Growth in nominal GDP between 2009 and 2011 turns out to be 500%. i.e., $\left(\frac{1200-200}{200} \times 100\right)$

On the other hand, growth in real GDP over this same time period amounts to 150% $\left(\text{i.e.,}\frac{500-200}{200} \times 100\right)$. Growth in real GDP is much smaller than growth in nominal GDP for the same time period because real GDP controls for changes in prices during the period under consideration. The dramatic price run-up that inflates nominal GDP is eliminated in the calculation of real GDP. Changes in real GDP constitute an accurate measure of what happens to economic output over time. We refer to changes in real GDP over time as **economic growth.**

Table 3.9a   Value of Production in Base-Year Prices

Year	Price of Hotdogs	Quantity of Hotdogs	Price of Hamburgers	Quantity of Hamburgers
2009	$1	100	$2	50
2010	$1	150	$2	100
2011	$1	200	$2	150

Table 3.9b   Real GDP for a Hypothetical Two-Good Economy

Year	Market Value of Hotdogs	Market Value of Hamburgers	RGDP
2009	$100	$100	$200
2010	$150	$200	$350
2011	$200	$300	$500

Table 3.9c   Nominal GDP versus Real GDP

Year	NGDP	RGDP
2009	$200	$200
2010	$600	$350
2011	$1200	$500

THE GDP DEFLATOR

Recall that the difference between growth in nominal GDP and growth in real GDP is the change in prices over the period under consideration. Nominal GDP does not control for changes in prices, while real GDP does. Therefore, increases in prices (inflation) would inflate nominal GDP relative to real GDP. This subsection presents one way to "deflate" nominal GDP to arrive at real GDP. The statistic used to deflate nominal GDP to account for price changes is the **GDP deflator**.

The GDP deflator is a price index that measures changes in the general price level. Therefore,

$$Real\ GDP = \frac{Nominal\ GDP}{GDP\ Deflator} \times 100$$

Equivalently,

$$GDP\ Deflator = \left(\frac{Nominal\ GDP}{Real\ GDP}\right) \times 100$$

From Table 3.9c, let's calculate the GDP deflator for 2009, 2010, and 2011.

For 2009:

$$GDP\ Deflator = (200/200) \times 100$$
$$= 1 \times 100$$
$$= 100$$

For 2010:

$$GDP\ Deflator = (600/350) \times 100$$
$$= 1.71 \times 100$$
$$= 171$$

For 2011:

$$GDP\ Deflator = (1200/500) \times 100$$
$$= 2.4 \times 100$$
$$= 240$$

Notice that the GDP deflator for 2009 is equal to 100. This results from the fact that 2009 prices are the base year prices. As a consequence, nominal GDP is equal to real GDP for that year. The base year will always have a GDP deflator of 100.

SUMMARY

- GDP is the market value of all final goods and services produced within a country in a given time period. We use market values in order to add up "apples and oranges." We use final goods in order to avoid double counting.

■ GDP is concerned only with new or current production. Old output is not counted in current GDP because it was already counted back at the time it was produced. GDP is only concerned with market value; goods and services not sold in the formal marketplace are not included in GDP. Not all market activity is included in GDP. The revenues from criminal enterprises, unreported tips, and unreported yard sale revenues are all a part of the underground economy and, as such, are not included in GDP.

■ The expenditure approach to measuring GDP can be expressed as

$$GDP = C + I + G + (X - M)$$

where **C** is personal consumption or consumer spending, **I** is investment (business spending), **G** is government spending, and **(X − M)** is exports minus import (net exports). Consumer spending **(C)** is by far the most important component of GDP in the United States, accounting for roughly 70% of national output.

■ Nominal GDP is calculated using current year prices and real GDP is calculated using constant prices. The year in which the prices are picked to be held constant is called the *base year,* and the corresponding prices are called base year prices. In the base year nominal and real GDP are equal. Positive changes in real GDP represent economic growth.

■ The GDP deflator is a price index used to measure changes in the general price level.

KEY TERMS

Gross Domestic Product (GDP)	Constant prices
Intermediate good	Base year
Value added	Base year prices
Recession	Economic growth
GDP per capita	Real GDP
Nominal GDP	GDP deflator

PROBLEMS

1. State whether GDP increases, decreases, or stays the same when:
    a. An individual sells her house on her own.
    b. An individual sells his house through a broker.
    c. Government increases Social Security payments.
    d. Government decreases Social Security payments.
    e. All households with kids decide to have one spouse stay home and take care of the kids.
    f. Stock prices rise by 20%.
    g. An unemployed worker gets a job and starts working
    h. The United States legalizes the sale and use of marijuana.

2. KFC purchases $1,000 worth of chicken from *Tyson Foods*. KFC then bakes this chicken and sells it to the public for a total of $1,500. Taking these transactions together, what is the effect on GDP?

3. Use the information in the table above to rank the 10 countries according to their per capita GDP.

Country Name	Nominal GDP in 2014	Population in 2014
United States	17,419,000,000,000	318,857,056
China	10,254,831,729,340	1,364,270,000
India	2,048,517,438,874	1,295,291,543
Canada	1,785,386,649,602	35,540,419
Mexico	1,294,689,733,233	125,385,833
Nigeria	568,508,262,378	177,475,986
South Africa	350,085,020,840	54,001,953
Qatar	210,109,065,934	2,172,065
Equatorial Guinea	15,529,729,677	820,885
Madagascar	10,593,147,381	23,571,713

4. Based on the following table answer the following questions.

	Prices and Quantities			
Year	Price of Hotdogs	Quantity of Hotdogs	Price of Hamburgers	Quantity of Hamburgers
2009	$1.00	50	$2.00	25
2010	$1.50	60	$3.00	50
2011	$2.50	80	$4.00	75

a. Calculate nominal GDP for 2009, 2010, and 2011.
b. How much did nominal GDP grow between 2009 and 2011?

5. Referring to the table in problem 4 and using 2010 as the base year, do the following:

a. Calculate real GDP for 2009, 2010, and 2011.
b. How much did real GDP grow between 2009 and 2011?

6. What explains the difference between your answers for 4b and 5b?

7. Again, referring to the table in problem 4 and using 2010 as the base year, answer the following questions:

   a. Calculate the GDP deflators for 2009, 2010, and 2011.
   b. What do you notice about the GDP deflator for 2010?

8. Based on the following table answer the following questions.

	2009	2010	2011	2012
Nominal Gross Domestic Product (NGDP)	?	13,398	14,077	14,443
Real Gross Domestic Product (RGDP)	12,638	12,976	13,255	?
Gross Domestic Product deflator (GDPD)	100	?	106.2	108.5

[Round to the nearest tenth]

a. Nominal GDP$_{2009}$ =
b. GDP Deflator$_{2010}$ =
c. Real GDP$_{2012}$ =
d. How much did the economy actually grow in percentage terms between 2009 and 2011?

4

Measuring the Cost of Living: Inflation

Why might it not be a good idea to put your money under your mattress for prolonged periods of time? Why is a $1,000-a-month fixed mortgage payment more of a financial burden in the first year of a 30-year mortgage loan than it is in the thirtieth year? Why might the burden of long-term public debt be overstated? Inflation is at least part of the answer to each of these questions. **Inflation** is defined as a persistent increase in the overall price level. Inflation infers that prices are rising in general. In the real world, even in periods of inflation, prices of some goods and services might actually be falling or stagnate; however, if prices are rising for most goods and services, in general we are experiencing inflation. We measure inflation by looking at a large number of goods and services and calculating the average increase in their prices during some period of time. This chapter provides a brief overview of the measures, cause, and uses of inflation statistics.

LEARNING GOALS

➤ Define and understand inflation.
➤ Understand the Consumer Price Index.
➤ Calculate the rate of inflation.
➤ Investigate the causes of inflation.
➤ Understand the impact of inflation.

MEASURING INFLATION

We use price indexes to measure inflation. A price index is a weighted average of prices of a select basket of goods. For exposition purposes, let us consider a hypothetical example in Table 4.1. Assume that a typical consumer buys the items shown in the Table. That is, these items constitute our basket of goods for purposes of calculating the price index. The amounts in which our typical consumer buys each of the goods are also indicated in the Table. Additionally, the unit price of each item is given for each of the two years (2011 and 2012) under consideration.

Table 4.1   A Hypothetical Price Index Example

	2011			2012		
Item	Quantity	Unit Price	Expenditure	Quantity	Unit Price	Expenditure
Hotdogs	10	$1.00	$10.00	10	$1.50	$20.00
Hamburgers	8	$2.00	$16.00	8	$2.80	$22.40
Movies	4	$10.00	$40.00	4	$12.00	$48.00
Apples (pounds)	6	$2.50	$15.00	6	$2.20	$13.20
Total			$81.00			$103.20

Let us assume that our interest is to calculate the price index in year 2012 using 2011 as the base year. Essentially, the price index compares the price of the basket of goods in the current year (2012) with the price of the same (or similar) basket of goods in the base year (2011). Therefore, the price index in this hypothetical example is given by the ratio of total expenditure on the basket of goods in the current year to the total expenditure on the basket in the base year (normalized by multiplying by 100). Thus,

$$Price\ Index = \frac{Current\ year\ price\ of\ a\ basket\ of\ goods}{Base\ year\ price\ of\ a\ basket\ of\ goods} \times 100$$

From Table 4.1, the price index for 2012 is equal to127.4 [(103.20/81) × 100]. So, what do we make of this number? What exactly does a price index of 127.4 mean? Notice that the basket of goods did not change between 2011 and 2012 and yet the expenditure on the basket increased from $81 to $103.20. This confirms that prices went up. But by how much did the price go up? The price increased by 27.4%. This increase in the price index is a measure of inflation. If the selected goods in the basket are a good representative of what households buy, we can say that the country, city, or region experienced inflation of 27.4% in 2012.

In general, if the price index increases from year to year we say that the economy is experiencing inflation. As we mentioned earlier, the GDP deflator is a price index. It measures the level of prices of all new, domestically produced final goods and services in an economy. Indeed, a year to year increase in the GDP deflator would represent inflation.

The most popular price index, however, is the **Consumer Price Index (CPI)**. The CPI is computed each month by the Bureau of Labor Statistics using a bundle of commodities and services that is meant to represent the "market basket" purchased monthly by the typical urban consumer or household. The CPI "market basket" consists of a number of broad categories of household expenditures including, apparel, education and communication, food and beverages, housing, medical care, recreation, and transportation (see Figure 4.1). Housing is by far the largest component of the market basket, accounting for more than two-fifths of monthly household spending. Transportation and the food and beverages categories account for another third of monthly household expenditures. Altogether, spending on housing, transportation, and food and beverages amounts to almost three-quarters of total monthly expenditures by households. It is important to keep in mind that the CPI is a *weighted* index. The weight that is applied to a category of goods and/or services depends on the share of consumer spending it claims. We weight goods and services that account for a large share of consumer spending more heavily than we do those that account for a small share of consumer spending. If we didn't weight prices for goods and services by their share of consumer spending, we would in essence be weighting the importance of all commodities equally. An index created in this manner would be meaningless. For example, it makes no sense to weight the price changes in regards to bread and automobiles equally since automobiles account for such a large share of consumer spending and bread for so little. If a hypothetical Automobile-Bread Price Index (ABPI) was not "weighted," a 10% increase in the price of automobiles could be completely offset by a 10% decrease in the price of bread, and, as a result, inflation would be nonexistent. Clearly, this hypothetical "unweighted" ABPI does not present consumers with a realistic indication of the general price level that they face. Intuitively, we would surmise that consumers in this example experienced inflation because of the dominance of automobiles in consumer spending habits. The CPI is a weighted price index that provides consumers with a good indication of the general cost of living.

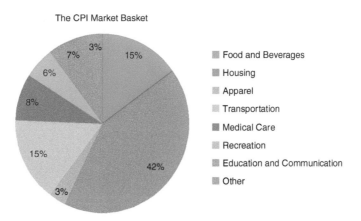

Figure 4.1   The CPI Market Basket

Based on the data provided in Table 4.2, overall inflation as measured by the CPI was negligible in 2015. In 2014, the CPI was 234.8 and in 2015 it was 236.5. This represents a 0.7% increase in the overall price level for 2015. However, when we look at the price trends for the individual components in the market basket, we see a wide variation. For example, while prices for food and beverage, apparel, and recreation changed little in 2015, the housing, medical care, education and communication, and other goods and services experienced significant price increases. At the same time, prices in the transportation category were down 4.2%. (Of course, the dramatic drop in the price of petroleum products no doubt impacted the substantial price decline in the transportation category.) Again, it is important to keep in mind that inflation is not concerned with the price of any one good or service in particular but with the general price level.

As shown in Figure 4.2, inflation has been ever-present in the U.S. economy. There have been periods in which inflation was relatively high. For instance, in the three-year period from 1978 through 1981, inflation averaged 11.7 % annually. On the other hand, there have been periods in which inflation was relatively low. We are currently experiencing one of those periods. From 2005 through 2015 inflation has averaged less than 2.0% a year. Only twice in the past 60 years or so did the CPI fall from one year to the next. When year-to-year CPI falls, we say that the economy is experiencing **deflation**. This usually occurs when the economy is slowing down and experiencing high levels of unemployment. However, not all economic downturns result in deflationary episodes. The most recent period of deflation was in 2009, which saw prices fall four-tenths of one percent from the previous year's price level.

Table 4.2:   Consumer Price Index for All Urban Consumers (1982–1984 = 100)

Expenditure Category	Annual Average 2014	Annual Average 2015	Percent change from 2014 to 2015
All items	234.8	236.5	0.7
Food and beverage	245.6	247.5	0.8
Housing	234.7	239.5	2.0
Apparel	123.9	122.8	−0.9
Transportation	199.8	191.5	−4.2
Medical care	439.7	451.1	2.6
Recreation	114.9	115.6	0.6
Education and communication	137.4	139.4	1.5
Other goods and services	410.6	418.3	1.9

Source: Bureau of Labor Statistics, United States Department of Labor

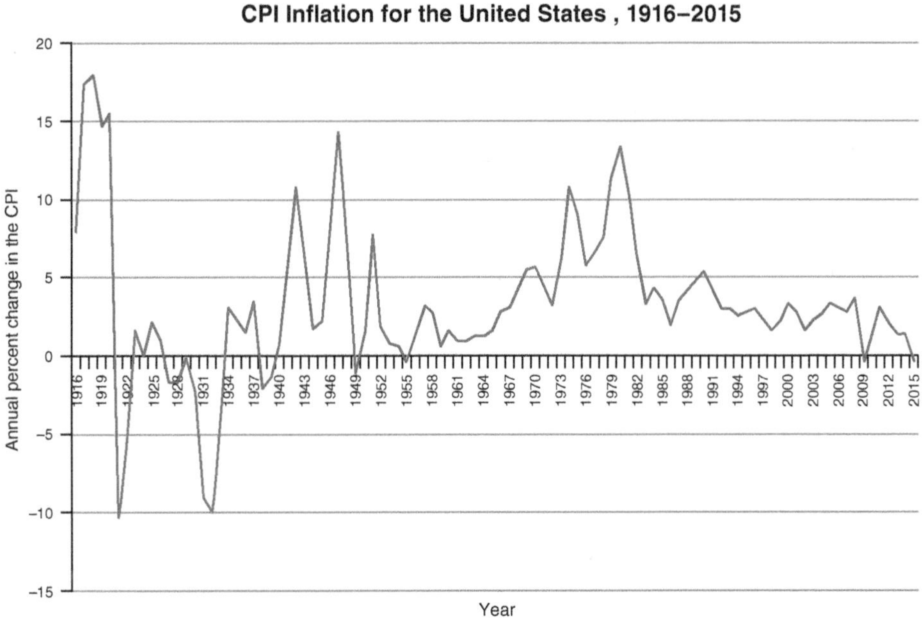

CPI Inflation for the United States , 1916–2015

Figure 4.2   United States CPI Inflation, 1916–2015 (1982–1984 = 100)
Source: By Authors using data from the U.S Bureau of Labor Statistics (BLS)

CALCULATING THE RATE OF INFLATION

The rate of inflation is represented by the year to year percentage increase in the price index. For instance, Table 4.3 below indicates that the CPI in year 2000 was 172.2 and the 2010 CPI was 218.1, inflation between 2000 and 2010 can be calculated as follows:[1]

$$\text{i.e.,} \left(\frac{218.1 - 172.2}{172.2} \right) \times 100 = 26.7\%$$

In other words, prices grew by 26.7% between 2000 and 2010. Another way of looking at this is that prices in general were on average 26.7% higher in 2010 than they were in 2000. If your goal were for your income to maintain its purchasing power over this period, it too would have had to increase by 26.7%. For example, let's say that your mom earned $50,000 in 2000. In order to maintain the same level of purchasing power in 2010 as she had in 2000, she would have be making $63,350 in 2010, which is 26.7 % more than she earned in the year 2000. Another way of determining this is to divide the later year's CPI (i.e., 218.1) by the former year's CPI (i.e., 172.2) and then multiply that result by the original salary of $50,000.

---

[1] Notice that we multiply by 100 in order to obtain the percentage change.

Table 4.3   Calculating the Rate of Inflation

Year	Price Index	Year	Price Index	Year	Price Index	Year	Price Index	Year	Price Index
1970	38.8	1980	82.4	1990	130.7	2000	172.2	2010	218.1
1971	40.5	1981	90.9	1991	136.2	2001	177.1	2011	224.9
1972	41.8	1982	96.5	1992	140.3	2002	179.9	2012	229.6
1973	44.4	1983	100.0	1993	144.5	2003	184.0	2013	233.0
1974	49.3	1984	103.9	1994	148.2	2004	188.9	2014	234.8
1975	53.8	1985	107.6	1995	152.4	2005	195.3	2015	236.5
1976	56.9	1986	109.6	1996	156.9	2006	201.6		
1977	60.6	1987	113.6	1997	160.5	2007	207.3		
1978	65.2	1988	118.3	1998	163.0	2008	215.3		
1979	72.6	1989	124.0	1999	166.6	2009	214.5		

1970–2015 Consumer Price Index for All Urban Consumers (1983 = 100)

So let's say that the starting salary for an accountant was $10,000 in 1975. What would be the equivalent 2015 salary? It would be nearly $44,000. See if you can figure this out.

WHAT CAUSES INFLATION?

Inflation can occur when demand for goods and services outpaces supply. This generally happens during periods of economic expansion. This type of inflation is often referred to as **demand-pull inflation**. Sometimes economists describe such inflation as "Too many dollars chasing too few goods." In the extreme, this type of inflation can occur when the economy is operating at or near full capacity and consumer demand for goods and services continues to increase. One way of thinking about this type of inflation is to imagine what would happen if an economy was producing at its limit (i.e., supply is fixed) and the money supply was increased. This increase in the money supply would lead to an increase in demand; however, since the economy was producing at its limit there would be nowhere for prices to go but up.

Inflation can also result from a large increase in the price of key intermediate products that are used extensively in an economy. When the price of a commodity like steel, oil, or even an input like labor increases, such price increases constitute increases to the cost of production. These higher input costs are then passed along to the final consumers in the form of higher product prices. This type of inflation is referred to as **cost-push inflation**.

The classic example of cost-push inflation is the "oil crisis" of the 1970s. The 10-year period from 1970 to 1980 saw unprecedented runups in the price of crude oil (petroleum) due largely to supply disruptions and political instability in the Middle East, the world's major supplier of crude oil.[2] In 1970, the price of a barrel of oil averaged $3.39, by 1980 it had ballooned to $37.42—a tenfold increase[3]. Products derived from oil are broadly used in many market sectors. Two petroleum-derived products—gasoline and diesel fuel—power our transportation sector. When the price of oil increases, anything that requires gasoline and diesel fuel to transport will be more costly. That means that not only do we pay more for our own personal motor vehicle travel, we also pay more for food that has to be transported to the grocery stores, for new housing where construction materials have to be shipped, for appliances and home furnishings that have to be delivered, and so forth. Keep in mind that gasoline and diesel fuel are only two of the many widely used products that are derived from petroleum. When one considers that others products like jet fuel, asphalt, kerosene, and plastics are also produced from petroleum, one begins to understand the extent of the impact of a dramatic increase in crude oil prices on a modern economy and why inflation results.

Typically, there is an inverse relationship between inflation and unemployment. Generally, when inflation is high, unemployment is low, and when inflation is low, unemployment is high. In the 1970s, we experienced periods of high inflation and high unemployment. This situation is referred to as **stagflation** (**stag**nant economy + in**flation**), and normally it results from cost-push pressures. In the case of the 1970s, the oil supply shocks led to significant price runups for consumers and producers alike. On the consumer side, these price runups led to less overall demand for goods and services. On the producer side, higher prices resulted in higher costs and lower profits for producers. Together these developments resulted in less employment (i.e., higher unemployment).

In the extreme, the uncontrolled printing of money on the part of the government can lead to **hyperinflation**, a very severe form of inflation. In a sense, hyperinflation can be looked upon as a special case of demand-pull inflation. There is wide variation in what rate of inflation is considered to be hyperinflation. Some consider a 20 to 30% a month increase in the price level to be hyperinflation, while others contend that hyperinflation doesn't exist until the inflation rate has hit 50% a month. Nevertheless, hyperinflation represents an extremely high runup in prices and a concurrent rapid and continuous decline in the purchasing power of the local currency. As a result, hyperinflation is generally associated with the immediate exchange of the local currency for goods and/or nonmonetary assets. The world's most

---

[2] The Middle East is the geographic region where Europe, Africa, and Asia meet. It is an unofficial and imprecise term that now generally encompasses the lands around the southern and eastern shores of the Mediterranean Sea—notably Egypt, Jordan, Israel, Lebanon, and Syria—as well as Iran, Iraq, and the countries of the Arabian Peninsula. Afghanistan, Libya, Turkey, and the Sudan are sometimes also included (Merriam-Webster) In the mid-1970s the major oil producers in this region accounted for as much as two-thirds of world crude oil exports. Today, they account for roughly a third.

[3] Even in real terms (i.e., controlling for inflation) oil prices during this period experienced more than a four-fold increase.

recent episode of hyperinflation occurred during 2007–2009 in Zimbabwe. By July 2008, when Zimbabwe's Central Statistical Office released its last inflation Figures for that year, the month-over-month rate had reached 2,600.2%—more than 231 million percent on a year-over-year basis (The Federal Reserve Bank of Dallas 2011). Zimbabwe's largest currency denomination in 2009 was the Z$100 trillion note. By comparison, at independence in 1980 the largest currency denomination was the Z$20 note.

WHY ARE WE CONCERNED WITH INFLATION?

Two concerns that we have with inflation is that it erodes purchasing power and it arbitrarily redistributes real income and wealth. In regards to the *erosion of purchasing power*, when the price level increases, each dollar is worth less. In other words, goods and services cost more, and it takes more dollars to purchase the same amount of goods and services than in the absence of inflation. A good way to think about this is to imagine that you had a nest egg of $10,000. Assume also that you had an aversion to placing your money in financial institutions so you decide to store your $10,000 under your mattress. Let's say you kept this money under your mattress for a year and that during this year the general price level increased by 10%. As a result, a bundle of goods and services that cost $10,000 at the beginning of the

year now costs $11,000. At the beginning of the year, your nest egg would have been able to purchase this bundle, but by year's end, your nest egg was insufficient to purchase the same bundle. Thus, the purchasing power of your $10,000 nest egg has been eroded. In fact, each dollar that you had under your mattress at the beginning of the year is now worth 91 cents,[4] so there is an opportunity cost to holding money during times of inflation. The higher the rate of inflation, the higher is your opportunity cost of holding cash.

As you may have figured out by now, people who live on a fixed income are particularly hard-hit by inflation. The purchasing power of their income is much reduced. The loss of purchasing power during periods of inflation also explains why labor unions always push for cost-of-living adjustments (COLAs) in their contracts. These COLAs protect the purchasing power of union members' income. In essence, COLAs ensure that real incomes remain unchanged by guaranteeing that nominal incomes keep pace with the rate of inflation.

It is important to keep in mind that inflation creates winners and losers. There is an arbitrary **redistribution in real income** and wealth associated with inflation. This redistribution is caused by three influences; the *price effect*, the *income effect*, and the *wealth effect*. The **price effect** results from the fact that when inflation occurs, some prices increase faster than others and, as a result, some people are impacted more than others. For example, if the prices of pharmaceuticals increase faster than prices of other goods, the impact on the elderly will be substantial, but it will matter little for healthier younger people. Conversely, if the price of beef goes up relative to vegetables, beef eaters are affected but vegans are not. In regard to the **income effect**, rising prices for you mean growing income for someone else. For example, during the first quarter of 2012 the price of regular gasoline went from $3.27 a gallon to $3.90 a gallon. While this 63 cents a gallon increase represents growing costs to the average automobile driver, it also represents considerable income gains for gasoline producers and their shareholders.

The **wealth effect** is concerned with the redistribution of income between borrowers and lenders that is caused by inflation. For example, let's assume that you have a 30-year fixed rate mortgage with monthly payments of $1,000. So in the first month you pay $1,000 to the lender and in the 360th month, you make your last payment of $1,000. Clearly, if there has been inflation during this 30-year period, the $1,000 you pay in the 360th month is probably worth only a fraction of the amount you paid in the first month. If inflation is high enough, the amount of principal and interest that you paid over the life of the loan could very well be worth less in real terms than the initial borrowed amount. So the sage advice from Shakespeare's *Hamlet*, "Neither a borrower nor a lender be," is only half correct in this instance. If loan payments are indeed fixed during periods of inflation, it can be beneficial to borrow; however, lenders will be harmed. From a national perspective, the real impact of debt is often overstated because over time a country is paying off its debt with an inflated currency. In this case, inflation is an ally.

---

[4] At the beginning of the year $10,000 could buy $10,000 worth of goods and services and hence, $1 was equal to $1 worth of goods and services. By the end of the year $10,000 can only purchase $10,000 / $11,000 worth of goods and services. So each dollar is now worth 90.9 cents.

SUMMARY

- Inflation means that prices are rising in general, and it occurs when *many* prices increase simultaneously. Technically, even in periods of inflation, prices for some goods and services could actually be falling or stagnant; however, if prices are rising for most goods and services, in general the economy is experiencing inflation.
- We measure inflation by looking at a large number of goods and services and calculating the average increase in their prices during a given period of time. We use price indexes to measure inflation.
- The most popular price index, however, is the *Consumer Price Index* or *CPI*. The CPI is computed each month by the Bureau of Labor Statistics (BLS) using a bundle of commodities and services that is meant to represent the "market basket" purchased monthly by the typical urban consumer.
- Only twice in the past 60 years or so did the CPI fall from one year to the next. When the CPI falls, we say we are experiencing **deflation**. This usually occurs when the economy is slowing down and experiencing high levels of unemployment. However, not all economic downturns result in deflationary episodes.
- Inflation can occur when demand for goods and services outpaces supply. This generally happens during periods of economic expansion. This type of inflation is often referred to as *demand-pull inflation*.
- Inflation can also result from a large increase in the price of a commodity that is used extensively throughout the economy. This type of inflation is referred to as *cost-push inflation*. The classic example of cost-push inflation is the "oil crisis" of the 1970s.
- In the extreme the uncontrolled printing of money on the part of the government can lead to *hyperinflation*. Hyperinflation represents an extremely high runup in prices and a concurrent rapid and continuous decline in the purchasing power of the local currency. As a result, hyperinflation is generally associated with the immediate exchange of the local currency for goods and/or nonmonetary assets.
- Generally, when inflation is high, unemployment is low and vice versa. In the 1970s we experienced periods of high inflation and high unemployment. This development is referred to as *stagflation* and normally results from cost-push pressures.
- Two concerns that we have with inflation is that it erodes purchasing power and it arbitrarily redistributes real income and wealth.

KEY TERMS

Inflation	Stagflation
Consumer Price Index (CPI)	Redistribution in real income
Deflation	Price effect
Demand-pull inflation	Income effect
Cost-push inflation	Wealth effect
Hyperinflation	Deflation

PROBLEMS

1. When the first Ford Mustang was introduced in 1964, the base model V6 sold for about $2,400.

   a. What is the price of a Ford Mustang today?
   b. What might explain the difference between the price in 1964 and today?

2.

   Table 4.3   Calculating the Rate of Inflation

Year	Price Index	Year	Price Index	Year	Price Index	Year	Price Index	Year	Price Index
1970	38.8	1980	82.4	1990	130.7	2000	172.2	2010	218.1
1971	40.5	1981	90.9	1991	136.2	2001	177.1	2011	224.9
1972	41.8	1982	96.5	1992	140.3	2002	179.9	2012	229.6
1973	44.4	1983	100.0	1993	144.5	2003	184.0	2013	233.0
1974	49.3	1984	103.9	1994	148.2	2004	188.9	2014	234.8
1975	53.8	1985	107.6	1995	152.4	2005	195.3	2015	236.5
1976	56.9	1986	109.6	1996	156.9	2006	201.6		
1977	60.6	1987	113.6	1997	160.5	2007	207.3		
1978	65.2	1988	118.3	1998	163.0	2008	215.3		
1979	72.6	1989	124.0	1999	166.6	2009	214.5		

   1970–2015 Consumer Price Index for All Urban Consumers (1983 = 100)

   Based on the price index Table, answer the following questions:

   a. What is the base year?
   b. Which decade 1970–1979, 1980–1989, 1990–1999, or 2000–2009 exhibited the highest rate of inflation?
   c. Based on your year of birth and 2015, what is the rate of inflation? (If you were born before 1970, use 1970 as your birth year.)
   d. If someone was earning $9,860 annually in 1971, how much would she have to earn in 2015 to maintain her purchasing power?

3. Who is hurt during periods of inflation? Who benefits during periods of inflation?
4. Explain the difference between demand-pull and cost-push inflation.

5

The Production Possibilities Frontier and the Rationale for Trade

According to the World Trade Organization, the dollar value of world merchandise trade reached an all-time peak of $18.4 trillion in 2014. This is greater than the entire GDP for the United States. Why do nations trade? Why do large economies, who can produce more of everything, still find it advantageous to trade with small, less productive economies? This chapter introduces one of the classical theories of trade and the associated economic concepts. First, the chapter introduces the concept of production possibilities. Second, we use the countries' production possibilities to illustrate the concept of comparative advantage. Finally, we show that when countries trade based on comparative advantage, they experience gains from such trade.

LEARNING GOALS

➤ Understand the Production Possibilities Frontier (PPF).

➤ Depict economic growth with the PPF.

➤ Understand increasing marginal opportunity cost.

➤ Calculate opportunity cost.

➤ Understand absolute advantage.

➤ Understand comparative advantage.

➤ Recognize gains from trade.

PRODUCTION POSSIBILITIES

In order to investigate why nations engage in trade, we should first introduce an important economic concept—production possibilities. A production possibility refers to a

Table 5.1   Production Possibilities for a
Hypothetical Two-Good Economy

Grapes	Beef
0	50
10	37.5
20	25
30	12.5
40	0

combination of goods and services a country is capable of producing at full employment of its resources and technology. To make the illustration tractable, let us assume a hypothetical economy that produces only two goods—grapes and beef. In this example, given the country's resources and technology, we can determine the different possible combinations of grapes and beef the country could produce. Table 5.1 provides the production possibilities for our hypothetical two-good economy.

In Table 5.1, our hypothetical economy could choose to produce 50 units of beef and no grapes (0 units of grapes; 50 units of beef). Similarly, the other extreme would be producing 40 units of grapes and no beef (40 units of grapes; 0 units of beef). Between these two extremes, there are a multitude of other production possibilities.

The production possibilities in Table 5.1 can be presented graphically by a **Production Possibilities Frontier (PPF)**. It shows the combinations of the two goods that can be produced with available resources and existing technology.

In Figure 5.1, we plot the production possibilities (combinations of grapes and beef) in Table 5.1. The resulting graph is the economy's PPF. We assumed that if we devoted all of our resources to the production of grapes, we could produce 40 units (i.e., no beef is

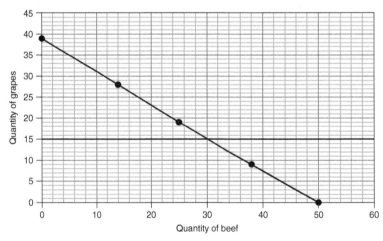

Figure 5.1   The Production Possibilities Frontier (PPF)
for Two-Good Economy

produced). This production possibility is represented by point A in Figure 5.1. On the other hand, if we devoted all of our resources to the production of beef, we could produce 50 units (i.e., no grapes are produced). This production possibility is represented by point E in Figure 5.1. Out of the multitude of other production possibilities in Figure 5.1, we labeled only a few of them—represented by points B, C, and D. Unlike production possibilities represented by points A and E, production possibilities represented by points B, C, and D (as well as any production possibilities between points A and E) involve the production of both grapes and beef.

The PPF in Figure 5.1 indicates the maximum amount of grapes and beef, alone or in combination, that our hypothetical economy can produce given our existing resources and the current state of our technology. At point A we are producing only grapes, while at point E, we are producing only beef. However, if the economy devoted half of the resources to grape production and half to beef production, our economy would be at point C on the PPF and we would be producing 20 units of grapes and 25 units of beef. Our hypothetical economy in Figure 5.1 could also produce any other combination of grapes and beef along the PPF.

OPPORTUNITY COST AND THE PPF

The PPF illustrates the tradeoffs in production facing our two-good economy. The PPF illustrates an inverse relationship between the amount of one good (say, grapes) that can be produced in an economy and the amount of the other good (say, beef) the economy is capable of producing.[1] In order to produce more of one good, the economy has to trade off some production of the other good. Let's refer back to Figure 5.1. Assume that the economy is currently producing 20 units of grapes and 25 units of beef (point C). Further assume that the country decides to increase the production of grapes to 30 units. This goal can only be achieved by reducing production of beef from 25 units to 12.5 units. The economy would then produce at point B (30 units of grapes and 12.5 units of beef).

In a way, you can think of the PPF as a graphical depiction of **opportunity cost**. It shows directly how much of one good must be given up in order to produce more of the other. In our example, in order to produce 40 units of grapes, we must give up 50 units of beef (producing at point A in Figure 5.1). So the opportunity cost of producing one unit of grapes is 5/4 units of beef. Putting it differently, for every one unit of grapes we produce we must give up one and a quarter units of beef. Conversely, when we produce 50 units of beef we must trade off 40 units of grapes (producing at point E in Figure 5.1). As a result, the opportunity cost of producing one unit of beef is 4/5 units of grapes. Keep in mind that, unless otherwise noted, opportunity cost in this context refers to how much of a good is given up when *one unit* of another good is produced. There are a number of ways to

---

[1] Don't confuse the demand curve with the PPF. Even though both curves exhibit a negative slope, the demand curve depicts the inverse relationship between the price of a good and the quantity demanded of that same good while the PPF represents the inverse relationship between the production of one good and the production of another good.

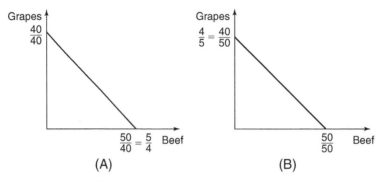

Figure 5.2   The PPF and Opportunity Cost

figure out opportunity cost with straight line PPFs. For example, we could use graphical approaches. Figure 5.2 depicts one such approach. Panel A is concerned with the (marginal) opportunity cost of grapes, so it divides the endpoint quantities by 40. Dividing 40 units of grapes by 40 yields one unit of grapes, while dividing 50 units of beef by 40 yields 5/4 or 1.25 units of beef. So for every unit of grapes we produce, we must give up 5/4 units of beef. On the other hand, Panel B is concerned with the opportunity cost of beef, so it divides the endpoint quantities by 50. The end result now is that in order to produce one unit of beef we must give up 4/5 or .8 units of grapes. Another graphical approach for calculating opportunity cost with straight line PPFs involves calculating the slope of the PPF.[2] The absolute value of the slope of the straight line PPF yields the opportunity cost of the commodity that is on the horizontal or X-axis.[3] In our example the slope is $-4/5$ (the *rise* is equal to 40 and the *run* is equal to -50). As a result, the absolute value of the slope is 4/5 and the opportunity cost of producing beef (the commodity on the X-axis) is 4/5 grapes. So how do we calculate the opportunity cost for the commodity on the vertical or Y-axis? Well, with a straight line PPF we just take the reciprocal of the result we got for the opportunity cost of the commodity on the horizontal axis. Thus, the opportunity cost for producing grapes (the commodity on the Y-axis) is 5/4 beef. Would the results be any different if we had placed the quantities for beef on the vertical axis and the quantities for grapes on the horizontal axis? The answer is no.

We can also calculate the (marginal) opportunity cost using algebra. In our example, we know that 40 units of grapes are equivalent (in terms of the amount of resources required to produce them) to 50 units of beef. Needless to say, 50 units of beef are also equivalent (in terms of resources required to produce them) to 40 units of grapes. If we use the letters G and B as abbreviations for grapes and beef, respectively, we can reduce the above relationships to either of the two following equivalent equations.

---

[2] The slope is calculated by dividing the change in the Y-axis variable by the change in the X-axis variable. Sometimes we refer to this as "*the rise over the run.*"

[3] The slope of the PPF is always negative because it depicts an inverse relationship. By taking the absolute value of the slope, we are essentially ignoring the negative sign.

$$(1)\ 40G = 50B \quad\text{or}\quad (2)\ 50B = 40G$$

Solving equation (1) for G yields the opportunity cost of a unit of grapes (in terms of amount of beef forgone) as follows:

$$(1)\ 40G = 50B$$
$$40G/40 = 50B/40$$
$$1G = 5B/4 = (5/4)B$$

Solving equation (2) for B yields the opportunity cost for beef as follows:

$$(1)\ 50B = 40G$$
$$50B/50 = 40G/50$$
$$1B = 4G/5 = (4/5)G$$

Once again, the opportunity cost of producing a unit of grapes is 5/4 units of beef and the opportunity cost of producing a unit of beef is 4/5 units of grapes.

EFFICIENCY AND THE PPF

The PPF also graphically illustrates the concept of **productive efficiency**. Productive efficiency is getting the maximum amount of output with a given amount of resource. In other words, no more output can be obtained from a resource. *The PPF represents the maximum possible output given the economy's resources and technology.* Therefore, a point on the frontier represents efficient use of resources. It shows that, given the current state of our technology, resources are being used to their fullest capacity. In other words, resources are not being wasted.

On the other hand, production possibilities represented by points below the PPF indicate inefficient use of resources. So in Figure 5.3, points A, B, and C on the graph each represent a productively efficient use of resources. To the contrary, point D represents inefficient use of resources. At point D, 10 units of grapes and 25 units of beef are being produced. However, considering the current state of technology and the amount of resources available, this economy could produce 20 units of grapes, and at the same time produce 25 units of beef (point C in Figure 5.3). Production at point D implies that resources are being employed inefficiently. One real-world way of thinking about point D is to consider the case of gender discrimination in a society. If women are systematically prevented from obtaining employment or even promotions to more responsible positions based on their gender alone, then many will be prevented from obtaining their highest level of production and society would be operating at a point below its PPF.

It should be noted that the points outside of the PPF represents unattainable combinations of goods. For example, based on Figure 5.3, we would love to be able to produce at point F. However, at point F we would be producing 40 units of grapes and 50 units of beef, a combination that is well beyond our production possibilities.

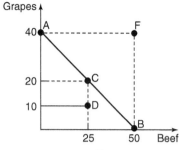

Figure 5.3   Efficiency and the PPF

ECONOMIC GROWTH AND THE SHIFTS IN THE PPF

The PPF can also be used to illustrate long-run economic growth. Economic growth simply means that the economy produces more. An outward movement of the PPF signifies that the economy can produce more. Assuming a productively efficient economy, increased capacity to produce does translate into increases in actual production. Thus, this outward movement of the PPF represents economic growth.

As a result of economic growth, combinations of goods that were once considered to be unattainable may now be attainable. Figure 5.4 illustrates this point. In Figure 5.4(a), we have an outward shift of the entire PPF. Such a shift could result from technological advancements in the production of both grapes and beef. Now if the economy devotes all of its resources to the production of grapes, we can now produce 80 units of grapes versus 40 units before the shift. Similarly, if the economy devotes all of its resources to the production of beef, we can produce 100 units instead of 50 units before the shift in the PPF. In addition, we can produce more grapes and beef in combination than we could before. For example, consider *point A* in Figure 5.4(a), which represents a combination consisting of 40 units of grapes and 25 units of beef. This combination of grapes and beef was unattainable before the shift in the PPF. Before the outward shift in the PPF, our two-good economy could only afford to produce 40 units of grapes if it did not produce any beef. All the economy's resources would have to be devoted to grapes production in order to produce 40 units. However, with an outward shift in the PPF, the economy does much better—the 40 units grapes and 25 units of beef combination, although better than the best achievable results under the old PPF, represents an inefficient use of resources under the new PPF.

Figure 5.4(b) represents an outward movement of the PPF that pivots from the vertical intercept (the combination of 40 units of grapes and zero units of beef). Such a shift may occur when there is a technological advancement in the production of beef alone. In this instance, for any given amount of grapes produced (with the exception of the case where we devote all of our resources to the production of grapes), the economy produces more units of beef and vice versa relative to production before the outward rotation of the PPF. In other words, we can produce more grapes and beef in combination than we could before the shift in the PPF. Consider *point B* in Figure 5.4(b), which represents a combination consisting of 20 units of grapes and 50 units of beef. (Notice that this combination represents *efficient* use of resources. Why?) This combination was unattainable before the shift in the PPF, but now it is attainable.

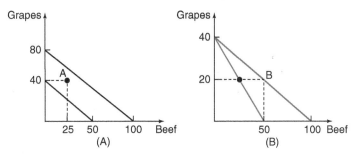

Figure 5.4   **Shifts in the PPF and Economic Growth**

SOURCES OF ECONOMIC GROWTH

How do you get the economy to grow? In other words, what factors cause the PPF to shift out or to rotate outward? We have already alluded to technological advances in the above example. *Technology* is indeed an important source of economic growth. Technology is defined as new and/or better ways of doing things. It typically results in greater efficiency, higher productivity, and lower cost. Because of technological advances, we can produce more with the same amount of resources, or we can produce the same amounts with fewer resources. Even in the case where there is technological improvement in just one sector of production, it allows us to produce more of all other goods. This sounds strange, but it makes sense when you think about it. For example, let us revisit the PPF in Figure 5.4(b) before the technological improvement in beef production. If we devoted half of our resources to the production of grapes and half of our resources to the production of beef we would have produced 20 units of grapes and 25 units of beef (*point A* in Figure 5.5). After the technological improvement in beef production, a 50–50 split in the use of the economy's resources would lead to 20 units of grapes being produced and 50 units of beef being produced (*point B* in Figure 5.5). However, if we decided to keep our production of beef at 25 units, it will allow us to produce at *point C*. At *point C,* we are producing the same amount of beef as before; however, we are now producing more grapes. So the technological improvement in beef production has led to greater amounts of grapes being produced. Why? Because it now takes fewer resources to produce 25 units of beef than it did before the technological improvement and, as a result, more resources can be devoted to the production of grapes.

The acquisition of new resources can also lead to economic growth. *Resources* are composed of *land, labor,* and *capital. Land* is defined as the earth and its assets (i.e., minerals and bodies of water). Other things constant, acquiring more land should cause the economy to grow, resulting in an outward shift of the PPF. For example, during the 19th century the United States experienced significant westward expansion. In fact, the land area of the United States actually doubled with the Louisiana Purchase in 1803.[4] By acquiring this land, the production possibilities of the United States were greatly expanded. *Labor* is

---

[4] In 1803 President Jefferson bought the Louisiana Territory from the French for $15 million. The total land area, which ranged from the Mississippi River to the Rocky Mountains and from New Orleans to Canada, was more than 800,000 square miles (greater than twice the size of the original 13 colonies).

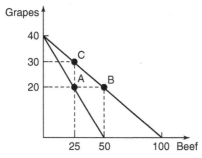

Figure 5.5 **Technological Advances and the PPF**

defined as human power—both physical and mental. Labor generally expands with growth in population. In other words, the larger the population, the larger the labor force and the greater the production possibilities for a nation. Between 1900 and 2010 the U.S. population experienced more than a three-fold increase, growing from 76 million people to 309 million people during this time period.[5] This added population greatly expanded the production possibilities in the United States throughout the 20th century. *Capital* is defined as goods that are used to produce other goods. Capital can either be physical or human. *Physical capital* consists of buildings, materials, and equipment.[6] When a nation acquires more *physical capital,* its production possibilities are expanded. *Human capital* is the skills that are represented in workers. These skills are acquired through education, experience, and on-the-job training. As a nation acquires more human capital, its labor force becomes more productive and its economic growth potential expands. Land, labor, and capital are referred to as *factors of production.*

INCREASING MARGINAL OPPORTUNITY COSTS

In our depiction of the PPF so far we have used straight line graphs to illustrate the relationship between the outputs of two goods. In other words, the slope of the line stays unchanged regardless of which combination of the goods we decide to produce. For instance, in our example involving the production of grapes and beef, we initially had a straight line PPF that extended from the point of 40 units of grapes and no beef on the Y-axis to the point of 50 units of beef and no grapes on the X-axis.

The slope of this PPF was (–)4/5 regardless of the combination of grapes and beef being produced. This implies that the tradeoffs that this economy faces were also unchanging. No matter where production occurred on the PPF, the economy has to give up 5/4 units of beef to produce 1 unit of grapes. Similarly, in order to produce 1 unit of beef the economy gives

---

[5] A significant portion of U.S. population growth is accounted for by foreign born immigrants. In 2010 the foreign born population in the U.S. amounted to 40 million people, accounting for nearly 13 percent of the population.

[6] Physical capital that is owned by the public is often referred to as infrastructure or *social capital.*

up 4/5 units of grapes. As a result, the economy faces *constant marginal opportunity costs*. Since this economy consists of only two types of workers, grape harvesters and ranchers, what this is really saying is that grape harvesters are just as good as ranchers at producing beef. Likewise, ranchers are just as good as grape harvesters at picking grapes. This is unrealistic because grape harvesters and ranchers are not equally productive at doing the other's job. In reality, as the economy produces ever-increasing units of beef, it will reach a point where it will exhaust the number of ranchers and will have to start employing comparatively less-productive grape harvesters in the raising of beef. As more and more grape harvesters are devoted to beef production, the economy loses ever-increasing amounts of grapes. In other words, more beef will be produced only at the expense of increasing amounts of grapes that are given up. Conversely, as the economy produces ever-increasing units of grapes, it will reach a point where it will exhaust the number of grape harvesters and will have to start increasingly employing comparatively less-productive ranchers in the grapes sector. As more and more ranchers are devoted to grape production, the economy loses ever-increasing amounts of beef. In other words, more grapes will be produced only at the expense of increasing amounts of beef that is forgone. This phenomenon that we have just described represents the *law of increasing marginal opportunity cost*. It results from the fact that not all resources are equally suited to the production of both goods (grapes and beef in our case). The **law of increasing marginal opportunity cost** states that opportunity cost (the value of foregone production) increases as more of a good is produced. As a result, the PPF should be represented by a *concave* curve that is flatter at the top and steeper at the bottom(see Figure 5.6).

Consider Table 5.2, which is a nonlinear version of Table 5.1.

Let us assume that the economy is initially producing 50 units of beef and no grapes (Row A). If the economy now wishes to produce 10 units of grapes, it needs shift some resources away from beef production to grapes production. In Table 5.2 we show that the production of the 10 units of grapes (from Row A to Row B) necessitates a reduction in beef production of 5 units (from 50 units to 45 units). Therefore, on average, the opportunity cost of producing each of the 10 units of grapes is 0.5 units of beef (5/10).

If the economy decides to further increase the production of grapes by 10 units (Row B to Row C), the additional 10 units of grapes necessitate a 10-unit reduction in beef production.

Table 5.2   Increasing Marginal Opportunity Cost

Row	Grapes	Beef	Average Opportunity Cost of a Unit of Grapes
A	0	50	—
B	10	45	0.5 units of beef
C	20	35	1.0 unit of beef
D	30	20	1.5 units of beef
E	40	0	2.0 units of beef

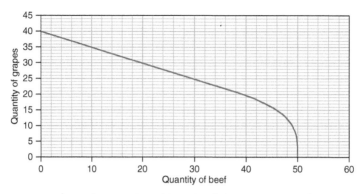

Figure 5.6   Increasing Marginal Opportunity Cost
and the PPF

This implies an average opportunity cost of one unit of beef for each if the 10 units of grapes produced. Clearly, as demonstrated in Table 5.2, the average opportunity cost of producing a unit of grapes is increasing as the economy devotes more and more resources to the production of grapes. Figure 5.6 is a graphical representation of the production possibilities in Table 5.2.

ABSOLUTE ADVANTAGE, COMPARATIVE ADVANTAGE AND TRADE

The simple Production Possibilities Model described in this chapter offers an important tool for illustrating gains from trade. However, before we delve deeper into the idea of specialization and trade, we need to be familiar with two important concepts—*absolute advantage* and *comparative advantage*. **Absolute advantage** can be defined as the ability to produce more with a given amount of resources or producing a given amount of output with a smaller amount of inputs. **Comparative advantage**, on the other hand, refers to producing something at lowest opportunity cost. We say that a nation has an absolute advantage over another nation if it can produce more of a good or service with a given amount of resources than another country. Oftentimes, we just say that a country has an absolute advantage if it can produce more (implicitly assuming that the countries have the same amount of resources). We say that a nation has a comparative advantage over another nation if it can produce a good or service at a lower opportunity cost. As we explain in this chapter, comparative advantage is more relevant to explaining trade patterns than absolute advantage.

One way to conceptualize the usefulness of comparative advantage over absolute advantage is to consider two countries—say, the United States and Bangladesh. The United States imports ready-made garments from Bangladesh. However, it is conceivable that the United States could produce these garments more efficiently. In other words, the United States likely has an absolute advantage over Bangladesh in the production of ready-made garments. If so, why does the United States not produce the garments here but instead choose to import them from Bangladesh? The answer is comparative advantage!

In choosing between producing a good at home or importing the good, the United States considers the opportunity cost of producing the good locally. Recall that opportunity cost of producing a good is measured by the amount (or value) of some other good that is sacrificed. If the United States chooses to produce more ready-made garments instead of importing them from Bangladesh, it might have to produce fewer semiconductors. On the other hand, Bangladesh may not be sacrificing as much since it may not have the technology to produce semiconductors anyway. In this example, although the United States has an absolute advantage over Bangladesh in the production of ready-made garments, Bangladesh has a comparative advantage in the production of ready-made garments. The concept of comparative advantage allows us to understand why technologically advanced rich countries trade with poor less developed countries. Absolute advantage, on the other hand, does not.

Let us now consider a numerical example—two regions, Bovinia and Merlot, each have 200 workers equally divided between the production of beef and the production of grapes (see Table 5.3). In the case of Bovinia the 100 workers devoted to beef production can produce 50 units of beef per month, and the 100 workers devoted to grape production can produce 25 units of grapes per month. In the case of Merlot, the 100 workers devoted to beef production can produce 30 units of beef per month and the 100 workers devoted to grape production can produce 75 units of grapes per month. Their combined monthly output is 80 units of beef and 100 units of grapes.

Now if we assume that workers in Bovinia and Merlot are equally productive in producing beef and grapes, we can derive the following production possibilities table (see Table 5.4) and the corresponding PPF (see Figure 5.7).

Clearly Bovinia has an absolute advantage in beef production. If it devoted all of its resources to beef production, it could produce 100 units of beef, while Merlot could produce 60 units of beef if it devoted all of its resources to beef production. On the other hand, Merlot has an absolute advantage in the production of grapes. By devoting all of its resources to grape production, Merlot can produce 150 units of grapes per month while the corresponding level of output for Bovinia is just 50 units of grapes per month. Simply looking at these levels of production, it is clear that if the two regions specialized in the production of the good in which each region enjoys an absolute advantage, total production of beef and grapes would exceed the combined monthly outputs in Table 5.3.

Table 5.3   A Hypothetical Two-Economy, Two-Good Example

	Bovinia		Merlot		
Product	Workers	Monthly Output	Workers	Monthly Output	Combined Monthly Output
Beef	100	50	100	30	80
Grapes	100	25	100	75	100

Table 5.4   Production Possibilities for Bovinia
and Merlot

Bovinia		Merlot	
Beef	Grapes	Beef	Grapes
100	0	60	0
0	50	0	150

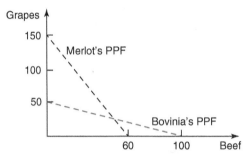

Figure 5.7   The PPFs for Bovinia
and Merlot

Compared to total monthly outputs of beef and grapes in Table 5.3 (pre-specialization), post-specialization combined production levels are higher. Total beef production increases by 20 units, while total production of grapes increases by 50 units. These are gains from specialization.

However, as we will see later in this chapter, absolute advantage is only helpful in understanding patterns of specialization and trade when it coincides with comparative advantage (when the economy that has an absolute advantage in the production of a good also has a comparative advantage in the production of that good). This is not always the case in the real world. Often we have trade partners where one of them enjoys an absolute advantage in all the trade goods (such as the U.S.–Bangladesh example described above).

For this reason, the most reliable way to understand patterns of trade is to determine the economy with a comparative advantage in the production of a given good. Recall that an economy enjoys a comparative advantage in the production of a good if its opportunity cost of producing a unit of that good is lower than in other economies.

Therefore, in order to figure out which region has a comparative advantage in the production of beef and grapes, we have to calculate opportunity costs. What must the region of Bovinia give up in order to produce one unit of beef? From Figure 5.7, the region of Bovinia can produce 100 units of beef by giving up all the 50 units of grapes that the region could otherwise have produced. Thus, for every unit of beef, the region gives up 1/2 a unit of grapes (i.e., 100B:50G → 1B: 1/2G). What must the region of Merlot give up in order to produce one unit of beef? In Figure 5.7, the region of Merlot can produce 60 units of beef by giving up all the 150 units of grapes it could otherwise have produced. In other words, the opportunity cost of 60 units of beef is the 150 units of grapes that are sacrificed. Thus, for every unit of beef produced, *Merlot* must give up 5/2 units of grapes (i.e., 60B: 150G → 1B:5/2G). In the case of beef production, we observe that the opportunity cost of producing beef is lower for Bovinia than it is for Merlot (1/2 units of grapes versus 5/2 units) and, as a result, we conclude that Bovinia has a comparative advantage in beef production. In regards to grapes, Merlot has the comparative advantage because it only has to give up 2/5 units of beef in order to produce one unit of grapes as opposed to Bovinia, which has to give up 2 units of beef. *It is important to keep in mind that, in a two-economy, two-good case, an economy cannot have a comparative advantage in both goods.*[7] Table 5.5 summarizes our opportunity cost calculations.

Table 5.5   **Opportunity Costs and Comparative Advantage**

	Bovinia	Merlot
Beef	1/2G	5/2G
Grapes	2B	2/5 B

According to the British economist David Ricardo (1772–1823), everyone could be better off if they concentrate their production on the good for which they have a comparative advantage and trades it for the good for which they do not have a comparative advantage. With Bovinia specializing in beef production and Merlot concentrating on grape production, we get the output table in Table 5.6.

The combined output is now 100 units of beef and 150 units of grapes, which is significantly more than the original combined monthly output as illustrated in Table 5.3. This means that both countries now have an incentive to specialize in production and engage in trade. There are gains to be made from trade. *Gains from trade* mean that economies or

Table 5.6   **Gains from Specialization**

| | Bovinia | | Merlot | | |
Product	Workers	Monthly Output	Workers	Monthly Output	Total Output Monthly output
Beef	200	100	0	0	100
Grapes	0	0	200	150	150

[7] If Region 1 has a comparative advantage in one good, Region 2 will have a comparative advantage in the other. Only in the case where the slopes of the PPFs for the two regions are the same (i.e., implying identical opportunity costs) will we not be able to determine comparative advantages.

people can get more of what they want through trade than they could if they decided to be self-sufficient. In other words, specialization and trade makes it possible for economies to consume at levels beyond their PPF. However, it is one thing to increase total production of a good through specialization; it is another to ensure that the increased production benefits both trading partners. In other words, can we show that, at some exchange rate between beef and grapes, both Bovinia and Merlot would experience gains from trade? The answer is yes. We demonstrate this by extending our example.

Let us assume that the two regions have agreed to exchange one unit of beef for one unit of grapes and that Bovinia trades a total of 40 units of beef for 40 units of grapes from Merlot. Will both countries be able to consume at levels beyond their own PPF? Well, let's see. After trading 40 units of beef, Bovinia is left with 60 units of beef and 40 units of grapes. This combination of beef and grapes is beyond its PPF. Likewise, after trade Merlot is left with a combination of 110 units of grapes (having sold 40 units to Bovinia in exchange for beef) and 40 units of beef, a consumption possibility that is beyond its PPF. Figure 5.8 illustrates this important conclusion: **gains from trade**.

What would happen if Bovinia experienced a technological improvement in grape production that quadrupled its output of grapes to 200 units per month? Clearly, now Bovinia has an absolute advantage in both commodities (see Figure 5.9). Does it still make sense for Bovinia to continue to trade with Merlot? In order to answer this question, we must once again calculate the opportunity costs. Table 5.7 gives us the new opportunity costs for Bovinia and Merlot. The table shows that Bovinia has a lower opportunity cost in beef production because it only has to give up two units of grapes to produce one unit of beef, while Merlot has to give up 5/2 units (2.5 units) of grapes to produce one unit of beef. Hence, Bovinia maintains a comparative advantage in beef production. Merlot, on the other hand, maintains its comparative advantage in grape production because it has a lower opportunity cost of producing a unit of grapes. Merlot gives up 2/5 units of beef in order to produce one unit of grapes, which is less than the 1/2 unit of beef that Bovinia must give up to produce one unit of grapes. This suggests that gains from trade are still possible even when one region has an absolute advantage in the production of both goods. We have, therefore, confirmed our earlier assertion that absolute advantage is not a reliable way to determine patterns of specialization and trade. Richer industrialized nations (with absolute advantage) can benefit from trade with smaller, less developed nations.

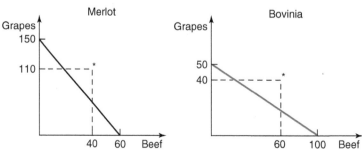

Figure 5.8   **Gains from Trade**

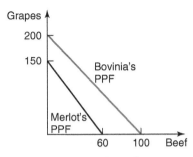

Figure 5.9   **PPFs after a Technological Improvement in Bovinia's Grape Sector**

Table 5.7   **Opportunity Costs Following Technological Improvement**

	Bovinia	Merlot
Beef	2G	5/2G
Grapes	1/2B	2/5 B

SUMMARY

- The Production Possibilities Frontier (PPF) illustrates the tradeoffs facing an economy that produces only two goods. It shows the maximum combinations of the two goods that can be produced using all available resources and existing technology.
- The PPF can be looked upon as a graphical depiction of opportunity cost. It shows how much of one good must be given up in order to produce more of the other.
- The PPF also graphically illustrates the concept of *productive efficiency*. Any point on the frontier represents an efficient use of resources. It shows that, given the current state of our technology, resources are being used to their fullest capacity. In other words, there are no idle resources.
- The PPF can also be used to illustrate long-run economic growth. Economic growth simply means that our economy can produce more. Indeed, any outward movement of the PPF signifies that we can produce more and, thus, this outward movement of the PPF represents potential long-run economic growth. As a result of economic growth, combinations of goods that were once considered to be unattainable may now be attainable.
- Advances in technology and the acquisition of new resources can lead to economic growth. Technology is defined as new and/or better ways of doing things. Resources are composed of land, labor, and capital. Land is defined as the earth and its assets, labor is defined as human power—both physical and mental—and capital is defined as goods that are used to produce other goods.

- The straight-line PPF implies constant marginal opportunity cost. In reality as more and more resources are devoted to the production of one commodity, ever-increasing amounts of the other commodity must be given up. The phenomenon is known as the *law of increasing opportunity cost* and results in a PPF that is bowed out (concave to the origin).
- A nation has an *absolute advantage* in the production of a good over another nation if it can produce more of a good or service with a given amount of resources than another country. A nation has a *comparative advantage* over another nation if it can produce a good or service at a lower opportunity cost.
- Comparative advantage provides the motivation for trade. Everyone could be made better off if we would all concentrate our production on goods for which we have comparative advantages and trade these goods for those for which we do not enjoy a comparative advantage. As a result, *gains from trade* can be realized. In other words, people, regions, and nations could consume at levels beyond their own PPF if they specialize in those goods in which they hold a comparative advantage and traded for the rest.

KEY TERMS

Production Possibilities Frontier (PPF)   Law of increasing marginal opportunity cost
Opportunity cost   Absolute advantage
Productive efficiency   Comparative advantage
Economic growth   Gains from trade

PROBLEMS

1.

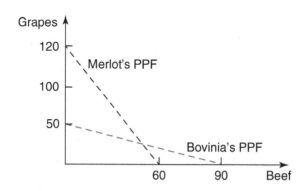

a. Based on the above PPFs for the regions of Merlot and Bovinia, which region has an *absolute advantage* in grape production?

b. Based on the above PPFs for the regions of Merlot and Bovinia, which region has an *absolute advantage* in beef production?

c. If Merlot produces and consumes 80 units of grapes, how much beef is it able to produce and consume?

2. Based on the PPFs in problem 1, complete the following opportunity cost table. (**Hint:** In order to produce one unit of beef, how many grapes must Bovinia/Merlot give up? And in order to produce one unit of grapes, how much beef must Bovinia/Merlot give up?)

Opportunity Cost Table

	Bovinia	Merlot
Beef	—	—
Grapes	—	—

  a. Based on the completed Opportunity Cost Table, which region has a *comparative advantage* in grape production?
  b. Based on the completed Opportunity Cost Table, which region has a *comparative advantage* in beef production?
  c. Which region should concentrate its production on grapes and trade for beef?
  d. Which region should concentrate its production on beef and trade for grapes?

3. If Bovinia now offers to trade 40 units of beef for 40 units of grapes from Merlot, will Merlot be better or worse off than before? Will Bovinia be better or worse off than before?

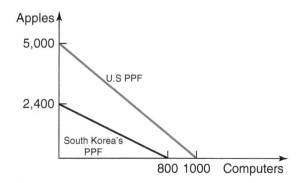

4.

  a. Based on the above PPFs for the United States and South Korea, complete the following Opportunity Cost Table:

Opportunity Cost Table

	United States	South Korea
Computers	—	—
Apples	—	—

b. Now assume that the United States experiences a technological breakthrough in the production of computers that allows it to double computer production to 2,000 if it devoted all of its resources to the production of computers. Based on this information complete the following Opportunity Cost Table:

Opportunity Cost Table

	United States	South Korea
Computers	—	—
Apples	—	—

c. Do you notice any changes in opportunity costs? Would these changes alter the pattern of specialization and trade?

5. Given the following Production Possibility Frontier table, answer the subsequent questions.
   a. What's happening to opportunity costs as output of bananas increases?
   b. What is the opportunity cost of bananas as we go from producing zero bananas to six bananas?
   c. What is the opportunity cost of bananas as we go from producing 20 bananas to 21 bananas?
   d. What's happening to opportunity costs as output of apples increases?

Output of Apples	Output of Bananas
30	0
25	6
20	11
15	15
10	18
5	20
0	21

PART 2

GLOBALIZATION: AN INTRODUCTION

6

Globalization: Definition and Measures

n 2011, ABC World News ran a series of reports titled "Made in America." In one of the reports, correspondents David Muir and Sharyn Alfonsi asked a Dallas family to remove all foreign-made items from their home. When they did, the house was left virtually empty. They report that only a few items—a vase, a candle, and some pottery—were left in the house. This Dallas family is not an exception in the United States and in many other countries. We suspect that many of us would have a similar experience if we attempted to remove foreign-made items from our homes. Over the past few decades, foreign-made goods have become increasingly accessible and cheaper for U.S. consumers. This is the reality of the new global economy. Is this trend desirable? How does it affect American workers and workers elsewhere around the world? Is it time for a "buy American" campaign? A clear understanding of the way this new global economy works helps to answer these and other questions. This chapter opens the discussion on globalization—a process that is symbolized by situations similar to that in the ABC World News series noted above.

LEARNING GOALS

➤ Define and explain the concept of globalization.
➤ Understand and appreciate the multidimensional nature of globalization.
➤ Describe the various indicators of globalization.
➤ Articulate the arguments for and against globalization.

GLOBALIZATION DEFINED

Globalization describes a process by which economies of the world are becoming increasingly integrated; societies and cultures are increasingly interconnected; and governments are increasingly interdependent.

The current wave of globalization is primarily fueled by major advances in transportation and communication technologies. These advances have considerably reduced the cost of exchanging goods and transmitting information. In regard to transportation, the extensive use of super cargo ships has substantially increased freight volumes. Moreover, containerization has reduced costs by standardizing the transshipment of goods from one mode of transportation to another. Regarding communication, advances in satellite communications and electronic signal transmission have considerably reduced the cost of transmitting sound and data over long distances. In essence, technological advancement has made the world virtually smaller.

Image © jokerpro, 2013. Used under license from Shutterstock, Inc.

The world has become smaller not physically, but in terms of ease of access to different parts of the world. We think of distance more in terms of time it takes to get from point A to point B as opposed to miles or kilometers. We also think of distance in terms of ease of communication with friends, family, or business partners in geographically distant places. Increasingly, technology is making the world a single virtual neighborhood that makes it easier to interact socially, economically, and politically.

MEASURING GLOBALIZATION

Globalization is a multidimensional process that includes economic, social, and cultural dimensions. Although most aspects of globalization are observable, measuring the degree of globalization poses significant challenges. For example, we observe cultural interconnectedness through the spread of languages, music, fashion, ethnic foods, etc. However, quantifying the strength of such interlinks is difficult. As such, researchers and policymakers have resorted mainly to **proxy measures** (indicators that approximate a particular aspect of globalization that we wish to measure). Below we discuss some of these indicators or measures of globalization.

Measuring the Economic Dimension of Globalization

Economic globalization refers to integration and interdependence of economies around the world. This interdependence is mainly seen in cross-country trade in goods and services as well as cross-border flows of capital.

Trade in goods and services takes place in the sector of the global economy referred to as the **real sector**. Participants in the real sector are either selling goods and services to other countries (exporting) or buying goods and services from other countries (importing). Therefore a country's imports and exports (also known as trade flows) provide a reasonably good measure of a country's interdependence with the rest of the world.

A second measure of economic integration is based on **cross-border capital flows**. Capital flows is what we commonly refer to as international investment. For any given country

CONTAINERIZATION AND ECONOMIC GLOBALIZATION

A major contributor to economic globalization has been the dramatic increase in international trade volumes, which resulted in large measure from the widespread adoption of containerships and intermodal container transport systems. It goes without notice today that the rustic goods-carrying container that we see on ships is the same as those that we see on trains and on trucks. The seamless movement of goods from faraway places by way of containers on ships, rail, and truck is something we take for granted. However, this development in the extensive modernization of freight transportation is only about fifty years old. It was the mid-1960s when containerships and intermodal container transport systems began to be widely introduced. This development revolutionized freight transport by dramatically improving efficiencies and reducing transportation costs. More importantly, it allowed for regions to exploit their comparative advantages and, as a result, the volume of world trade increased precipitously. For example, according to data from the *World Trade Organization*, the value of world exports of goods increased from $190 billion in 1965 to roughly $6.5 trillion in 2000. There is

no doubt that other contributors, such as the advent of free trade agreements and the general reduction in trade barriers during this time period, also impacted world trade volumes. However, it is generally accepted that containerships and intermodal container transport systems have generally played the major role.

such as the United States, a flow of investment in and out of the country to (or from) other countries is a good indicator of the country's economic interdependence with other countries. International capital flows take two forms.

a. **Foreign Direct Investment (FDI):** Foreign direct investment refers to ownership of at least a 10% interest in a company located in a foreign country. A 10% stake in a business venture is considered sufficient to allow direct control of the operations of the business. For example, Ford Motor Company's production plants in Mexico are an FDI inflow for Mexico, and an FDI outflow for the United States. Foreign direct investment is typically a long-term investment, the size of which indicates the strength of countries' economic ties.

b. **Portfolio investment:** Portfolio investment refers to investment in stocks (shares) of companies in foreign countries. It also includes investment in bonds issued by foreign governments or foreign companies. Unlike FDI, portfolio investment is usually short-term. In other words, investors constantly buy and sell different assets, thus changing their investment portfolios. The degree of portfolio investment also indicates the extent of economic interdependence among countries.

Finally, **restrictions on trade and capital flows** that countries impose could also indicate how much a country deals with other countries. Countries with more economic barriers to trade and cross-border capital flows are considered less globalized. Barriers to trade include taxes on imports (also known as import tariffs) and export taxes (export taxes are unconstitutional in the United States but legal in some countries). Taxes make the taxed goods expensive relative to the untaxed goods. For example, if government imposed a heavy tax on imports of computers, foreign producers of computers would have to sell their computers at a higher price and therefore less competitive against domestic producers of computers. This would reduce the country's imports of computers.

The KOF Swiss Economic Institute has combined all these indicators of economic globalization to assign a score of economic globalization to most countries in the world. The second column of Table 6.1 shows a list of 25 most economically globalized countries according to the KOF Index. The index uses 2012 data.[1]

The ranking in Table 6.1 may surprise you due to the absence of some major economies among the top economically globalized countries. For example, the United States, Japan, and major economies of Western Europe such as Germany, France, and the United Kingdom are not ranked among the top 25!

The reason for this seemingly unexpected ranking lies in the data used to compute the indexes on which the rankings are based. As discussed earlier, the index of economic globalization is based on flows (values) of exports and imports as well as international capital flows. All these are measured as a percentage of Gross Domestic Product (GDP), which makes the percentages smaller for countries with larger GDP figures.

For example, consider Singapore and the United States. Singapore's GDP for 2014 is estimated to have been $307.86 billion. Singapore's exports and imports in 2014 are estimated at $410 billion and $366 billion, respectively. Therefore, the sum of exports and imports expressed as a percentage of GDP is given by:

$$[(410 + 366)/307.86] \times 100 = 2.52 \times 100 = 252\%$$

For the United States, the estimated GDP for 2014 is $17,419 billion. The U.S. exports and imports in 2014 were $1,621 billion and $ 2,413 billion, respectively. Therefore, the sum of exports and imports expressed as a percentage of GDP is given by:

$$[(1621 + 2413)/17,419] \times 100 = 0.23 \times 100 = 23\%$$

---

[1] The KOF index of Globalization is developed by the KOF Swiss Economic Institute and explained in detail in Axel Dreher, "Does Globalization Affect Growth? Evidence from a New Index of Globalization." *Applied Economics*, 38 (2006): 1091–1110.

Table 6.1   **The Top 25 Globalized Countries (2012 data)**

Rank	Economic	Social	Political
1	Singapore	Austria	Italy
2	Ireland	Singapore	France
3	Luxembourg	Switzerland	Austria
4	Netherlands	Netherlands	Belgium
5	Malta	Ireland	Spain
6	Belgium	Belgium	United Kingdom
7	United Arab Emirates	Cyprus	Sweden
8	Estonia	Canada	Brazil
9	Hungary	Denmark	Netherlands
10	Finland	France	Egypt, Arab Rep.
11	Bahrain	United Kingdom	Switzerland
12	Czech Republic	Portugal	Portugal
13	Mauritius	Sweden	Canada
14	Austria	Norway	Turkey
15	Sweden	Germany	Argentina
16	Slovak Republic	Slovak Republic	United States
17	Portugal	Finland	Germany
18	Denmark	Spain	Norway
19	Georgia	Australia	Denmark
20	New Zealand	Czech Republic	India
21	Cyprus	United Arab Emirates	Finland
22	Panama	Kuwait	Hungary
23	Latvia	Hungary	Greece
24	Malaysia	Greece	Australia
25	Qatar	Liechtenstein	Nigeria

Source: Compiled by authors based on the KOF Globalization Index

In our simple USA–Singapore example, although the United States has much larger values of exports and imports compared to Singapore in absolute terms, relative to the country's GDP, Singapore has a much larger percentage of exports and imports relative to GDP. The intuitive interpretation of such a measure is that smaller countries are more dependent on other countries. Larger economies such as the United States have large domestic markets to consume a lot of their production. This reduces its exports relative to total production. At the same time, larger economies, as measured by GDP, produce a lot of goods and services to meet most of its domestic demand. This reduces large-country imports relative to GDP. Smaller economies on the other hand, with smaller domestic markets, have to go out of their own borders to seek markets for their exports and also to buy imports.

Using the same KOF index of economic globalization, we observe that the world has become more globalized over the past four decades. Figure 6.1 shows the trend of economic globalization from 1970 to 2012. The graph shows a steeper ascent beginning early 1990s. Not surprisingly, this coincides with a period of dramatic advances in information technology. We also observe a drop in economic globalization beginning 2008. This is likely attributed to the global financial crisis of 2008–2009.

Measuring the Social Dimension of Globalization

Social globalization refers to social and cultural interconnectedness across countries. Social globalization is facilitated by personal travel and sharing of information and ideas. Information flows are facilitated by communication through personal telephone contacts, travel, Internet, and other modes of communication. Information and ideas are also transferred by multinational companies (companies with business operations in more than one country).

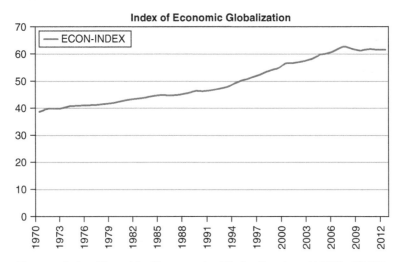

Figure 6.1   Trend in Economic Globalization (1970–2012)
Source: By authors using data from the KOF Swiss Institute Index of Globalization dataset

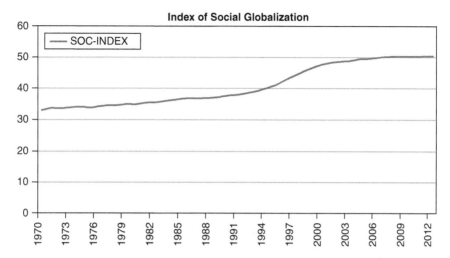

Figure 6.2   Trend in Social Globalization (1970–2012)
Source: By authors using data from the KOF Swiss Institute Index of Globalization dataset

Therefore, the index of social globalization[2] uses data on indicators of the extent of cross-border social and cultural interactions. Such indicators include

a. The number of international telephone calls.
b. International travels.
c. International population.
d. Internet users.

The KOF Swiss Institute combines these and a few more indicators of social integration to come up with an index of social globalization. Column 3 of Table 6.1 presents a ranking of the top 25 most socially globalized countries. It's worth noting that the top 25 socially globalized countries are mostly Western European countries.

Similar to the trend in economic globalization, the world is increasingly becoming more socially and culturally integrated. Again, this seems to be driven by improvements in communication technology that allow people, businesses, and societies to reach places far away from their homes via the Internet and travel. This trend is shown in Figure 6.2.

Measuring the Political Dimension of Globalization

Political globalization refers to interdependence among national governments. This is observed mainly through international relations. Indicators of political globalization include:

a. Membership in international organizations such as the United Nations (UN), the World Trade Organization (WTO), the World Bank, and the International Monetary Fund (IMF).

---

[2] Also from the **KOF index of globalization**

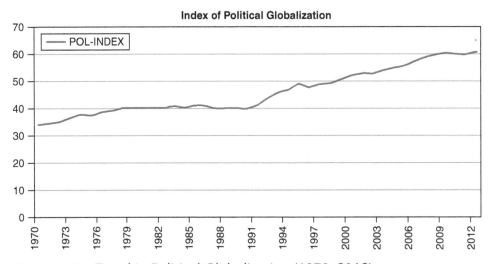

Figure 6.3   **Trend in Political Globalization (1970–2012)**
Source: By authors using data from the KOF Swiss Institute Index of Globalization dataset

b. Treaties (agreements) signed by sovereign governments with legally binding obligations. Countries are considered more politically globalized if they are members of many international organizations and/or signatories to more international treaties.

Figure 6.3 shows the trend in political globalization from 1970 to 2012. The average score of political globalization dropped in the 1980s and picked up in the 1990s. The late 1980s and early 1990s also happen to coincide with the end of the cold war. This might explain the sudden increase in political globalization.

IS GLOBALIZATION DESIRABLE?

Globalization is said to have made the world wealthier. Yet, it remains a very controversial topic in popular discussions as well as among policymakers. This section of the chapter discusses the arguments for and against globalization.[3]

Arguments for Globalization

1. **Increased wealth of nations:** Globalization provides larger markets for countries' exports. This allows countries to produce more, sell more, and expand employment. This has been especially true for high-income and middle-income countries that are in a position to compete in a globalized market.

---

[3] A more detailed discussion of pros and cons of globalization can be found in Joyce S. Osland, "Broadening the Debate: The Pros and Cons of Globalization." *Journal of Management Inquiry*, 12 (137) (2003).

2. **Efficient production due to specialization:** Globalization makes it unnecessary for each country to produce every good or even most goods it consumes. As discussed in Chapter 5, all countries have more goods and services to consume when they specialize in producing goods for which they have a comparative advantage and trade with other countries to obtain what they do not produce on their own. This allows consumers to have access to a variety of goods and likely pay lower prices for the goods and services they consume.

3. **Transfer of technology and knowledge:** Globalization is associated with closer economic integration among countries. This, among other channels, takes the form of increased foreign direct investment (see the section on economic globalization). Foreign investment is one of the ways technology and knowledge is transferred from affluent countries to less-developed countries that lack resources to invest in Research&Development (R&D). When multinational companies invest in less-developed countries, they take their production technology with them. With time, the technology spills over to local entrepreneurs and/or producers. Moreover, foreign firms hire local workers ranging from factory workers to middle managers. This provides an opportunity to learn a new and better work ethic as well as managerial skills. All this, together, increases the productivity of local workers.

4. **Foreign direct investment increases employment:** More jobs are created in the new foreign-owned firms. More jobs and income improve people's well-being; help to reduce poverty, and increase government revenue through taxation of income and consumption. A responsible government with more resources would then provide more public services to improve the welfare of the country's residents.

5. **Growing strength of the civil society:** Civil society organizations that advocate for various causes, such as environmental activists and human rights organizations, have been strengthened by easier access to information, which is associated with globalization. For example, due to the existence of global media houses, and now social network websites, global companies that do not adhere to acceptable working conditions or to good environmental practices in developing countries are pressured to institute corrective measures. A spotlight is also kept on human rights abuses in all countries. This important role of the global communication network has been termed as the **CNN effect**.

6. **Reduced possibility of armed conflicts among nations:** It may not seem realistic to suggest that globalization reduces wars given the various wars that started at the beginning of the 21st century and continue on today. However, it makes sense to expect that countries with strong economic ties are more likely avoid war in favor of settling political disputes through diplomatic means. To the extent that this is true, globalization deters war.

7. **Increased cultural exposure:** Globalization has allowed more exposure to different cultures and lifestyles. This is achieved through migration, tourism, and shared information on the Internet and other sources of information. This awareness of the world outside our own breeds more understanding and tolerance for our differences.

Arguments against Globalization

Much as globalization may have created more wealth and improved lives through greater awareness, it has also been a source of a great deal of controversy. Protests against institutions that are perceived to be major agents of globalization are a testament to the level of discontent caused by the growing global collective influence on national affairs. This section of the chapter describes some of the key arguments against globalization.

- **Income inequality:** Globalization has been associated with an increasing income gap between the poor and the rich. This is reflected in the income gap between the least developed countries and the high-income countries as well as in income inequality within countries. So, what does globalization has to do with income inequality?
- Between countries: Imagine two countries. One country has a well-developed infrastructure, advanced technology, well-functioning financial markets, and a well-educated labor force. On the other hand, the other country is an underdeveloped country with poor infrastructure, mostly rudimentary technologies, and mostly uneducated labor force. When these two countries are forced to compete for resources and markets, it should not be surprising that the richer, more developed country wins. This is what happens in a global competitive economy. The less-prepared countries lose, and the more prepared countries win. Empirically, we observe that high-income and middle-income countries have been the major beneficiaries of this recent wave of globalization. We observe more convergence in average incomes between middle-income and high-income countries. To the contrary, we observe a divergence in average incomes between the low-income and high-income countries.
- Within countries: Over the past two or three decades, high-income individuals have become richer at a faster rate than the middle-income or the low-income. For example, according to a paper by the Economic Policy Institute, most of the gains in U.S. household income has accrued to the top 1% of households (approximately 60% of gains), while the top 0.1% took home 36% of the gains.[4] What explains this trend? Many have convincingly argued that free trade associated with globalization has a lot to do with it.
- Opening national borders to trade (i.e., eliminating or significantly reducing barriers to trade) encourages producers to seek out low-cost countries. As a result, we have seen factories relocated from developed countries to less-developed countries where labor costs are relatively low. Some cities in the United States have been totally devastated after losing some of their biggest employers. In such cases, unemployment rises to exceptionally high levels, while families, entire neighborhoods, and local governments are severely hurt. It is important to note that in rich countries like the United States, it is mostly the low-income, the low middle-income, and the middle-income sections of the population that are disproportionately hurt by a situation such

---

[4] Lawrence Mishel and Josh Bivens, "Occupy Wall Streeters Are Right about Skewed Economic Rewards." Economic Policy Institute Briefing Paper #331, October 26, 2011.

as one described above. For example, factory workers in the United States have to compete with significantly lower wages in Central American countries and other parts of the developing world. To the contrary, sectors of the economy that mostly employ the highly educated and skilled labor including the service sector (finance, insurance, legal services, etc.) are unlikely to move production to less-developed countries due to the relative scarcity of skilled workers in the developing world. As a result, the highly educated and skilled will experience an increase in income due to the concentration of employers that demand their skills. This is believed to be a major source of the growing income inequality within developed countries such as the United States. In the absence of corrective measures, this trend should be expected to continue or even worsen.

THE BURGER KING INVERSION

In 2014, the U. S. fast food Company Burger King acquired the Canadian doughnut Company Tim Horton in a deal worth roughly $11 billion. This acquisition allowed Burger King to change its corporate headquarters on paper from Miami, Florida to Oakville, Ontario. This simple move enabled Burger King to not only take advantage of Canada's lower corporate tax rates, it will also—more importantly—shield any of Burger King's future overseas profits from being taxed by U.S. authorities. In the United States, once profits from American companies' overseas operations are repatriated they are taxed at the corporate rate. Since Canada does not tax company profits earned outside its borders this move will significantly boost Burger King's bottom line. Indeed, Burger King has already received an immediate windfall from its actions. According to the *Forbes* magazine article, *"The Tax Inversion Rush—In One Handy Graphic"* by Janet Novack, Burger King had about $500 million in unrepatriated foreign profits at the time of the Tim Horton acquisition that will now be spared from U.S. taxes. While these developments are good news for Burger King and other U.S. companies that have undergone inversion, it represents a substantial loss of government revenues.

© Mark Van Scyoc/Shutterstock

© Niloo/Shutterstock

- **The growing power of multinational companies:** Multinational companies are corporations that have business operations in several countries.[5] These corporations are very big and financially powerful as measured by total turnover (or revenues). In fact, some are larger than the economies of most countries in which they operate. As a result of globalization, these corporations have immense influence over public policy in most countries. This reduces the sovereign power of government and the people it represents to decide on public policy priorities of their countries without undue influence. Besides, multinational companies are able to avoid paying corporate income (profit) taxes especially through a business practice called "*corporate inversions.*" A *corporate inversion* occurs when a company sells its assets to a foreign company located in a country with a relatively low corporate tax rate. The goal of this practice is to reduce the company's overall tax burden. This causes loss of revenue to governments, and thus limits the ability of government to provided important public services.

- **Globalization and competition for foreign direct investment (FDI):** Increased competition among countries to attract FDI can result into a **"race to the bottom."** Governments are eager to make concessions to major potential foreign investors so as to win them over from competitor countries. Such concessions include different incentive packages that offer tax holidays, but may also include more lax enforcement of environmental and labor laws. This could lead to dire working conditions for workers in the developing world and potential health effects of increased pollution.

- **Loss of cultural identity:** Under arguments for globalization, we discussed the importance of cultural exposure. However, there are two sides to this argument. Some have argued that the influence of Western culture is destroying indigenous cultures in developing countries. The young in these countries have little to no knowledge of their own indigenous cultures and traditions. They associate themselves more with Western culture. Many social conservatives are very offended by this cultural trend. Additionally, the *Walmarts* of the global economy have driven local stores from their local markets and introduced more standardized fashion trends. As a result, uniquely local products are gradually disappearing and becoming a thing of the past.

- **Environmental degradation:** A more affluent global economy demands more production. More production comes at a cost of increased use of energy and more pollution. Although there have been efforts to develop more "greener" sources of energy, fossil fuels are still a dominant source of energy. The use of fossil fuels in production, travel, and shipping is associated with carbon emissions, which in turn are associated with global warming. Additionally, globalization is associated with mass agricultural production controlled by large commercial agri-businesses. Making room for such production has necessitated higher rates of deforestation.

- **Undesirable international flows:** Globalization allows countries to share a lot of good things—trade, investments, knowledge, technology, and culture. However, it could

---

[5] We discuss multinational enterprises in detail in the next chapter. The terms *multinationals, multinational companies, multinational enterprises,* and *multinational corporations* will all be used to mean the same thing.

APPLE IN CHINA

An audit of Apple's Chinese factories details concerns over excessive working hours and a series of other poor working conditions including health and safety concerns. The following are excerpts from a March 2012 article by Juliette Garside for The Guardian.

Excessive work hours

"In the most detailed public investigation yet into conditions at Foxconn factories in China, which assemble millions of iPhones and iPads each year, the independent Fair Labor Association found that more than half of employees had worked 11 days or more without rest." "In December, 46% of the workforce clocked up to 70 hours per week, although Chinese labor laws say employees should work no more than an average of 49 hours per week, including overtime."

Health and safety concerns

More than 43% of workers reported experiencing or witnessing an accident at the three plants audited." "Health and safety breached found by the auditors and published on Thursday include blocked exits, lack of or faulty personal protective equipment and missing permits, which the FLA said was remedied when discovered. Despite several suicides, which raised alarm two years ago, and an explosion that killed three workers last year, Foxconn still failed to consult workers on safety."

Source: Copyright Guardian News & Media Ltd 2012.

also lead to unwelcome flows. Examples of such flows are numerous, and they include diseases (HIV/AIDS, SARS, and other viral diseases like the Ebola virus). Unwelcome flows also include crime by international criminal cartels that smuggle illicit drugs, arms, etc. into countries, which in turn have negative consequences on the general welfare. International terrorism is also included on this list of undesirable flows. All this is aided by advances in communication technology and the strong integration of economies and cultures. Additionally, economic integration allows easy spread of economic and/or financial crises. For instance, the 2007–2009 financial crisis that started with the housing market troubles in the United States quickly spread to a number of European countries that had strong financial ties with the U.S. financial sector.

SUMMARY

- *Globalization* is a multidimensional process that refers to the growing integration of economies and the interconnectedness of cultures and governments.
- Economic integration includes increased flows of goods and services across countries (the *real sector*) as well as international capital flows (the financial sector).

- Cross-border capital flows take two forms—*foreign direct investment (FDI)* and *portfolio investment.*
- Foreign direct investment (FDI) refers to a controlling interest in a firm located in a foreign country. A 10% stake in a foreign firm is considered foreign direct investment.
- Portfolio investment refers to mostly short-term investment in stocks issued by foreign firms. Such an investment typically represents less than 10% interest in the foreign firm.
- In addition to trade flows and capital flows, restrictions on trade and capital flows also indicate the extent of economic integration.
- Relatively small rich countries tend to have higher levels of economic integration as measured by trade and capital flows. This is, at least in part, explained by lack of sufficient domestic markets. Thus, they have to rely more on external import and export markets as well as external sources of capital.
- *Social globalization* refers to the growing interconnectedness of societies and cultures. Indicators of social globalization include international telephone calls, international travels, international population, and the number of Internet users.
- *Political globalization* refers to the increasing interdependence among national governments. Indicators of political globalization include membership in international organizations and the number of legally binding sovereign treaties.
- Globalization offers a number of advantages to countries. The major ones include access to larger export markets, access to better technology and knowledge, more foreign capital inflows that creates more domestic jobs, and increased cultural exposure.
- The benefits of globalization come at a cost. Arguments against globalization include increase in income inequality, resulting from the fact that free trade that is associated with globalization creates losers and winners. Globalization increases the power of the big "global players" (including multinational corporations and global financial institutions) over national governments. Additionally, through the greater influence of the Western culture, globalization has progressively led to the erosion of indigenous cultures in developing countries. This has been especially true among the youth in the developing world.

KEY TERMS

Globalization	Economic globalization
Proxy measures	Social globalization
Real sector	KOF index of globalization
Cross-border capital flows	Political globalization
Foreign direct investment (FDI)	CNN effect
Portfolio investment	"Race to the bottom"
Restrictions on trade and capital flows	

PROBLEMS

1. Define *globalization*.

   a. List and *briefly explain* three benefits (advantages) of globalization.
   b. List and *briefly explain* two costs (disadvantages) of globalization.

2. In the opening paragraph of this chapter, we briefly described ABC World News report series titled "Made in America." In the news reports, a few people interviewed vowed to pay closer attention to the tags on items they buy to make sure that they buy U.S.-made goods. Would you recommend that American consumers insist on "buying American"? Why or why not?

3. Describe the measures or indicators of the three dimensions of globalization discussed in this chapter.

4. In Table 6.1, relatively small high-income countries top the list of most globalized countries. Why not the (economically and demographically) larger countries?

5. In recent decades, middle-class real wages in the United States have either fallen or stagnated. In contrast, profits have more than doubled during the same period of time. Many have suggested that globalization has something to do with this growing income inequality. Do you agree? Why or why not?

6. Many people (especially older people) in developing countries dread the spread of Western culture. They see Western culture as eroding their own traditions (mostly among the younger generation). On the other hand, many view Western influence in developing countries as a positive influence that has the potential to transform developing economies through a better work ethic and respect for the rule of law. What is your opinion about the advantages and disadvantages of such cultural influence that results from globalization?

7. Define, explain, and compare/contrast the following terms:

   a. Globalization *versus* "CNN effect"
   b. Real sector *versus* financial sector
   c. Economic globalization *versus* multinational companies
   d. Foreign direct investment (FDI) *versus* portfolio investment
   e. Social globalization versus political globalization

7

Globalization: Some Major Agents

The process of globalization is driven by a multitude of interactions across geopolitical boundaries. These interactions take the form of business transactions conducted by business entities such as transnational corporations, social interactions between individuals, and policy discussions among governments and other institutions. This chapter identifies the key "actors" driving globalization. The institutions described in this chapter are considered by many as the face of globalization and have been a subject of immense criticism by the so-called anti-globalists.

LEARNING GOALS

➤ Understand the history of international organizations such as the World Bank, the International Monetary Fund (IMF), and the World Trade Organization (WTO), describe their structures, and articulate their roles in the global economy.

➤ Understand the agreements on which the WTO is founded.

➤ Understand the principles that guide the work of the WTO.

➤ Articulate the main criticisms of the World Bank, the IMF, and the WTO.

➤ Understand the scope and influence of multinational corporations in the global economy.

INTERNATIONAL FINANCIAL ORGANIZATIONS: THE WORLD BANK AND THE INTERNATIONAL MONETARY FUND (IMF)

Following the end of World War II, governments of major economic powers set out to tackle a number of significant challenges. Prominent among them was the reconstruction of European and Asian economies devastated by the war; ensuring a stable monetary and financial system; and promoting international trade.

In July 1944, representatives from 44 countries convened a UN conference at a hotel in Bretton Woods, New Hampshire. The goal was to discuss ways to address these major global economic challenges. The three-week conference recommended the establishment of multilateral institutions that have since become a major force in global policymaking. Two of these institutions are the so-called **Bretton Woods institutions**: the International Monetary Fund (IMF) and the International Bank for Reconstruction and Development (IBRD). A third proposed institution, the International Trade Organization (ITO), never materialized until about 21 years ago.

The leading voices at the conference were the UK delegation led by John Maynard Keynes, and the U.S. delegation led by then-Assistant Secretary of the Treasury, Harry Dexter White. During the conference, the IMF and the IBRD were established.

International Monetary Fund (IMF)

The **International Monetary Fund (IMF)** was founded in 1944 (and became operational in 1946) to support global financial stability and economic development. Primarily, the IMF was charged with ensuring stable currency exchange rate systems in order to facilitate international transactions. As we note in chapters 11 and 12 of this book, a country runs a trade deficit when the value of its imports exceed the value of its exports. In order to reverse the trade deficit, a country may resort to devaluation of its currency (see chapter 12) in order to make its exports more competitive. The IMF was charged with providing the necessary financial support to member countries in order to avoid such destabilizing currency devaluations.

Currently, the IMF consists of 188 member nations and is headquartered in Washington, DC. Each of these member countries has one seat on the board of governors, the IMF's top decision-making body. A governor and/or an alternate governor represent each member country on the board. In practice governors tend to be the countries' ministers of finance, commerce or the head of the country's central bank.

An executive board consisting of 24 members does the day-to-day administration of IMF activities. The executive board of the IMF is chaired by the executive director who is also the top official of the IMF. By convention, the managing director of the IMF has always been European. Eight of the 24 seats on the executive board are held by countries that make the biggest financial contribution (known as quotas) to the IMF. These include the United States, Japan, China, Germany, the United Kingdom, France, the Russian Federation, and Saudi Arabia. The remaining 16 seats are assigned to the rest of the IMF members in groups. For example, a group of 15 European and middle eastern countries has one seat on the executive board. Similarly, a group of more than 20 African countries has one seat on the executive board. This has often led to complaints of unequal representation of developing countries on the IMF executive board.

The IMF's mandate is derived from its Articles of Agreement. Section I (iii) lays out the IMF's initial primary purpose. It states: "To Promote exchange rate stability, to maintain orderly exchange arrangements among members, and to avoid competitive exchange depreciation". Additionally, the IMF was charged with helping to establish a multilateral system of payments (Section I (iv)), to provide temporary funding to countries with balance of payments problems (Section I (v)), and to lessen the severity and duration of balance of payments disequilibrium.

Since countries' economies are linked to each other through trade and transnational investments, balance of payments imbalances would have implications for the global economy. The founding of the IMF as a supranational institution was intended to oversee global financial stability and prevent or contain problems arising out of exchange rate misalignments and consequent balance of payments imbalances.

It's clear from the Articles of Agreement that the IMF was not intended to deal with long-term economic development issues but rather short-term problems that threaten the stability of the global monetary system. In its first 2 decades, the focus of the IMF activities was primarily in developed nations with countries including France, United States, Belgium, Finland, and the United Kingdom obtaining IMF loans through its primary lending facility, the Stand-By Arrangement (SBA). The SBA is one of several arrangements to borrow from the IMF. Financial assistance obtained through the SBA is typically short-term and should be repaid quarterly within a period of 3.25 years to 5 years.

With increasing economic fortunes in emerging economies and the 1980s sovereign debt crises in major developing countries in Latin America, the IMF's focus sharply turned to developing nations. IMF activities as measured by the number of programs undertaken as well as the dollar amounts in loans significantly increased in the 1980s and 1990s. In addition to the growing number of programs, the duration of programs (the time between the start of the program to the end of the program) substantially increased. The longer duration of programs has been attributed to the changing nature of crises that the IMF deals with.

In the early decades, the IMF dealt primarily with short-term balance of payments problems and currency exchange instabilities associated with such balance of payments problems. However, today's IMF is increasingly confronting sovereign debt and banking crises that tend to take much longer to resolve. Over the past decade the focus of IMF activities has shifted back to developed nations. The 2008 global financial crisis and consequent sovereign debt problems are responsible for the refocusing of IMF programs.

THE IMF AND THE EUROZONE SOVEREIGN DEBT CRISIS

The *Maastricht Treaty* of 1993 established the European Economic and Monetary Union. The treaty provided for a three-stage process to establish the union, the first of which was to adopt a single currency. The single currency that was launched on January 1, 1999 is called the *Euro*.

The *Euro* is a common currency for 19 of the 28 members of the European Union. However, fiscal policy (government budgets and taxation) is still within the purview of national governments. The adoption of the single currency required countries to maintain fiscal discipline among other conditions. For example, countries' budget deficits were not to exceed 3% of GDP and the national stock of public debt was not to exceed 60% of GDP.

However, without a strict enforcement mechanism, the single currency served to incentivize fiscal indiscipline. With a single currency, domestic banks can obtain funds from foreign countries in their own currency, which eliminates the risk associated with changes in exchange rates. The increased access to foreign funds reduces interests rates and motivates more borrowing, both private and public. Moreover, there may be an incentive to bailout countries that borrow excessively and end up in a debt crisis. To the extent that this is true, the monetary union promotes fiscal indiscipline at the country level. Greece, which joined the *Eurozone* in 2001, was, by 2009, running structural budget deficits exceeding 12% of GDP while its stock of national debt exceeded 110% of GDP—both figures way larger than the limits established in the *Maastricht Criteria*.

With the housing market collapse in the United States, and the ensuing global financial crisis in 2007–2009, European banks that were heavily invested in U.S. *mortgage-backed* securities were exposed to big losses. Further, U.S. money markets were a big source of financing for many European banks. The resulting *credit crunch* caused economy-wide downturns and reduced government revenues. Budget deficits grew well above established limits and debt levels became unsustainable.

The epicenter of this Euro debt crisis is, undoubtedly, Greece. In 2010, Greece revised its 2009 budget deficit upward to 13.6% of GDP. This led to a credit worthiness downgrade by Standard and Poor's and consequently limited access to international financial markets. In May of 2010, the IMF, the Greek government, the European commission, and the European central bank agreed on a bailout package for Greece. The bailout would provide €110 billion (about $145 billion). The package was intended to help stabilize the Greek economy and restore the confidence of private actors. The IMF's contribution to the bailout package was €30 billion to be provided over a three-year period under the IMF's *Stand-by Arrangement*. Unfortunately, the Greek economy is far from stable. In January of 2016, Greek unemployment rate exceeded 24%.

It is important to note that in addition to Greece, several other Eurozone countries experienced and continue to experience heavy sovereign debt burdens. The other countries include Ireland, Portugal, Spain, and Italy. In November of 2010, Ireland sought bailout funds from the IMF and the EU. Portugal followed with a request in April 2011. The bailout programs demanded implementation of severe austerity policies (reducing government spending and increasing taxes) that threaten the social and political stability of the region. Massive protests against the bailout *conditionalities* have brought down governments in quick succession.

How Does the IMF Carry out Its Mandate?

a. The IMF monitors macroeconomic policies in member countries for any vulnerability that exposes the countries' economies to potential crises. The IMF conducts regular *surveillance* and economic analysis of all its member countries and produces an annual report of the findings. The annual member country reports may include suggested policy adjustments deemed necessary for the country's economic stability.

b. The IMF provides *technical assistance*. In pursuing its goal of maintaining a stable global monetary system, the IMF offers training and technical assistance to member country governments. Such technical assistance and training spans a number of areas thought to be important for economic stability. These include design and implementation of monetary policy, tax policy and administration, management of the national debt, and budget formulation and implementation.

c. The IMF provides *financial assistance* to countries facing severe balance of payments problems. Despite the constant monitoring and technical assistance by the IMF, economic and/or financial crises still occur. When a member country is faced with such a crisis, the IMF provides a source of funds necessary for economic recovery. Such funding is conditional on effective implementation of a set of policies designed and agreed to by the country's authorities and the IMF.

In recent years, following the global financial crisis of 2007–2009, the IMF is playing a vital role in helping to restore economic stability in the troubled Eurozone countries such as Greece, Portugal, Ireland, and Cyprus.

How Are IMF Activities Funded?

Quotas: IMF activities are mostly funded by member country contributions known as *quotas*. Each country is assigned a quota based on the relative size of its economy and sets the country's maximum resource commitment to the IMF. Quotas also determine the country's voting power and access to IMF loans.

Borrowing: If the IMF's financial resources from *quotas* fall short of its financial demands, it may utilize its Multilateral Borrowing Arrangements to raise funds. Currently, the IMF has a borrowing capacity of about US$250 billion.

Gold Reserves: The IMF is one of the largest official holders of gold with more than 2,800 tons of gold. Despite some limitations provided for in its Articles of Agreement, the IMF may sell gold to finance its activities.

The World Bank

The **World Bank** is a multilateral institution established in 1944 along with the IMF. The World Bank, like the IMF, is an independent agency of the United Nations. The World Bank is owned by 188 member countries.

The original mission of the World Bank was to finance post-war reconstruction of Europe and finance long-term development, hence the name **IBRD**. The IBRD is now one of five development agencies that form the **World Bank Group**. The other four include the International Finance Corporation (IFC), the International Development Association (IDA), the Multilateral Investment Guarantee Agency (MIGA), and the International Center for Settlement of Investment Disputes (ICSID).

The World Bank Today: Post-war reconstruction was completed by early 1960s. Although reconstruction remains a part of the World Bank activities, since the 1960s, its main focus has been on alleviating poverty and fostering sustainable development in middle-income and low-income countries. To achieve this "new" mission, a number of institutions were established to complement activities of the IBRD. As noted earlier, together these organizations form the World Bank Group.

With the supporting organizations, the IBRD primarily focuses on extending short-term policy development loans and technical assistance to middle-income countries. Such loans are intended to finance economic and institutional policy reforms deemed necessary for sustainable growth and development. Most of the IBRD financing comes from funds paid in by member countries and the Bank's own funds accumulated over time. The IBRD can also raise funds on private capital markets through issuance of its AAA-rated bonds.

The **International Finance Corporation (IFC)** was established in 1956 to complement the activities of the IBRD by investing in private firms to promote economic growth and alleviate poverty. Typical business ventures supported by the IFC are those that are profitable and offer the most economic and social benefits to the country as a whole. In addition to private sector loans, the IFC provides technical assistance to governments in areas such capital markets development, privatization of state-owned enterprises, and policies to attract foreign investment. In FY2015, the IFC disbursed $17.7 billion.

The **International Development Association (IDA)** was established in 1960 to provide financial and technical assistance to low-income countries that are typically not served by the IBRD and/or have difficulty obtaining financing from private capital markets. Unlike IFC loans, IDA and IBRD loans are provided directly to governments. IDA loans (referred to as *credits*) are typically long-term (30-plus years), no-interest development loans to countries with per capita Gross National Income (GNI) not exceeding US$1,215 for financial year 2016. This threshold income level is subject to annual review. Currently, 77 poorest countries are eligible for IDA loans; 39 of them are in Africa.

In the financial year 2015, the IDA disbursements totaled $19 billion. IDA activities are funded by contributions from richer member countries (donors) and transfers from IBRD and IFC. Donor countries meet every three years to review IDA activities and replenish its resources.

The IDA and the IBRD share the same board of governors and executive board. Their organizational structure is similar to that of the IMF described earlier. The Board of Governors is the top policymaking body of the World Bank and is made up of representatives from all member countries. However, the 25-member board of directors, whose meetings are chaired by the World Bank President, does the management of the Bank's activities. Six seats on executive board are reserved for the largest shareholders, which currently include China, Japan, the Unites States, the United Kingdom, France, and Germany.

The **International Center for Settlement of Investment Disputes (ICSID)** is another one of five institutions that form the World Bank Group. The ICSID was established by the World Bank executive board's convention on settlement of investment disputes between states and nationals of other states. The convention took effect on October 14, 1966, and has now been ratified by over 140 World Bank member nations. The ICSID simply provides a forum for arbitration and conciliation. The ICSID secretariat is headquartered in Washington, DC. While the World Bank provides funding for ICSID secretariat and administrative functions, parties that bring a case before the ICSID panel of arbitrators cover the rest of the costs related to a particular case. The ultimate goal of ICSID is to foster international investment.

The last, but not least, organization within the World Bank Group is the **Multilateral Investment Guarantee Agency (MIGA)**. In a way, MIGA complements the objectives of the ICSID. MIGA was established in 1988 to encourage long-term investment in developing economies. This is achieved through providing noncommercial risk insurance (known as *guarantees*) to transnational enterprises that invest in other countries. Countries eligible for MIGA guarantees are typically members of the IDA. Guarantees are also issued for investment projects in post-conflict countries with high political risk to private investors. Since its inception, MIGA has issued guarantees exceeding US$28 billion for several hundred thousand projects in about 100 countries. In FY2015, MIGA's issuance totaled $2.8 billion. MIGA activities are funded by member-country contributions and transfers from the IBRD.

Criticisms of the World Bank and the International Monetary Fund

The World Bank and the IMF play a substantial role in global economic governance. As one might imagine, any organization with as much power and influence as these two institutions cannot escape criticism. Critics of the World Bank and the IMF include various civil society organizations, academics, as well as some developing country governments. Criticisms range from policy issues to management issues.

Opposition to policies of major international financial and policy institutions is also reflected in massive protests at major summits hosted by these organizations. For example, protesters disrupted the 2000 IMF/World Bank summit in Prague, the capital of the Czech Republic. Attempts to disrupt or shutdown the 2006 IMF/World Bank summit in Singapore were effectively thwarted by law enforcement authorities. There have also been numerous protests in Washington, DC against the activities of the IMF and the World Bank.

Policy-Related concerns: World Bank and IMF policies have been criticized for their adverse effects on the poor in developing countries. In the 1980s, the World Bank and IMF developed a set of policies required to be implemented by developing countries that sought financial support from the two institutions. This was especially true for low-income countries and middle-income countries experiencing crises. The World Bank and the IMF believed that these countries faced structural problems that prevent long-term economic growth and stability. Commonly referred to as Structural Adjustment Programs (SAPs), this set of policies demanded austerity measures, more openness to trade, liberalized financial markets, and privatization as well as other conditions.

Critics argue that such policies have serious implications for the world's poor. For example, austerity measures undermine the governments' ability to provided much-needed social services. The private sector in most less-developed countries is underdeveloped and incapable of effectively providing employment at levels sufficient to offset public sector layoffs resulting from austerity policies. As a result, efforts to eradicate poverty have been unsuccessful.

In a book published in 2002, economics Noble laureate Joseph Stiglitz argues that the IMF has implemented inconsistent macroeconomic policies in developing countries in order to support major financial interests in developed countries.

For example, the IMF insists that countries should maintain a flexible currency exchange rate. As we will learn in Chapter 12 of this book, this simply means allowing market forces (demand and supply) to determine the value of a country's currency relative to currencies of other countries.

Although most major countries now maintain some form of flexible exchange rate regime, in the not-so-distant past, some countries (especially middle-income countries such as Mexico) have chosen to ignore the IMF's directives and instead implemented what is called a *fixed* exchange rate regime.

Contrary to a flexible exchange rate regime, under a fixed exchange rate, government (typically through the country's central bank) sets the value of a country's currency relative to other countries' currencies. Usually, such an exchange rate regime artificially maintains a strong currency that is not supported by market fundamentals. In a number of occasions when countries have been unable to sustain the fixed exchange rate, the IMF has stepped in to bail out the country and avoid a total collapse of the country's currency. Some have wondered why the IMF would insist on a flexible exchange rate regime and yet support countries that have insisted on doing the exact opposite. This is the policy contradiction.

This contradiction, Stiglitz argues, is an attempt to support major Western financial institutions invested in middle-income countries. Financial interests like multinational companies of various sorts would lose huge sums of money if the currency of a major emerging economy collapsed. Although this assertion is hard to prove, it is not implausible.

Governance concerns: Critics of the Bretton Woods institutions argue that the process of determining the leadership of the World Bank and the IMF is undemocratic. This is true to a good extent. First, by an unwritten convention, the president of the World Bank has always been an American citizen, while the head of the IMF has always been European. Although the board of governors/directors of the World Bank and IMF take a vote for their respective leadership nominees, candidates from the developing world are not considered for the two top positions in the two organizations.

Many view this as unfair given that most of the activities of these organizations are indeed in developing countries. Further, allocation of votes among member countries depends on the countries financial contribution to the organizations' capital. For example, the United States has about 17% of the total votes in the IMF's board of Governors—the organization's top policymaking body. Since major decisions at the IMF require a majority of 85% voting power, the United States effectively has veto power over IMF decisions. This also implies that the United States and other major contributors to the IMF and the World Bank can pressure the organizations to push for policies that serve the interests of the rich world at the expense of other member countries.

Many have argued for more involvement of civil society organizations (such as nonprofit organizations) in policy decisions of the World Bank and the IMF. It does seem true that decision-making at these major international institutions is far removed from the intended beneficiaries of the policy proposals. However, given the multitude of civil society organizations, it might be impractical to get all of them involved in high-level decision-making. Even selecting a few to represent the civil society is itself a potentially controversial process.

THE GENERAL AGREEMENT ON TARIFFS AND TRADE (GATT) AND THE WORLD TRADE ORGANIZATION (WTO)

The **General Agreement on Tariffs and Trade (GATT)** is a multilateral treaty originally signed by 23 countries in 1947 with the main objective of fostering freer trade. Having failed to agree to the establishment of the ITO at the Bretton Woods Conference of 1944, the GATT emerged as an acceptable compromise to deal with issues of global trade in goods. The goal was to promote trade liberalization in a mutually beneficial manner.

Although the GATT was not a full-fledged organization, it did maintain a secretariat in Geneva with several hundred staff. Countries that signed the GATT were not referred to as "members" but rather as "signatories." By 1994, the number of the GATT signatories had risen from the original 23 to 128. The GATT established rules that governed international trade in goods. Back in the 1940s, trade in services was relatively insignificant. Countries traded mostly merchandise (tangible goods). As such, the GATT only provided for trade in goods and not services.

In earlier years of the GATT, the focus was almost exclusively on reducing tariffs. **Tariffs** are taxes imposed by a country on its imports. The goal of such taxes is to make imports expensive relative to domestically produced goods, and therefore expand the market share of domestic producers. Other types of trade barriers (see Chapter 9) have similar effects on domestic market prices. As we will discuss in Chapter 9, the GATT was largely successful in reducing trade barriers.

Table 7.1   **GATT Trade Rounds**

Year	Place/Name	Subjects Covered	Countries
1947	Geneva	Tariffs	23
1949	Annecy	Tariffs	13
1951	Torquay	Tariffs	38
1956	Geneva	Tariffs	26
1960–1961	Geneva (Dillon Round)	Tariffs	26
1964–1967	Geneva (Kennedy Round)	Tariffs and anti-dumping measures	62
1973–1979	Geneva (Tokyo Round)	Tariffs, nontariff measures, "framework" agreements	102
1986–1994	Geneva (Uruguay Round)	Tariffs, nontariff measures, rules, services, intellectual property, dispute settlement, textiles, agriculture, creation of the WTO	123

Source: Printed by permission of the World Trade Organization (WTO)

To achieve progressive reductions in trade barriers, several multilateral trade negotiations were held under the GATT. These negotiations are commonly referred to as **trade rounds**. Trade *rounds* under the GATT lasted anywhere between less than a year and eight years. Specifically, between 1947 and 1994, eight *rounds* of multilateral negotiations were held under the auspices of the GATT. Table 7.1 presents a summary of these trade *rounds*. Later rounds leading to the establishment of the WTO lasted longer than earlier ones. This, in part, is due to the scope of issues addressed in later rounds—extending beyond import tariffs to nontariff measures, trade in services, and intellectual property rights. These are more contentious issues and would take longer to get negotiating countries to agree.

As shown in the table, the first several rounds of multilateral negotiations dealt with tariff reduction, but later included **anti-dumping** measures and other forms of trade barriers. **Dumping** refers to selling a good or service in another country (i.e., exporting) at a price below the cost of production or at a price below the domestic market price. This is considered unfair trade because it puts producers in the importing country (where the good is sold) at a competitive disadvantage. The GATT rules aim to reduce or eliminate such "unfair" trading practices among its member countries.

The World Trade Organization (WTO)

As indicated above, the idea of an international organization to foster rules-based multilateral trade was conceived at the Bretton Woods conference in July 1944. The ITO was intended to be the third pillar of the Bretton Woods multilateral economic system. However, the idea lacked support from major players at the conference, including the United States and the United Kingdom. The establishment of the ITO was deferred to a later time.

Fifty years after the Bretton Woods conference, the **WTO** was established at the conclusion of the last trade *round* under GATT—the Uruguay Round—in 1994. The final treaty that established the WTO was signed in the Moroccan city of Marrakesh in April 1994. The WTO became operational in January 1995. Until this point, the GATT had guided the multilateral trading system.

Establishment of the WTO was motivated by two important facts:

1. Although the GATT (WTO's predecessor) was simply an agreement rather that a formal organization, over the years, it evolved into an informal organization. In a way, we can think of the WTO as a formalization of the GATT secretariat. The GATT evolved into the WTO.
2. However, the WTO is much more than simply a formalization of the GATT. Recall that the GATT only dealt with trade in goods. Changes in the composition of trade, as well as new trade-related issues, necessitated expanding the scope of trade rules to cater for these changes. Thus, the WTO was founded on a number of agreements that reflect changes in multilateral trade. Broadly, these agreements include

   a. **GATT 1994**: This consists of rules/agreements governing trade in goods (merchandise). It's referred to as GATT1994 to differentiate it from the original GATT1948. All agreements signed under the GATT are enforced by the WTO.
   b. **GATS** (General Agreement on Trade in Services): This consists of rules governing multilateral trade in services.

    c. TRIPS (Agreement on Trade-Related Issues of Intellectual Property Rights): This consists of rules and agreements related to copyrights and patents in multilateral trade. These include protection of copyrights on literary and art works, computer programs, and guarding against trade in counterfeit goods.

What the WTO Does and How Its Objectives Are Achieved: The overriding goal of the WTO is to foster freer trade through negotiated agreements. Additionally, the WTO provides a forum for settlement of trade-related disputes among its member nations. Ultimately, it is hoped that achievement of these key objectives would in turn enhance economic growth and development through trade. These main objectives are manifest in all the WTO agreements. In the 5th edition of *Understanding the WTO* (2010), by the WTO, the comprehensive WTO agreements are reduced to a number of principles that guide its work. These principles are:

1. **Trade without Discrimination**: This principle of nondiscrimination takes two forms.

    a. **Nondiscrimination across countries**: The WTO ensures that countries do not discriminate among their trading partners. This is achieved through the **most-favored-nation (MFN)** principle. Under the *most-favored-nation* principle, if a country offers preferential treatment to one of its trading partners, it is obliged to offer the same treatment to all its trading partners.
    For example, if the United States reduces its customs duty (also known as import tariff) on Japanese bicycles from 10% to 7%, the MFN principle would require the U.S. government to offer the same tariff reduction on bicycles imported from India. The objective is to ensure that WTO member countries treat their trade partners impartially.
    It is important to note that the WTO agreements provide for a few exceptions to the most-favored-nation principle. One of these exceptions relates to countries that enter into bilateral and multilateral free trade agreements. Such agreements establish free trade areas among the members of (or signatories to) the agreement (see Chapter 10). In such cases, members of the free trade area are not obliged to extend the same preferences to all WTO member countries. For example, the United States, Mexico, and Canada signed the North American Free Trade Agreement (NAFTA) back in 1993. The agreement establishes free trade among the three countries. However, the three countries are not required to extend the same benefits to all WTO members.
    Another exception involves benefits extended exclusively to less developed countries. Wealthier members of the WTO may extend preferential treatment to imports from less-developed countries in an effort to uplift the standards of living in the less developed countries. One example of this is the **African Growth and Opportunity Act (AGOA)**. AGOA was signed into law by U.S. President Bill Clinton in May 2000 and offers preferential treatment to imports from a select group of African countries. About 40 African countries have benefited from AGOA. The benefits enjoyed by these African countries need not be extended to the entire WTO membership.

b. **Nondiscrimination between foreign and locally produced goods**: Foreign and domestic goods should be given equal treatment in the domestic market. In other words, once a foreign product has reached the domestic market, there should not be a difference in treatment of such a product that is sanctioned by the authorities. For example, national or local consumption taxes should be the same for foreign-produced products and domestically produced goods, services or intellectual property.

2. **Moving toward freer trade through negotiations**: Multilateral negotiations are regularly held under the auspices of the WTOs (under GATT for earlier rounds). The main focus of these negotiations is to reduce barriers to trade and gradually move toward a free flow of goods and services across countries. Since the establishment of the GATT, nine such rounds of multilateral negotiations have been held. The degree of success varies by round. The most recent round of negotiations, **"The Doha Development Agenda,"** has been a disappointment. However, since the inception of the GATT shortly after World War II, barriers to trade have significantly fallen and trade volumes across countries have increased substantially as a result of multilateral negotiations.

3. **Binding tariffs and transparency**: When a country agrees to lower tariffs, it is important that the market views such a move to be credible. Credibility and predictability is important for investors and other market participants. The WTO encourages policy credibility and certainty through a process known as "binding." **Binding a tariff** refers to a promise not to rise it in the future.

4. **Fair competition**: This principle supplements that of nondiscrimination discussed above. The WTO rules are designed to ensure not only freer trade but also "fair" trade. National policies that give unfair advantage to a country's producers over other producers are discouraged.

    For example:
    Developed countries, including the United States and the European Union, provide substantial production subsidies to agricultural producers. This gives the recipients of such financial support an unfair advantage over producers in countries that do not provide production subsidies. WTO rules are designed to discourage such policies. American and European agricultural producers are able to sell produce on world markets at remarkably low prices, thus unfairly gaining market share. In such circumstances, WTO rules offer a remedy to the importing countries. The rules provide for a *countervailing duty*. A **countervailing duty** is a special type of import tariff intended to counter the unfair trade advantage resulting from a subsidy or other policies in the exporting countries.

5. **Development and Economic Reform**: The WTO rules recognize the challenges faced by the least developed countries in implementing trade liberalization reforms. To this end, the rules provide for an extended period for such developing countries to implement the necessary reforms under the WTO agreements. At the same time, developed countries are expected to provide easier market access to goods exported from least developed countries. For instance, as we noted above, trade concessions offered to the least-developed countries are exempt from the WTO's *most favored nation* rules.

The Doha Development Agenda: The latest round of multilateral trade negotiations began in 2001 in Doha, the capital city of Qatar. Agricultural trading was at the center stage of negotiations. One of the contentious issues related to distortions in global agricultural markets. Primarily, these distortions are attributed to trade-distorting domestic support provided to producers by governments. Agricultural producers who are subsidized by the government are able to price their produce below the free market price and thus unfairly gain market share over the unsubsidized producers. Developing countries that claim comparative advantage over their developed-country counterparts in agricultural production consider this to be unfair trade. Farm subsidies in developed countries are often supplemented with export subsidies (as is the case in the European Union) and higher tariffs on imports in order to protect domestic producers.

Are agricultural subsidies in rich countries such as the United States and EU countries good for developing countries? The answer to this question depends on which developing country you ask. For example, large developing countries like China are net importers of food. This means they import more food than they export. For such countries, subsidized agricultural production in the United States and Europe offers them lower import prices. However, for many of the least developed countries, agricultural production constitutes a substantial proportion of their countries' exports. These countries are hurt by subsidized production in rich countries because their farmers are unable to compete with the low-priced subsidized products from developed countries.

In addition to agricultural production and trade, another major subject of negotiation was the Trade-Related Aspects of Intellectual Property Rights (TRIPS). The specific concerns related to patented pharmaceutical products from developed countries. The negotiations were intended to strike a balance between the financial interests of the pharmaceutical industry in developed nations and the public health needs of developing countries.

The Doha Development Agenda was intended to address these (and other) issues. Negotiations were initially planned to end by January 1, 2005. This deadline was not met. An extended deadline of end of 2006 was missed as well.

Since the Doha Ministerial Conference in 2001, a number of ministerial meetings have ended in a stalemate due to disagreement on a number of different issues. Negotiations broke down in 2003, resumed in 2004, and broke down again in 2006. After resuming in 2007, negotiations stalled again in 2008. The impasse is mostly attributed to disagreements related to production and trade of agricultural products. Although, the future of the Doha round is still uncertain, it is hard not to be pessimistic. The likelihood of ever reaching an agreement on the contentious issues being negotiated seems to be dwindling by the day. As we write, the Doha Development Agenda has stalled once again.

Why has the Doha Development Agenda been unsuccessful?
As we noted above, trade negotiations under the GATT were largely successful as measured by tariff reductions by signatory countries. However, trade negotiations under the WTO have not been as successful. There are a number of plausible reasons for this:

i) Trade negotiations under the GATT were largely negotiations among developed countries (primarily, the United States, Western European countries, Canada, and

Japan). By the late 1990s, more developing countries had become members of the WTO and were much more forceful and vocal in demanding that their interests be addressed. The sheer number of developing countries coupled with increasing economic power of emerging economies such as china, reduced the dominance of developed countries in trade negotiations. Moreover, most provisions in WTO agreements are approved by consensus. This gives developing countries an effective way to block any provisions that would go against their national interests.

ii) The rapid growth of regional trade agreements in the 1990s may also have reduced the urgency of multilateral agreements. After all, most regional agreements go deeper than multilateral agreements. For example, some regional agreements may include investment treaties, which allow easier capital flows among the signatory nations. Better still, others may reduce restrictions on movement of people. In contrast, multilateral agreements under the WTO rules do not offer these "deep" provisions. Additionally, WTO agreements are not legally enforceable.

iii) A recent paper by Richard Baldwin published in the *Journal of Economic Perspectives* noted that a change in the approach to industrialization in developing countries may have affected the success of the WTO trade negotiations.[1] The paper noted that the paradigm shift from the import substitution approach to industrialization to "offshoring" led developing countries to unilaterally reduce import tariffs. The unilateral import tariff reduction, made multilateral trade negotiations less appealing.

Criticism of the World Trade Organization: The WTO ministerial meeting in the U.S. city of Seattle in November 1999 was met with massive protests by so-called anti-globalists. Those opposed to activities of the WTO make the following arguments:

1. The WTO encourages free trade, which in turn results in industries either closing down due to global competition or relocating to low-cost countries. Workers in relocating industries or industries that cease to exist lose their jobs. It is not surprising that labor unions are some of the most vocal groups opposed to activities of the WTO.

2. Environmentalists have also come out against the WTO's mission to liberalize trade. They argue that free trade encourages mass production and transportation. Mass production increases pollution through emission of harmful gases into the atmosphere, increases the risk of water pollution, and destroys natural forests. Additionally, transportation of goods and people across countries increases the use of fossil fuels, which are associated with carbon emissions and global warming.

3. Least-developed countries around the world have not been happy with the WTO's agreements on Trade-related Aspects of Intellectual property. Many look at the WTO enforcement of intellectual property rights as unfair. Particularly, intellectual property rights issues related to pharmaceutical products are viewed as immoral because they make it harder for developing countries to deal with public health challenges.

---

[1] Richard Baldwin, "The World Trade Organization and the Future of Multilateralism." Journal of Economic Perspectives, 30 (1) (2016).

MULTINATIONAL ENTERPRISES (MNES)

A **multinational corporation** is formed when a company owns at least a 10% stake in a company located in another country. For example, if a U.S.-based company owns at least 10% of the stock of shares of a Canadian company, the U.S. firm would be considered a U.S.-based multinational corporation. In this case, the U.S. firm would be referred to as a **multinational parent** while the Canadian firm would be referred to as a **multinational affiliate**.

An investment constituting ownership of 10% or more of the stock of a foreign-based company is referred to as **foreign direct investment (FDI)**. In our United States-Canada example, the U.S. firm's investment in the Canadian affiliate is an FDI *outflow* for the United States; while at the same time is an FDI *inflow* for Canada.

Foreign direct investment takes two forms—**greenfield** FDI and **brownfield** FDI. In *greenfield* investment, a firm in one country builds an entirely new production facility in another country. For example, if Ford Motor Company builds a new production plant in Mexico, such an investment would be considered *greenfield* FDI. On the other hand, *brownfield* investment refers primarily to mergers and/or acquisitions. For example, a European automobile company acquiring an American automobile company is *brownfield* investment.

The United Nations Conference on Trade and Development (UNCTAD) 2011 World Investment Report shows a substantial drop in global FDI flows between 2007 and 2009, a period that coincides with a severe global financial crisis. FDI inflows dropped from a high of $1.97 trillion in 2007 to $1.19 trillion in 2009. There was a modest increase in FDI inflows in 2010 and 2011. However, this annual uptick was short-lived. In 2014, FDI inflows dropped by about 16% to $1.23 trillion from $1.47 trillion in 2013.

The modest FDI inflow growth between 2009 and 2011 is largely due to a substantial increase in inflows to developing and transition countries. FDI inflows to developing and

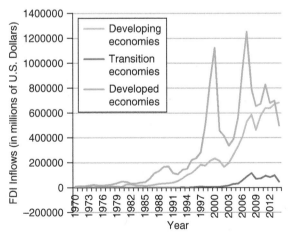

Figure 7.1   FDI Inflows by economy
category, 1970–2014
Source: By authors using data from UNCTAD

transition countries accounted for more than one-half of total FDI inflows in 2014. FDI inflows to developed countries continued to decline through 2014. Most of the decline is attributed to the economic and geopolitical uncertainty that ensued from the 2007–2009 global financial crisis.

The fact that the developing world is increasingly becoming an attractive center of international production is reflected in the growing FDI inflows. Half of the top 20 host economies in 2014 were developing economies. Developing countries such as Indonesia, Chile, and Mexico that did not make the list in 2009 made it to the top 20 host countries in 2010 and continued to make the list through 2014. In contrast, some developed countries such as the United Kingdom, although still on the list of top 20 host countries, have dropped in rank.[2]

Vertical versus Horizontal FDI

Foreign direct investment is also categorized as either *vertical* or *horizontal* FDI. **Vertical FDI** refers to a situation where the multinational affiliates produce parts of the finished product as opposed to a complete product. For example, a Dell laptop computer may be designed in Austin, Texas, while the production of the parts and assembling of the computer may be done in Malaysia, China, or Ireland. In this case, the production process is broken up into several parts, each of which may be done in a different country by both the *multinational parent* and international *affiliates*.

Why would firms engage in vertical FDI? The answer is, simply put, cost effectiveness. Due to differences in comparative advantage across countries, it is less costly to perform different parts of the production process in different countries. For example, in general it is cheaper to do skill-intensive parts of the production process in developed countries where skilled labor is relatively abundant while labor-intensive parts of the production process are done in labor-abundant developing countries. Put differently, vertical FDI is driven by the firm's desire to access cheaper foreign resources (reflected in the foreign country's comparative advantage in producing parts of the final product).

Horizontal FDI refers to cases where the multinational parent and its international affiliates produce identical products as opposed to different parts of the same product. For example, General Motors producing automobiles in the United States while at the same time its European affiliates are replicating the same (or similar) automobiles. Horizontal FDI is mainly driven by the firm's desire to locate closer to its foreign market. A firm's decision to engage in horizontal FDI is based on trade costs (shipping costs and other costs incurred in delivering goods to a foreign market) relative to the cost of building a production facility in the foreign country. If trade costs are higher than the costs of a foreign production facility, other things constant, the firm should opt for horizontal FDI (build a production facility abroad). Otherwise, the firm should produce at home and ship goods to the foreign market.

---

[2] See UNCTAD World investment reports (2011, 2015) for details.

The Significance of Multinational Corporations in the Global Economy

Multinational corporations play a dominant role in the global economy. Not only are they responsible for trillions of dollars in FDI, they also play an important role in global trade as well as transfer of knowledge and technology across countries. The latter is especially important for developing countries. In Chapter 6, we noted the importance of technological transfer in enhancing labor productivity in developing countries. In Chapter 8, we discuss the importance of multinational corporations in global trade. Trade between any two countries is influenced by a number of factors, including the economic size of countries, the distance between the countries, geography, and cultural ties between countries. Multinational corporations are one of these influences on trade flows. Countries that host each other's multinational corporations are more likely to trade with each other (see Chapter 8).

However, as noted in Chapter 6, the immense financial resources of multinational corporations, with all the benefits that come with it, pose serious challenges to governments. Regulating multinational corporations that have the ability to move resources around the world is, indeed, a big challenge. For example, through various "accounting innovations," multinational corporations are able to avoid taxation. Some have expressed concern over multinationals' corporate social responsibility record, especially in developing countries. Other concerns about multinational corporations have come from environmental protection groups. The scale of production by multinationals as well as increased shipping of finished and intermediate products from all around the world has been associated with environmental degradation.

SUMMARY

- Key actors in the process of globalization include major international financial and policy institutions such as the World Bank, the IMF, and the WTO.
- The World Bank and the IMF were founded at the 1944 United Nations monetary conference in Bretton Woods, New Hampshire (USA). This is the reason they are referred to as *Bretton Woods* institutions.
- The World Bank was established to mobilize funding for the reconstruction of war-torn Europe following the end of World War II. This explains the official name of the original World Bank Group institution—the *International Bank for Reconstruction and Development* (IBRD).
- After completing the reconstruction of war-torn Europe and Japan, the World Bank embarked on a new mission (eradication of poverty in developing countries). The new mission led to the creation of additional organizations that now constitute the larger World Bank Group. The additional institutions include the International Finance Corporation (IFC, established in 1956), the International Development Association (IDA, established in 1960), the International Center for Settlement of Investment Disputes (ICSID, established in 1966), and the Multilateral Investment Guarantee Agency (MIGA, established in 1988).

- The International Monetary Fund (IMF) was charged with stabilizing exchange rates and the global monetary system. This remains the IMF's official mandate.
- The World Trade Organization (WTO), established in 1994, was intially intended to be the third pillar of the *Bretton Woods System*. However, major countries at the 1944 Bretton Woods conference were sceptical about ceding their soveriegn power to manage their trade policy to an international organization. Fifty years after the Bretton Woods conference, the WTO was finally established.
- Having failed to form a full-fledged trade organization, in 1947 a group of 23 countries signed a trade treaty called the General Agreement on Tariffs and Trade (GATT) as a tentative set of rules to govern international trade in goods.
- The WTO is founded on three main agreements. These include:
  - GATT 1994: This sets rules governing trade in goods (merchandise).
  - GATS (the General Agreement on Trade in Services): This includes a set of rules intended to govern trade in services.
  - TRIPS (Trade-Related Issues of Intellectual Property Rights): This spells out rules governing copyrights and patents.
  - A number of principles guide the work of the WTO. These include trade without discrimination, moving toward freer trade through negotiations, binding tariffs and transparency, fair competion, and development and economic reform.
- Multinational corporations play an important role in the global economy. A *multinational corporation* is one that owns at least a 10% stake in a foreign-based enterprise. The domestic firm that owns a stake in a foreign company is referred to as a *multinational parent*, while the foreign enterprise is referred to as a *multinational affiliate*.
- The 10% interest in a foreign subsidiary is called foreign direct investment (FDI). FDI can be greenfield or brownfield. *Greenfield investment* refers to the establishment of a new business venture in a foreign country. On the other hand, *brownfield investment* refers to mergers (with) and acquisitions (of) a foreign firm or at least 10% of a foreign firm.
- FDI is also categorized as horizontal or vertical. *Horizontal FDI* refers to a situation where the foreign affiliate of a multinational replicates the product produced by the parent multinational. Horizontal FDI is primarily driven by firms' desire to access a foreign market. *Vertical FDI* refers to a situation where the production chain is broken down into stages and different affiliates of a multinational corporation produce a component of the final product. Vertical FDI is primarily motivated by the firm's desire to access cheaper resources in different countries by exploiting countries' comparative advantage in producing different components of a good.

KEY TERMS

Bretton Woods institutions	International Bank for Reconstruction
The International Monetary Fund (IMF)	and Development (IBRD).
World Bank	World Bank Group

International Finance Corporation (IFC)
International Development Association (IDA)
International Center for Settlement of International Disputes (ICSID)
Multilateral Investment Guarantee Agency (MIGA)
General Agreement on Tariffs and Trade (GATT)
World Trade Organization (WTO)
Tariffs
Trade Rounds
Anti-dumping
Dumping
GATT1994
GATS

TRIPS
Most favored nation (MFN)
African Growth and Opportunity Act (AGOA)
The Doha Development Agenda
Binding of tariffs
Countervailing duty
Multinational corporations
Multinational parent
Multinational affiliate
Foreign Direct Investment
Greenfield investment
Brownfield investment
Vertical FDI
Horizontal FDI

PROBLEMS

1. Briefly describe the original objectives of the International Monetary Fund and the World Bank. Why are these institutions referred to as Bretton Woods institutions?
2. What are the current roles of the World Bank and the International Monetary Fund?
3. How does the International Monetary Fund (IMF) fund its activities?
4. Who owns the World Bank? How are its activities funded?
5. Name the five development agencies that form the World Bank Group and briefly discuss each agency's functions.
6. Discuss some of the criticisms that have been leveled against the International Monetary Fund and the World Bank.
7. Describe the three major agreements on which the World Trade Organization (WTO) is founded.
8. Discuss the key principles that guide the work of the World Trade Organization.
9. Some anti-globalists have accused the World Trade Organization of serving the interests of rich industrialized countries at the expense of the least developed countries. In what ways might the activities of the World Trade Organization hurt the least developed countries?
10. Define, explain, and compare/contrast the following terms

    a. Multinational corporations versus foreign direct investment
    b. Multinational affiliate versus multinational parent
    c. Greenfield investment versus brownfield investment
    d. Vertical FDI versus horizontal FDI
    e. GATT94 versus TRIPS
    f. Most favored national principle versus binding tariffs
    g. Dumping versus countervailing duty

PART
3

GLOBALIZATION: GLOBAL TRADE

8

Global Trade in Goods and Services

The value of specialization and exchange has been recognized for as long as humanity itself. The exchange of goods such as tools and food in the Stone Age era is well documented. Although present-day specialization and trade is substantially different in nature, scale, and scope, the principles that underlie the gains from such specialization and exchange are fundamentally the same as those in antiquity.

While Stone Age era specialization and trade was based almost entirely on natural abilities (where some people were better at producing food while others were better at producing tools) and relied on kinship and village networks, present-day specialization and trade is based on differences in technology (and therefore labor productivity), resource endowments, and the need to exploit economies of scale. Moreover, 21st-century trade relies on wider global networks made possible by advances in communication and transportation technology.

The goal of this chapter is not to discuss the history of specialization and exchange, but rather to provide a general overview of global trade in the present. We will discuss the importance of trade in the global economy, present the top trading countries, and describe the pattern of trade (who trades with who). We discuss the relationship between economic size of countries and the value of trade between any pair of countries—a relationship known as the *gravity model* of trade—and discuss some impediments to international trade. The chapter will also describe the growing importance of trade in services. Finally, we will briefly discuss the rising influence of developing countries in the global economy.

Image © Igor Plotnikov, 2013. Used under license from Shutterstock, Inc.

LEARNING GOALS

➤ Describe the importance of trade in the global economy.

➤ Understand and describe the role of economic size in bilateral trade flows.

➤ Understand and describe the effect of proximity (distance) on bilateral trade flows.

➤ Describe other factors influencing bilateral trade flows.

➤ Understand the growing importance of trade in services.

➤ Understand the growing role of emerging economics in global trade.

THE IMPORTANCE OF TRADE IN THE GLOBAL ECONOMY

Based on the World Bank's World Development Indicators, total world output of goods and services (world GDP or gross world product) in 2014 was estimated at about $77.8 trillion. Total world exports were about 20.3% of this total world output. In other words, out of the $77.8 trillion, about $15.8 trillion worth of goods and services was consumed in countries other than the country of production.

These figures highlight the importance of trade to most economies that make up the global economy. Many countries export a substantial portion of their production to consumers outside their own national borders. Similarly, many economies satisfy their excess demand for some goods or services by importing them from other countries. As should be expected, some countries rely on trade more than others. However, all countries either lack a large enough domestic market to absorb their total production or lack enough production capacity to meet the demand for goods and services in the domestic market.

Figure 8.1 shows the value of trade (imports) as a percentage of Gross Domestic Product (GDP) for a selected group of countries. With the exception of Japan, U.S. imports to GDP ratio is smaller relative to other countries represented on the graph. Also important to note is that relatively smaller countries on the graph (South Korea and Canada) have higher trade to GDP ratios. Larger countries have larger domestic markets and tend to have more diverse resources that allow for more self-reliance. Smaller countries, on the other hand, have

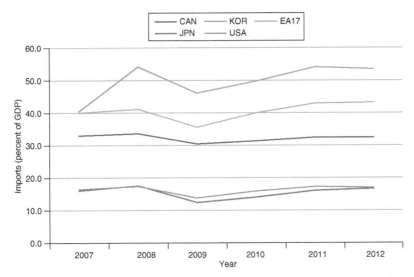

Figure 8.1   International Imports in Goods and Services for Selected Countries (as a percentage of GDP), 2007–2012
Source: By authors, using data from the OECD Factbook

to find markets for their exports (and a source for goods and services that the country does not produce in sufficient amounts) outside their national boundaries. The EA17 (Euro Area 17) shown on the graph is the combined imports to GDP ratio for 17 countries that form the Eurozone (the countries that use a common European currency called the *euro*).

Figure 8.2 includes a larger sample of countries. The general trend is the same—larger countries (as measured by GDP) tend to have lower trade–GDP ratios.

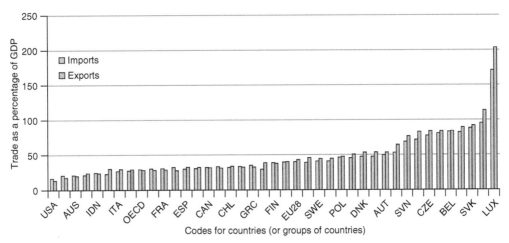

Figure 8.2   International Imports and Exports in Goods and Services (as percentage of GDP), 2014
Source: By authors, using data from the OECD Factbook

THE BIGGEST TRADERS: ECONOMIES MEASURED BY VOLUME OF MERCHANDISE TRADE

Our discussion in the preceding section showed that larger countries have a smaller trade to GDP ratio compared to smaller economies. However, this should not be understood to mean that larger countries trade less than smaller ones. In fact, the absolute value of trade (both exports and imports) should be positively correlated with the country's Gross Domestic Product (GDP).

Table 8.1 presents trade statistics for the top 10 exporters and top 10 importers. With only a few exceptions, the countries on both lists are large economies. The United States, the second largest exporter and number one importer, is the world's largest economy. China, Japan, and Germany are the second, third, and fourth largest economies in the world. France, Italy, and the United Kingdom are also among the top 10 largest economies based on 2014 GDP data. Later in the chapter, we will attempt to explain the exceptional cases of relatively smaller countries among leading exporters and importers.

BILATERAL TRADE OF THE UNITED STATES

As shown in Table 8.1, the United States is the number one importer in the world and second only to China in terms of the value of exports. In this section, we present an overview of U.S. trade. We consider the composition of U.S. trade in regard to the type of merchandise

Table 8.1   Leading Exporters and Importers of Merchandise, 2014

		Exports				Imports	
Rank	Country	Value ($ billions)	Share (%)	Rank	Country	Value ($ billions)	Share (%)
1	China	2342	12.3	1	United States	2413	15.6
2	United States	1621	8.5	2	Extra-EU (28)[a]	2232	14.7
3	Germany	1508	7.9	3	China	1959	12.9
4	Japan	684	3.6	4	Japan	822	5.4
5	Netherlands	672	3.5	5	Hong Kong, China[b]	601	4.0
6	France	583	3.1	6	Republic of Korea	526	3.5
7	Republic of Korea	573	3.0	7	Canada	475	3.1
8	Italy	529	2.8	8	India	463	3.0
9	Hong Kong, China	524	2.78	9	Mexico	412	2.7
10	United Kingdom	506	2.7	10	Singapore [c]	366	2.4

Source: World Trade Organization, International Trade Statistics 2015; the shares refer to the economy's share in world exports/imports.
[a] Extra-EU exports (and imports) refer to transactions between EU member countries and nonmembers of the EU.
[b] Only $151 billion of the $601 billion imports is retained. The reminder is re-exported.
[c] $173 billion of the $366 billion is retained.

imported and exported as well as trade in services. We also present a ranking of U.S. trade partners based on total bilateral trade flows between the United States and each of the countries on the list of top 12 trade partners.

What Do We Trade?

The U.S. exports and imports a wide range of goods and services. Table 8.2 presents the value of U.S. exports, imports, and the trade balance (exports minus imports) on goods in 2015. The values are by broad categories of goods and the data used are collected by the U.S. Customs and Border Protection and reported by the U.S. Bureau of Economic Analysis.

U.S. exports of "foods, feeds, and beverages" include a wide range of commodities. Examples include soybeans, corn, frozen fruits, oilseeds, rice, fish, and alcoholic beverages of different kinds. As shown in Table 8.2, this category constitutes a relatively small part of U.S. trade. However, in 2015, it is the only category of goods where the United States exported more than it imported. In other words, the United States had a positive trade balance or a surplus in this category, albeit a relatively small one.

The second category of exports and imports—industrial supplies and materials—includes items ranging from logs and lumber products to nuclear fuel materials. Crude oil, other fuel and chemical products, as well as all sorts of mineral products, are all included in this category. The third category—capital goods—includes agricultural machinery, industrial machines and engines, and civilian aircrafts. Then we have a narrower category—automotive vehicles, their parts and engines. The last category—consumer goods—includes consumer electronics such as cellphones and television sets, apparel, household appliances, cosmetics, and jewelry.

We note from Table 8.2 that the United States ran a negative trade balance (i.e., a trade deficit) in all but one category of goods. In fact, the United States has run an overall trade deficit for decades and continues to do so (see Figure 8.3). The question is: How much should we worry about this trend? Before we answer this question, it helps to understand potential effects of sustained trade deficits.

Table 8.2   U.S. Exports and Imports of Goods by End-Use Category ($ millions, Balance of Payments Basis), 2015

End-Use Category	Exports	Imports	Balance
Foods, feeds, and beverages	127,704	127,689	15
Industrial supplies and materials	428,172	485,908	(57,736)
Capital goods (except automotive)	538,341	599,156	(60,815)
Automotive vehicles, parts, and engines	151,563	348,283	(196,720)
Consumer goods	197,817	595,175	(397,358)
Other goods	61,317	84,721	(23,404)

Source: U.S. Bureau of Economic Analysis NEWS, April 5, 2016

A country that persistently buys (imports) more than it sells (exports) has to be funded by inflows of resources from foreign countries. In other words, when we import goods and services worth hundreds of billions of dollars in excess of export earnings, the deficit is offset by inflows of either foreign investment (sale of assets to foreigners) or borrowing (international indebtedness). These concepts are discussed further in Chapter 11. Pessimistic observers have expressed concerns about the possibility that foreign investors will stop funding our trade deficit. Although this does not seem likely at the moment, the potential shock to the United States and the world economy that might result is certainly a cause for worry.

Possible Causes of Trade Deficits

A stronger domestic currency: A stronger U.S. dollar relative to trade partners' currencies makes U.S. exports expensive relative to foreign products (imports). To understand the link between the value of a country's currency and the cost of a country's exports, it helps to imagine ourselves in the position of the foreign potential buyer of the country's export.

As an example, suppose that Air Canada wants to buy a new passenger jet. Air Canada has two potential suppliers—*Airbus* based in Europe and Boeing in the United States. Among other factors, Air Canada will consider in choosing a supplier is the price. If we assume that the prices are denominated in the currency of the countries where the potential supplier is based, then we can conceptualize the transaction in two distinct steps. The first step involves changing Canadian dollars into either euros or U.S. dollars. The second step is the purchase of the aircraft. If the U.S. dollar has appreciated (gained in value) against the Canadian currency, this would mean that Air Canada requires relatively more Canadian dollars to obtain a U.S. dollar and therefore makes Boeing an expensive option, other things constant.

Foreign Trade Practices: At times, **unfair trade practices** may benefit the country engaged in such practices at the expense of trading partners. For example, if a U.S. trade partner devalues (deliberately decreases the value of its currency relative to other currencies) its currency, U.S. exports would be less competitive against its trade partner. The effects of the foreign currency devaluation would be similar to those described in the preceding paragraph. Unfair trade practices also include lax labor and environmental policies that give some countries an advantage. In the 21st century so far, these issues seem to be dominating public discussions on U.S. trade policy.

Loss of Competitiveness: Some have suggested that the United States has simply lost its competitive edge in manufacturing. In other words, other countries are better producers of what we like to consume. This is, however, a questionable argument. The U.S. labor force is highly productive and U.S. companies continue to account for a substantial part of global production.

The Growth of Multinational Companies: A 2001 article by Joseph Quinlan and Marc Chandler[1] argues that the trade balance is no longer an appropriate measure of a country's competitiveness. Globalization has made it possible for companies to expand beyond national borders. American multinational companies such as Coca Cola, Walmart, General Motors,

---

[1] Joseph Quinlan and Marc Chandler, "The U.S. Trade Deficit: A Dangerous Obsession." *Foreign Affairs*, 80 (3) (2001): 87–97.

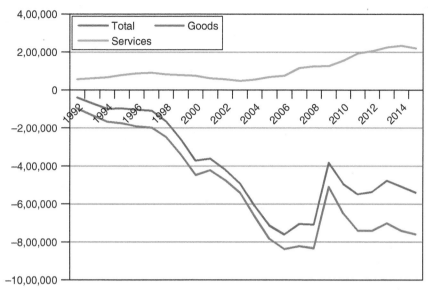

Figure 8.3   **U.S. International Trade in Goods and Services**
Source: By authors using data from the Bureau of Economic Analysis *NEWS*,
April 5, 2016

and Ford Motors have all established foreign affiliates to serve foreign markets. This eliminates U.S. exports to these markets and thus contributes to the country's trade imbalance.

Intra-Firm Trade: A substantial amount of imports could be attributed to the fragmentation of production processes. American multinational companies are increasingly importing intermediate products from their affiliate companies in foreign countries. This adds to the U.S. import bill and contributes to the trade imbalance.

Therefore, much as there are risks to running sustained trade deficits, popular discussions of the U.S. trade imbalance tend to focus on loss of export competitiveness to emerging economies such as China while ignoring the other contributing factors to this imbalance.

WHO TRADES WITH WHOM?

In Table 8.1, we presented leading exporters and importers in the world economy. What makes these economies leading traders? To answer this question, we need to understand what determines a country's trade flows. In particular, we will focus on determinants of bilateral[2] trade flows and impediments to trade.

The Effect of Economic Size of Countries: The economic size of a country is measured by Gross Domestic Product (GDP)—the market value of a country's production of final goods and services. Economically large countries tend to trade more, other things equal.

---

[2] Bilateral means "two-sided." So "bilateral trade flows" refer to the value of trade between any two countries.

Large countries tend to have diverse resources to produce a variety of goods and services as well as large markets to import from other nations.

In Table 8.3, the top 12 trade partners of the United States account for 65% of all U.S. trade. Among these 12 countries are some of the world's largest economies—China, Japan, Germany, United Kingdom, Brazil, France, and India. This leads us to believe that economic size, indeed, has something to do with bilateral trade flows.

The Effect of Proximity: In Table 8.3, the top U.S. trade partner is Canada. The third largest U.S. trade partner is Mexico. These two countries have at least one thing in common—they are both neighbors to the United States. Although these two countries are not small economies, they are not as large as some of the other countries down the list in Table 8.3 such as Japan, Germany, Brazil, France, and the United Kingdom. What explains their high bilateral trade flows with the United States? The answer is proximity to the United States.

The empirical relationship between bilateral trade flows on one hand and economic size of countries and proximity on the other can be expressed in the following equation.

$$T_{ij} = \frac{A \times Y_i \times Y_j}{D_{ij}} \qquad [8.1]$$

Table 8.3 **Top Trade Partners of the United States (2015)**

Country	Imports ($ millions)	Exports ($ millions)	Total Trade ($ millions)	Percent of Total U.S. Trade	Trade Balance
Canada	332,949	338,397	671,346	13.46	5,448
China	500,258	162,248	662,506	13.28	−338,010
Mexico	324,596	267,280	591,876	11.87	−57,316
Japan	163,975	107,221	271,196	5.44	−56,754
Germany	156,858	78,179	235,037	4.71	−78,679
United Kingdom	109,717	119,340	229,057	4.59	9,623
Korea, South	83,604	66,837	150,441	3.02	−16,767
France	65,213	49,459	114,672	2.30	−15,754
India	68,654	38,941	107,595	2.16	−29,713
Brazil	34,770	59,372	94,142	1.89	24,602
Italy	55,926	23,927	79,853	1.60	−31,999
Saudi Arabia	23,432	29,787	53,219	1.07	6,355
All other countries	843,423	882,631	1,726,054	34.61	39,208
All countries	**2,763,375**	**2,223,619**	**4,986,994**	**100.00**	**−539,756**
Top 12 trade partners	**1,919,952**	**1,340,988**	**3,260,940**	**65.39**	**−578,964**

Source: Bureau of Economic Analysis

T_{ij} denotes the value of trade between countries i and j; Y_i is the Gross Domestic Product of country i; Y_j is the Gross Domestic Product of country j; D_{ij} is the distance between countries i and j, and A is a constant. Equation [8.1] is referred to as the **gravity equation of trade**.[3]

The value of bilateral trade between country i and country j is directly proportional to the product of the countries' Gross Domestic products and inversely proportional to the distance between the two countries. We should expect that advances in communication and transportation technology will diminish the effect of distance on trade flows. However, it is inconceivable that the negative effect of distance on trade flows could be entirely eliminated.

Distance may have two distinct effects on trade flows. First, longer distances mean higher transportation/shipping costs and hence an impediment to trade. This effect of distance could be lessened by improvements in transportation technology. Second, societies that are far apart may be socially and culturally detached. This may also impede trade, other things equal. The social and psychological effect of distance on trade flows is harder to mitigate. It should be noted though that advances in communication technology across the global economy has helped to break down some of these social and cultural barriers. For example, the role of the Internet in general and social media in particular in enhancing cultural interconnectedness cannot be overstated.

Other Factors Affecting Bilateral Trade Flows

Geography: Geography affects trade flows through its influence on accessibility. For example, remote landlocked countries are more costly to trade with due to lack of access to sea, a major mode of shipping goods across the globe.

Cultural affinity: Societies that share cultures, including language, have a higher propensity to trade with each other. For example, the United States may trade more with some countries in Europe because of the shared history and cultural identity.

Multinational corporations: Multinational corporations account for a substantial amount of global trade and could explain some bilateral trade flows. For instance, American multinationals are located all over the world. However, due to several factors ranging from variation across countries in resource endowments to tax policies, some countries host relatively more American multinational corporations. Ireland is a good example of such countries. Moreover, U.S. multinational companies have easier access to the U.S. market and hence more trade between host countries and the United States.

Government policy: Government policy may impede or encourage more trade. A range of policy instruments such as import tariffs, import quotas, bureaucratic regulations of different sorts, and export subsidies all have substantial effects on bilateral trade flows.[4]

Trade agreements: Free trade agreements, discussed in Chapter 10, establish preferential trading arrangements among participating nations. This typically takes the form of partial or total elimination of trade barriers among member nations. As a result, trade flows among member countries are expected to increase.

---

[3] The name is borrowed from *Newton's Law of Universal Gravitation* where the gravitational force between two objects is directly proportional to the product of their masses and inversely proportional to the distance between them.

[4] Details on how these policies work are discussed in Chapter 9.

CHANGING PATTERNS AND COMPOSITION OF GLOBAL TRADE

Not only has the total volume and value of international trade flows grown over the years, but also the composition of trade has changed in profound ways. For instance, trade in services is increasingly taking a prominent share of global trade. These changing patterns of trade are mostly associated with technological advances that limit the effects of distance on trade flows. Table 8.4 (taken from a World Trade Organization publication) highlights this growing importance of trade in services. The number of countries reporting exports of various categories of services has substantially increased. The growing role of global trade in services is further demonstrated in Figure 8.4.

Table 8.4   Increase in the Number of Countries Reporting Exports of Selected BoP Services Components between 1997 and 2010

Service Category	Growth (percent)
Total commercial services	25
Transportation	20
Travel	21
Other commercial services	20
Communication services	174
Construction services	233
Insurance services	66
Financial services	221
Computer and information services	600
Royalties and license fees	143
Other business services	14
Miscellaneous business, professional, and technical services	97
Legal, accounting, management, consulting, public relations	508
Advertising, market research, and public opinion polling services	393
Research and development services	370
Architectural, engineering, and other technical services	409
Agricultural, mining, and on-site processing services	517
Other services	146
Personal, cultural, and recreational services	420

Source: From *Measuring Trade in Services*, World Trade Organization. Copyright © 2010 World Trade Organization. Reprinted by permission.

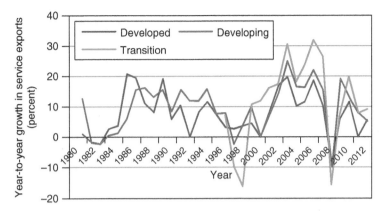

Figure 8.4 Growth in Service Exports, 1980–2013
Source: Data are from *the United Nations Conference on Trade and Development (UNCTAD)*. Data can be accessed at *http://unctadstat. unctad.org/*

Despite the big drop in exports of services during the 2007–2009 financial crisis, Figure 8.4 shows a significant recovery in 2010. The recovery was however short-lived owing to sovereign debt troubles in Europe.

Trade Patterns: The Growing Importance of Developing Countries' Economies

Developing economies are playing an increasingly significant role in global trade. This is especially true for a subset of developing economies commonly referred to as *emerging market economies*. **Emerging market economies** are typically developing countries that are transitioning from predominantly closed economies to open economies and are potential major markets for other countries' products as well as supplying exports to the rest of the global economy.

The list of such countries is quite long and includes both large economies such as China, India, and Brazil as well as relatively small economies such as Tunisia. Although the smaller economies on the list are considered less viable markets, they have undergone significant reforms toward free and more open market systems that qualify them to be categorized as emerging markets. Only a select group of emerging economies is regularly mentioned in policy and academic discussions. This "short list" of emerging economies includes Brazil, Russia, India, and China (the so-called **BRIC Bloc**). These are raising economic powers that have the potential to challenge the West's global economic leadership but also offer opportunities for investment and new export markets. The share of global production accounted for by developing countries has substantially grown over the past two decades. A 2014 OECD report on global development shows that non-OECD countries' share of the global economy (GDP, purchasing power parity basis) surpassed that of OECD countries in 2010.[5] The rapid economic growth in non-OECD countries is attributed to China and India.

---

[5] OECD (2014), "Perspectives on Global Development 2014: Boosting Productivity to Meet the Middle-Income Challenge."

Figure 8.5 shows the merchandise exports for selected economies as a share of total global merchandise exports between 1983 and 2014. With the exception of the United States, the countries represented on the graph are emerging economies. We note from the graph that the U.S. share of merchandise exports fell to 8.8% in 2014 from 11.2% in 1983.

In contrast, the huge growth in China's share of merchandise exports during the period 1983–2014 is impressive—rising to 12.7% in 2014 from just 1.2% in 1983. A similar, although not as dramatic, trend is observed in other Asian countries. The **"Asian Six"** on the chart represents six East Asian economies—Hong Kong (China), Malaysia, Republic of Korea, Singapore, Chinese Taipei (Taiwan), and Thailand. Collectively, these six economies' share of merchandise exports grew from 5.8% in 1983 to 9.6% in 2014. This reflects a substantial contribution to global trade by these emerging market economies.

Not all developing countries have performed as well as East Asian emerging economies. Figure 8.6 sorts countries by region and plots regional shares of global merchandise exports for the period 1948–2014.

Both the significance of the regional shares as well as the trend is revealing. Although Europe commands a larger share of global merchandise exports, Asia seems poised to take the lead in the not-so-distant future. Moreover, Asia's share of global merchandise exports had surpassed that of North America by 1983.

Of course, Asia is also home to another industrialized economic giant—Japan. It is true that Japan accounts for a substantial portion of Asia's share of merchandise exports. However, it is mainly China and the Asian Six that are responsible for the upward trend. In fact, Japan's share of global merchandise exports dropped to 3.6% in 2010 from 8% in 1983 and 9.9% in 1993.

In addition to growing trade shares of emerging developing economies—principally in Asia—a nontrivial portion of this increase can be attributed to the growing South–South

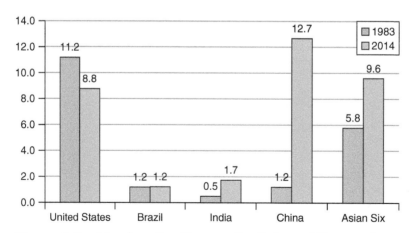

Figure 8.5   Merchandise Exports for Selected Economies as a Share of Global Merchandise Exports (1983, 2014)
Source: By authors using data from the WTO "International Trade Statistics 2015"

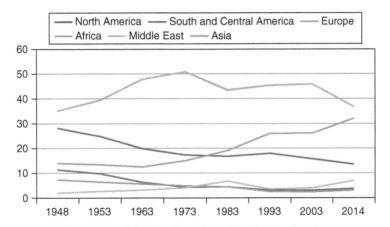

Figure 8.6   **World Merchandise Trade by Region as a Share of Total Merchandise Trade (1948–2014)**
Source: By authors using data from the WTO "International Trade Statistics 2015"

trade. The term *South* is used to refer to countries in the Southern hemisphere, which are predominantly developing nations. On the other hand, the *North* refers to industrialized nations in the northern hemisphere. South–South exports grew from $300 billion in 1990 to $3 trillion in 2008.[6] This is a tenfold increase over a period of 18 years. In 2013, the value of South–South trade had reached almost $5 trillion.[7]

SUMMARY

- Despite changes in the nature and scope of trade, specialization and trade in the present is fundamentally similar to specialization and exchange in antiquity.
- A substantial portion of global production of goods and services is consumed in places outside the country where the production took place. On average, countries export about 20% of their GDP.
- Trade (the sum of exports and imports) as a percentage of GDP is higher for smaller economies than larger ones. Larger economies typically have larger domestic markets and therefore a greater degree of self-sufficiency.
- The United States—the world's top importer—has imported more merchandise than it has exported over the past three decades.
- The U.S. imports and exports a wide range of commodities including foods and beverages, industrial supplies, capital goods, and consumer goods.
- The persistent U.S. trade deficit is funded by foreign investment—U.S. spending on foreign goods and services is offset by foreign capital inflows.

---

[6] Raymond J. Ahearn, "Rising Economic Powers and the Global Economy: Trends and Issues for Congress." Congressional Research Service, (2011).
[7] UNCTAD (2014), "Key Statistics and Trends in International Trade 2014."

- A trade deficit can be caused by a number of factors including a stronger domestic currency, foreign trade practices that give an unfair competitive advantage to foreign countries, activities of multinational companies, and loss of competitiveness.
- The top 12 trade partners of the United States account for 65% of all U.S. trade.
- Bilateral trade values are directly proportional to the countries' economic size and inversely proportional to the distance between the countries. This empirical relationship is known as the *gravity model* of trade.
- Other determinants of bilateral trade include geographical factors that affect accessibility to countries, cultural and/or historical ties between countries, multinational corporations, government policies/regulations, and trade agreements.
- The post–World War II period has seen a significant increase in the importance of global trade in commercial services. In the past two decades alone, the number of countries reporting exports of services has grown tremendously.
- Recent decades have also seen the raise of developing countries in global trade. Emerging market economies export substantially more today (as a share of global exports) compared to three decades ago.
- China, one of the emerging market economies, is now the leading exporter in the world, after surpassing the United States.

KEY TERMS

Trade balance	Emerging market economies
Trade deficit	Gravity equation of trade
Unfair trade practices	BRIC Bloc
Intra-industry trade	Asian Six

PROBLEMS

1. In Table 8.1, some relatively small economies such as the Netherlands and Hong Kong appear on the list of top trading countries. Although these two are high-income countries as measured by GDP per capita, they have relatively small economies (measured by GDP) relative to countries like Germany, France, the United Kingdom, and Italy. What might explain their relatively high values of trade? (*Hint*: determinants of bilateral trade flows other than economic size)

2. In 2000, Howard J. Wall of the Federal Reserve Bank of St. Louis did a study on Canada–U.S. trade. He paired each of six Canadian provinces with *a U.S. state* with comparable GDP and distance from British Columbia (another Canadian province). He found that the Canadian province of British Columbia traded substantially more with other Canadian provinces than U.S. states of the same economic size (GDP) and distance from British Columbia. This finding does not match the predictions of the gravity model. What might be the reason for this?

3. A classmate argues that because of technology, the world has become a big "global village." Therefore, distance between countries is irrelevant for trade among nations. Do you agree or disagree with her?

4. The United States has persistently run a trade deficit for about three decades. Should we be concerned about this trend? What are the possible causes of the persistent U.S. trade deficit?

5. Briefly discuss ways in which patterns and composition of global trade have changed in the past 30 years.

6. Define, explain, and compare/contrast the following terms:

   a. Trade balance versus trade surplus

   b. Merchandize trade versus the gravity model of trade

   c. BRIC Bloc versus "Asian Six"

   d. Trade deficit versus intra-firm trade

9

Regulating International Trade

In previous chapters, we highlighted the role of trade in the global economy (Chapters 5, 6, and 8) and potential gains to trading nations resulting from specialization. Countries engaged in trade have more goods and services available to consumers than they would have under autarky. Free trade promotes a more efficient use of resources because nations specialize in producing those goods and services for which they enjoy a comparative advantage over other nations. Further, free trade allows producers to exploit economies of scale resulting from large-scale production and industrial agglomeration.

Despite these benefits, about every country in the world has imposed some restriction on international trade. The justifications for limiting trade are numerous and somewhat varied across countries. Some of the reasons for protectionist policies make sense from a socio-economic point of view, but a vast majority of them are fallacious. Some of the widely acceptable justifications for protectionist policies relate to protection of infant industries, protection of domestic producers from unfair foreign trade practices (such as anti-dumping measures), and national security reasons.

A large part of this chapter will be devoted to discussing the various policy tools that governments use to regulate trade and their effects on a nation's welfare. We will start with a basic discussion of import tariffs and their effects and move on to discuss various nontariff barriers to trade.

LEARNING GOALS

➤ Define an import tariff and describe the effects import tariffs have on the market price of the good.

➤ Understand the types of import tariffs and the pros and cons of each type of tariff.

➤ Describe and graphically illustrate the costs and benefits of an import tariff.

➤ Understand the difference in welfare effects of a *small country* tariff versus a *large country* tariff.

➤ Define an import quota and describe its effect on the market price of a good.

➤ Understand the types of import quotas.

➤ Describe and graphically illustrate the welfare effects of an import quota.

➤ Understand and describe other nontariff barriers discussed in the chapter.

IMPORT TARIFFS

A **tariff** is a tax imposed on goods traded across countries. An **import tariff** is levied on imports by an importing country.[1] Tariffs are typically collected by customs officials at the country's ports of entry (seaports, airports, and border points). The obvious effect of an import tariff is to increase the price of the good in the importing country. A higher price is good for domestic producers but hurts domestic consumers. As a result, domestic production of the good increases while domestic consumption of the good falls. Consequently, the amount of imports decreases.

There are three types of tariffs—*ad valorem tariffs*, *specific tariffs*, and *combination (compound) tariffs*. An **ad valorem tariff** is levied as a fixed percentage of the value of imports. For example, a tariff of 10% is an ad valorem tariff. This means that $10 in taxes is paid for every $100 in import value. A **specific tariff** is levied as a fixed amount of currency units (such as U.S. dollars) per unit of imports. A $5 tariff on imported calculators is an example of a specific tariff. This means that for every calculator imported (regardless of the price), the importer must pay $5 in taxes. Finally, a **combination (compound) tariff** is a combination of an ad valorem and specific tariff. A $5 specific tariff on calculators in addition to a 20% ad valorem tariff is an example of a combination tariff. In this example, the total tax due on a $20 calculator is $9 ($5 + 0.2 × $20).

Specific tariffs are easy to understand and calculate. All one needs to do is count the number of units of the good imported and multiply that number by the tariff per unit. Thus, with a $10 specific tariff on calculators, someone importing 1,000 calculators would owe $10,000 ($10 × 1,000) in import taxes. However, with specific tariffs, taxes owed do not change with changes in the value of the imported good. This makes it inappropriate for goods where quality (and value) varies significantly as is the case with most electronics.

In contrast, with ad valorem tariffs, taxes owed change with the change in the price (or value) of the product. Let's assume a 40% ad valorem tariff is imposed on imported calculators. For a $20 calculator, tax owed to government is $8 (0.4 × $20). However, for a $30 calculator, tax owed increases to $12 (0.4 × $30). This is an advantage of an ad valorem tax

[1] Tariffs can also be imposed on exports. Taxes on exports are called export tariffs. This chapter will focus exclusively on import tariffs. Export tariffs are unconstitutional in the United States and hardly applied in any major industrialized countries. However, export tariffs are levied on some developing countries' commodity exports to raise government revenues and bolster export prices. Unless stated otherwise, in this chapter and elsewhere in this book, we use the word "tariffs" to mean "import tariffs."

because it is easier to tax goods of different values. However, ad valorem tariffs may be more costly for government to collect. Customs officials must be in a position to verify the values of imports declared by importers in order to reduce tax evasion (importers have the incentive to undervalue goods subject to tariffs so as to minimize their tax liability). Gathering all the necessary information can be quite costly.

Table 9.1 shows average ad valorem tariff rates for a select group of economies. Three of the economies are industrialized developed economies (European Union, United States, and

Table 9.1   Average Tariffs for Selected Countries by Product Groups, 2014

Product Category	Developed Countries			Developing Countries		
	European Union	Japan	United States	Brazil	China	India
Animal products	20.4	14.2	2.4	37.8	14.9	106.1
Dairy products	45.3	102.7	19.2	48.8	12.2	65.0
Fruit, vegetables, and plants	10.4	9.3	4.8	34.1	14.9	100.1
Coffee and tea	6.1	13.5	3.2	34.1	14.9	133.1
Cereals and preparations	19.4	61.0	3.5	42.9	23.7	115.3
Oilseeds, fats, and oils	6.8	7.5	4.2	34.6	11.1	169.7
Sugars and confectionary	25.6	27.1	16.9	34.4	27.4	124.7
Beverages and tobacco	20.8	16.1	16.3	37.7	23.3	120.5
Cotton	0.0	0.0	4.7	55.0	22.0	110.0
Other agricultural products	3.5	3.7	1.1	28.8	12.1	104.8
Fish and fish products	11.0	4.9	1.0	33.6	11.0	100.7
Minerals and metals	2.0	1.0	1.7	32.9	8.0	38.3
Petroleum	2.0	13.4	1.4	35.0	5.0	--
Chemicals	4.6	2.3	2.8	21.1	6.9	39.6
Wood, paper, etc.	0.9	1.0	0.4	28.4	5.0	36.4
Textiles	6.5	5.5	7.9	34.8	9.8	27.3
Clothing	11.5	9.2	11.4	35.0	16.1	37.4
Leather, footwear, etc.	4.2	9.6	4.3	34.6	13.7	34.6
Nonelectrical machinery	1.7	0.0	1.2	32.4	8.5	28.6
Electrical machinery	2.4	0.2	1.7	31.9	9.0	27.8
Transport equipment	4.1	0.0	3.1	33.1	11.4	35.7
Manufactures (unspecified)	2.5	1.1	2.1	33.0	12.2	34.0
Trade weighted average	3.6	2.1	5.2	10.0	4.6	6.2

Source: Data from "World Tariff Profiles 2015" by WTO, ITC, and UNCTAD (data cover years 2013 and 2014)

Japan), while the other three are emerging/developing economies. In general, tariff rates are higher in developing economies (with the exception of China). Further, developed economies have relatively higher tariff rates on agricultural products (especially animal products and dairy products), which might reflect the political influence of agricultural producers in these countries. Industrial products, on the other hand, are subject to relatively lower tariff rates.

Effects of an Import Tariff

As we noted above, an import tariff has the effect of increasing the price of the imported good in the country imposing the tariff (the importing country). A rise in price unambiguously hurts domestic consumers and benefits domestic producers (who also charge a higher price for import-competing goods). The extent of the increase in the domestic price of the imported good for a given tariff depends on the relative economic influence of the country imposing the tariff on the global market for the imported product. In particular, we distinguish between a *small country* tariff and a *large country* tariff.

A Small Country Tariff: A **small country** is defined as one whose consumption and/or production cannot affect the world price of the good it imports. This means that such a country can increase or decrease its demand for an imported product without affecting the price of that good on the global market. In other words, the country is such a small part of the global market for the imported good that its actions are insignificant. The small country takes the world price of the good as a given.

Figure 9.1 demonstrates the effect of a small country tariff on the domestic price of the imported good. In Figure 9.1, a small country imports widgets on the world market. The world market (free trade) price of a widget is $10. If this small country chose not to trade, the domestic price of a widget in the small country would have been, say, $18 (where domestic quantity demanded is equal to domestic quantity supplied).

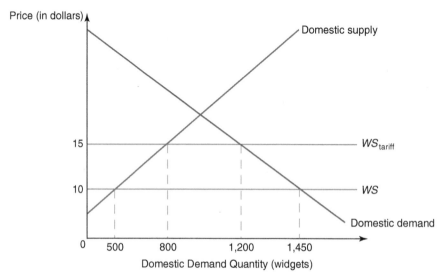

Figure 9.1   **A Small Country Import Tariff**

The horizontal line labeled *WS* represents the world supply of widgets to the small country. World supply is horizontal because the small country could consume as many widgets as it pleases without affecting the world (free trade) price of $10. At a price of $10, domestic quantity supplied (Qs) is equal to 500 widgets, while domestic quantity demanded is equal to 1,450 widgets. Since 500 of the 1,450 widgets demanded are domestically produced, the reminder (1,450 − 500 = 950 widgets) are imported.

Now suppose that the government of this small country imposes a specific tariff of $5 per widget. We know from the discussion above that this will increase the domestic price of widgets. The question is: By how much? Because the global price remains at $10 (for a *small country*), foreign producers of widgets will only sell (export) widgets to the small country if the domestic price net of taxes is as high as the world price of $10. Otherwise, foreign producers will shun the small country that imposed the tariff and instead ship their widgets to other countries. After all, a small country makes up a tiny part of the world market for widgets. This suggests that the domestic price of widgets in the importing small country has to be $15 (the world price ($10) + tariff ($5)). Domestic consumers in the small country pay the entire tariff. In this case, we say that the entire (100%) tariff (tax) is *forward-shifted* to domestic consumers. None of the tariff is *backward-shifted* to producers of widgets. A **forward-shifted tax** is the portion of the tax paid by the buyer (added to the price paid by the buyer). On the other hand, a **backward-shifted tax** is the portion of the total tax paid by the seller (subtracted from the seller's revenues).

A Large Country Tariff: A **large country** is defined as one whose consumption and/or production of a good affects the world price of the good. A tariff imposed by a large country reduces the world price of the imported good. As a result of the tariff, the domestic price of the good increases. A higher price increases domestic quantity supplied and reduces domestic quantity demanded. The volume of imports (domestic quantity demanded − domestic quantity supplied) falls. A decrease in imports by a large country leaves more widgets on the world market, which reduces the world price of widgets. As such, the domestic price of widgets increases by less than the amount of the tariff. Domestic consumers only pay a portion of the tariff (in the form of a higher domestic price), while the reminder of the tariff is paid by foreign producers (in the form of a lower net-of-tariff price). Figure 9.2 demonstrates the effect of a large country tariff on the price.

In Figure 9.2, the domestic price of widgets in the importing large country increases from $10 to $13 as a result of a $5 specific tariff. This suggests that domestic buyers of widgets pay $3 of the $5 tariff per unit. The $3 is the *forward-shifted* tax. Who then pays the remaining $2 tariff? Foreign producers. Note that at the world market price of $10, domestic producers of widgets supplied 500 widgets while domestic buyers demanded 1,450 widgets. Thus, at the price of $10, imports are equal to 950 widgets. However, the imposition of an import tariff changes things. The tariff-inclusive price of $13 per widget increases domestic production of widgets by 250 (750 widgets − 500 widgets) and reduces domestic demand for widgets by 150 (1,450 widgets − 1,300 widgets). Therefore, at the price of $13 per widget, imports shrink to 550 widgets (1,300 widgets − 750 widgets).

The reduction in imports of a large country leaves an excess amount of widgets in world markets and causes the world price of widgets to drop. In Figure 9.2, the world price of

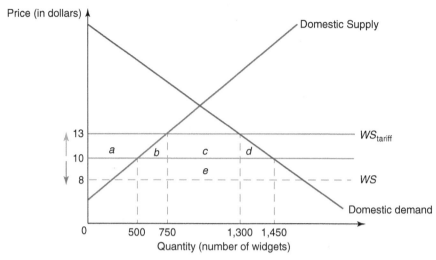

Figure 9.2   A Large Country Import Tariff

widgets has dropped from $10 to $8. Foreign producers who sell widgets to the large country represented in Figure 9.2 will sell their widgets at the domestic price of $13. However, $5 of the $13 collected by the foreign producers is transferred to government as tax. The sellers keep only $8.

Recall that in the absence of a tariff, buyers would pay $10 and foreign producers would keep the entire $10 (because without the tariff, they do not have to give anything to government). With a tariff, however, foreign producers keep only $8. This means that foreign producers pay a $2 tax (out of the $5 tariff) in the form of less revenue, while domestic buyers of widgets pay a $3 tax in the form of a higher price. The $2 portion of the tariff is the *backward-shifted* tax. As such, the burden of an import tariff imposed by a large country is shared between domestic consumers in the importing country and foreign producers of the taxed good.

Costs and Benefits of Import Tariffs

Tariffs, like any tax levied by government, help the importing government to increase its revenues. Moreover, domestic producers gain by charging a higher price than they would without the protection offered by the tariff. However, consumers pay the higher prices. Depending on the relative size of the country's market, consumers in the importing country may bear the full burden of the tax.

In this section of the chapter, we discuss the overall impact of an import tariff on national welfare. In other words, our interest is to determine if an import tariff is associated with a net gain (loss) to society as a whole. To analyze the costs and benefits of a tariff, we rely on two concepts discussed earlier in this book—*consumer surplus* and *producer surplus* (see Chapter 2). Next, we provide a brief review of these two concepts.

Consumer surplus is the difference between the maximum price the buyer is willing to pay for a good (or service) and what she actually pays (the market price). For example, say you are willing to pay $25 for a skateboard. If the seller offers you the same skateboard for

$15, your consumer surplus is $10 ($25 − $15). An increase in the market price of the good reduces consumer surplus (makes buyers worse off). Consumer surplus is graphically represented by the area (triangle) between the demand curve and the market price.

Producer surplus is the difference between the minimum price a seller is willing to accept and what he actually receives (the market price). For example, say you are willing to sell your 10-year-old car for $3,000. If a friend offers you $3,500, your producer surplus is equal to $500 ($3,500 − $3,000). An increase in the market price of the good increases producer surplus (makes sellers better off). On a graph, producer surplus is shown by the area (triangle) between the market price and the supply curve.

Geometric Illustration of Consumer Surplus and Producer Surplus: Figure 9.3 illustrates the concepts of consumer surplus and producer surplus. In Panel (a), willingness to pay is measured by the demand curve. At a market price of P_1, consumer surplus is given by the area of the triangle between the price and the demand curve (i.e., $\triangle CP_1A$). An increase in the market price to P_2 has the effect of reducing the consumer surplus to the area of the triangle between the new market price of P_2 and the demand curve (i.e., $\triangle BP_2A$). Clearly, $\triangle CP_1A$ is larger than $\triangle BP2A$, implying a decrease in consumer surplus as a result of the market price increase.

In Panel (b), producer surplus at market price P_1 is given by the area of the triangle between the price of P_1 and the supply curve (i.e., $\triangle EP_1F$). At a higher market price of P_2, producer surplus increases to the area of the triangle between the new market price of P_2 and the supply curve (i.e., $\triangle DP_2F$). Again, it is clear from Figure 9.3 that $\triangle DP_2F$ is larger than $\triangle EP_1F$, implying an increase in producer surplus as a result of a price increase.

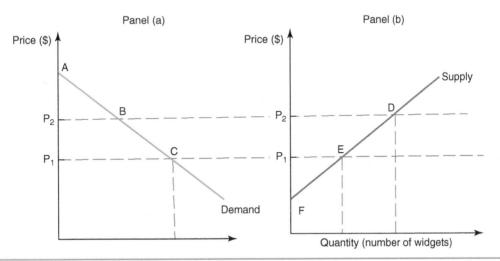

Panel (a): Consumer surplus at a price of P_1 is given by the area of triangle CP_1A. At a higher price of P_2, consumer surplus is represented by the area of triangle BP_2A.

Panel (b): Producer surplus at market price P_1 is equal to the area of triangle EP_1F. At a higher market price of P_2, producer surplus is given by the area of triangle DP_2F.

Figure 9.3 Geometric Illustration of Consumer Surplus and Producer Surplus

This description suggests a simple (and somewhat obvious) observation—an increase in the market price benefits producers (sellers) and hurts consumers (buyers). We are now beginning to see why an import tariff that raises the market price hurts consumers and benefits domestic producers.

Given that import tariffs create winners (producers/sellers) and losers (consumers/buyers), what is the net effect of the tariffs on the country as a whole? To answer this question, one needs to find out if the gains from tariffs more than offset the losses to consumers. Consider the case of a small country tariff described earlier in the chapter and demonstrated (once again) in Figure 9.4 below.

In Figure 9.4, the import tariff raises the domestic price of the good from $10 to $15. Recall that consumer surplus (shown graphically as the triangle between the market price and the demand curve) decreases with an increase in the market price. In Figure 9.4, this decrease in consumer surplus is given by the sum of areas labeled a, b, c, and d [i.e., *loss in consumer surplus* is equal to $(a + b + c + d)$]. How much is this loss? Well, all we need to do is calculate the size of the area on the graph that represents the loss in consumer surplus. That is: rectangle $(a+b+c)$ + triangle $d = (\$5 \times 1,200) + (0.5 \times \$5 \times 250) = \textbf{\$6,625}$. Alternatively, recognizing that $(a + b + c + d)$ forms a trapezoid,[2] the combined area should be equal to:

$$\$5 \times [0.5 \times (1,200 + 1,450)] = \textbf{\$6,625}$$

We should now know from our definition (and illustration) of producer surplus that area a (in Figure 9.4) is a *gain in domestic producer surplus*. Therefore, part of the loss in consumer surplus (area a) is transferred to domestic producers. This gain in producer surplus is equal to $3,250 [$5 \times 0.5 \times (500 + 800)$].

Further, as discussed earlier in this chapter, as a result of the tariff, imports fell from 950 widgets (1,450 − 500) to 400 widgets (1,200 − 800). The government collects $5 in taxes (tariff) per imported widget. Therefore, *government revenue* from the tariff is equal to $2,000 ($5 × 400). Therefore, some of the lost consumer surplus is transferred to government in the form of tax revenue. This is represented by the area of the rectangle labeled c in Figure 9.4.

Areas labeled b and d in Figure 9.4 are part of lost consumer surplus. However, no one receives this part of the consumer loss! This is called **deadweight loss** (also known as **efficiency loss** or **welfare loss**). Areas a and c as are simply a redistribution from consumers to domestic producers and the government of the importing country. These represent a loss to consumers but not to the economy as a whole. However, deadweight loss is, indeed, a loss to the economy as a whole.

Area (triangle) b is often referred to as a **production distortion**. Note from Figure 9.4 that the increase in the price of a widget is an incentive for domestic producers to increase production. Domestic production of widgets increases by 300 widgets (from 500 to 800 widgets). In other words, government intervention in the market by imposing a tariff has distorted domestic producers' production decisions. These 300 widgets were initially (before the imposition of the tariff) not produced domestically because the pre-tariff world price of

---

[2] The area of trapezoid $= h \times \dfrac{(l_1 + l_2)}{2}$; where, l_1 and l_2 are the two lengths of the trapezoid and h is the height of the trapezoid.

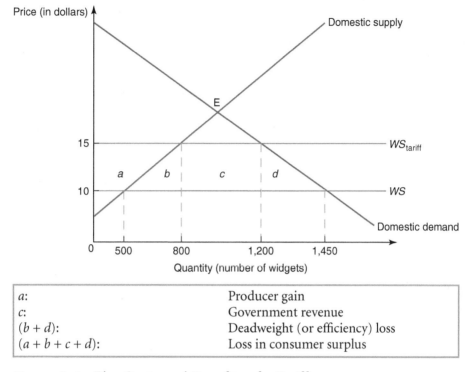

Figure 9.4   **The Costs and Benefits of a Tariff**

$10 is lower than the domestic cost of producing a widget (as shown by the supply curve) for output of widgets exceeding 500. The "artificial" increase in the domestic price to $15 (due to the tariff) makes the extra production viable. However, this distortion is not good for the economy because the cost of producing the extra 300 (from 500 to 800 widgets) exceeds the global price of $10. The economy is essentially spending more to produce the 300 widgets than it would cost to import them at a world price of $10 per widget. This is, obviously, an inefficient way to obtain these additional widgets, thus the label *efficiency loss*.

Area (triangle) *d* is often referred to as a **consumption distortion**. The increase in the domestic price as a result of the tariff leads to a 250-widget reduction in domestic quantity demanded (1,450 widgets − 1,200 widgets). Given the demand curve, consumers value each of these widgets anywhere between $10 and $15 (the value or benefit attached to each widget is reflected in the maximum price a consumer is willing to pay for the widget). The net benefit (equivalent to consumer surplus) for the consumer is given by the difference between the value attached to a widget (given by the demand curve) and the price a consumer will pay for it. By "artificially" increasing the price of a widget through the imposition of an import tariff, domestic consumers are deprived of the net benefit from each of the 250 widgets that they would have consumed at a world price of $10 per widget. This deprivation is a loss to the country or society as a whole.

You might be wondering if the above discussion would apply to a tariff imposed by a large country. The answer is "yes, for the most part." There is a small but profound difference between the effects of a small country tariff and those of a large country tariff. Once again, let's consider Figure 9.2. In addition to the loss in consumer surplus ($a + b + c + d$), we have area e. In the large country case, although the domestic price of a widget increases (as in a small country tariff), it does not increase by the full $5 tariff (as is the case in a small country tariff). The domestic price increased by $3. Therefore, domestic consumers only pay a portion of the tariff. The rest of the tariff ($5 − $3 = $2) is paid by foreign producers in the form of lower net-of-tax price (foreign producers keep $8 instead of the **pre-tariff** net price of $10).

As a result of the increase in price from $10 to $13, imports fall from 950 widgets (1,450 − 500) to 550 widgets (1,300 − 750). Therefore, for each of the 550 widgets imported, government collects $3 in taxes per widget from domestic buyers of widgets and $2 per widget from foreign producers of widgets (for a total of $5 tariff per widget). In Figure 9.2, total revenue to government is equal to the sum of areas c ($3 × 550 = $1,650) and e ($2 × 550 = $1,100). Area c represents total tax revenue to government from domestic consumers of widgets, while area e (sometimes referred to as **terms of trade gain**) represents tax revenue to government from foreign producers of widgets imported by the large country.

Notice that we still have deadweight/efficiency loss in the case of a large country tariff. The efficiency loss is defined just as in a small country tariff—equal to the area ($b + d$). In Figure 9.2, deadweight loss is equal to $600 {[3 × (750 − 500)/2] + [3 × (1,450 − 1,300)/2]}. Therefore, as a result of the tariff, the large country experiences a welfare loss equal $600 ($b + d$), but gains area e (revenues collected from foreign producers of widgets).

If $e > (b + d)$, the large country experiences a net welfare gain from the tariff. On the other hand, if $e < (b + d)$, the large country tariff causes a net welfare loss. There is no net welfare change when $e = (b + d)$. In the example illustrated in Figure 9.2, area $(b + d) = $600, while area e is equal to $1,100. Therefore the large country experiences a net welfare gain equal to $500 ($1,100 − $ 600).

NONTARIFF TRADE REGULATIONS

Nontariff regulations comprise an assortment of government policies intended to either reduce imports or increase exports. Such policies include import quotas, export subsidies, voluntary export restraints, bureaucratic procedures, and local content requirements.

In this section of the chapter, we discuss each of these policies in turn. Among these policies, import quotas are most widely used and discussed in most international economics textbooks. As such, we describe the effects of an import quota in a little bit more detail than the rest of the nontariff barriers to free trade.

Import Quotas

An **import quota** is a quantitative limit on the amount of a good that can be imported into a country. Import quotas are a more direct way to reduce imports relative to tariffs. Recall from our discussion of import tariffs that tariffs increase the price of the imported good in the importing country and indirectly reduces the quantity demanded of the good. Import quotas, on the other hand, explicitly regulate the amount of the good allowed into the country from a foreign country.

Types of Import Quotas: There are two types of import quotas. These are:

Absolute Quota: An absolute quota limits the amount of a good that may enter the country in a given period of time, usually one year. For example, a U.S. import quota on sugar of 4 million metric tons per year would be an example of an absolute quota. Import quotas could be worldwide (i.e., all exporting countries are subject to the quota limitation) or country-specific (designed to affect a particular trade partner or group of trade partners).

In the United States, import quotas are enforced by the U.S. Customs department but set by the department of commerce in conjunction with the Office of the U.S. Trade Representative (USTR). Import licenses may be issued to limit imports to the quota amount.

Tariff-Rate Quota: A tariff-rate quota allows a specified amount (quota) of a good to be imported into the country at a reduced tariff rate (could be zero percent tariff) and a higher tariff rate for imports exceeding the quota in a given quota period. In other words, a tariff-rate quota sets no strict limits on the quantity of a good that can be imported into the country. However, imports exceeding the quota during the quota period are subject to higher customs duties (tariffs). For example, if the United States allowed 2 million metric tons of sugar to be imported into the country per year at zero percent tariff-rate, and 10% for sugar imports exceeding the 2 million metric tons quota, this policy would be a tariff-rate quota.

The Effects of an Import Quota: By restricting imports, an import quota reduces the total supply of a good in the importing country. Given the demand for the good, a smaller supply means a higher domestic price of the imported good. As noted earlier in this chapter, a higher domestic price incentivizes domestic producers to increase production, while reducing domestic quantity demanded of the imported good. Therefore, an import quota hurts domestic consumers and benefits domestic producers in the importing country. Imagine a small country that imposes an absolute import quota on beef. Figure 9.5 demonstrates the effects of such a policy on the importing country.

In Figure 9.5, the world price of a ton of beef is $10,000. At this price, the country imports 250 (650 − 400) tons of beef. However, the government of the country restricts imports of beef to 75 tons (import quota = 75 tons). As result, the domestic price of beef increases until imports of beef match the quota of 75 tons. The new price in the domestic market is $12,000 per ton. Similar to the effects of an import tariff, the increase in price resulting from the imposition of an import quota reduces consumer surplus in the importing country and increases domestic producer surplus. In Figure 9.5, the loss in consumer surplus is given by the sum of areas labeled *a, b, c,* and *d.* These areas combined form a trapezoid whose area is equal to $1,250,000 [($12,000 − $10,000) × (600 + 650)/2].

A portion of the consumer loss is received by domestic producers. In Figure 9.5, domestic production of beef increases by 125 tons as a result of the import quota (from 400 tons to 525 tons). In addition to their increased share of the domestic market, domestic producers charge a higher price of $12,000 compared to $10,000 before the imposition of the quota. The gain in producer surplus is labeled *a* in Figure 9.5, and is equal to $925,000 [($12,000 − $10,000) × (400 + 525)/2].

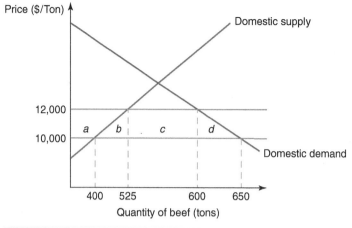

Figure 9.5   The Effects of an Import Quota

The effects of an import quota differ from those of an import tariff in one significant way: The importing country government does not collect revenue. An import quota is not a tax, and therefore does not raise revenue for the importing government.[3] On the other hand, an import tariff is a tax that increases government revenue. Therefore, area *c* in Figure 9.5 (which would have represented government revenue in the case of a tariff) represents *quota rents*.

Quota rents are additional revenues to holders of import licenses. When the domestic price of an imported good increases as a result of the quota, importers who hold import licenses collect a higher per unit price. Quota rents represent these additional revenues to importers. In Figure 9.5, holders of import licenses collect an extra $2,000 ($12,000 − $10,000) for each of the 75 tons of imported beef. Therefore, quota rents in this example (area *c*) are equal to $150,000 ($2,000 × 75 tons).[4] Areas labeled *b* and *d* represent deadweight (efficiency/welfare) loss resulting from the imposition of the import quota. In this example, deadweight loss (the sum of production and consumption distortions) is equal to $175,000 {[($12,000 − $10,000) × 0.5 × (525 − 400)] + [($12,000 − $10,000) × 0.5 × (650 − 600)]}. Refer to the preceding section (on import tariffs) for a discussion of the meaning of deadweight loss.

---

[3] Importing country government could potentially collect revenues through the sale of import licenses. This, however, is not typical.
[4] Quota Rents = Increase in Price × Quota

THE U.S. SUGAR POLICY

For over a century, the United States has had laws affecting imports of sugar from foreign countries. The first Sugar Act was enacted in 1934. Although these laws have evolved over the years, the current policies have barely changed for decades. Sugar imports into the United States are subject to a tariff-rate quota (TRQ). The tariff-rate quota allows a certain amount of sugar imports (the quota amount) at a low tariff rate and a higher tariff rate for any amount exceeding the quota amount. Each year, the United States Department of Agriculture (USDA) sets the quota amount subject to a minimum of 1.2 million tons (this minimum quota amount is in accordance with WTO provisions). The USDA then monitors domestic production of sugar and decides whether to adjust the quota amount during the quota period.

What are the effects of such a policy on U.S. national welfare? In December 2015, world raw sugar price was about $0.150/lb. In contrast, U.S. wholesale price of sugar was $0.26/lb. This price differential (of $0.11/lb.) between the U.S. price and world price may seem insignificant when not put in a proper perspective. However, consider that total sugar consumption in the United States in 2015 was about 10.2 million metric tons (1 metric ton = 2,000 pounds). This implies that the $0.11/lb price differential increased total annual U.S. sugar expenditure by approximately $2.244 billion, which is not insignificant at all.

As we saw in Figure 9.5, an import quota, just like other trade regulations, create efficiency losses (deadweight loss or welfare losses). These losses are a result of the policy's distortionary effects both on the consumption and the production side of the market. Studies in the late 1990s and early 2000s estimated that sugar import restrictions protect 2,260 jobs in the sugar industry while employment decreased in industries producing sugar-containing products (SCPs). Most of these jobs in the SCPs industries are lost as a result of companies relocating to other countries to access lower sugar prices. A 2006 study by the United States International Trade Commission (USITC) in the U.S. Department of Commerce reports an estimated annual cost of a job saved by sugar import restrictions at $826,000. A more recent (2011) USITC study reports that liberalizing the U.S. sugar market (removal of import restrictions) would increase U.S. welfare by $49 million in 2015.

Voluntary Export Restraints

Voluntary export restraints (VERs) are trade quotas imposed by the exporting country usually at the request of the importing country. Voluntary export restraints may result from agreements between producers in the importing country and their counterparts in the exporting country, specifying a limit on shipments of goods from the exporting country to the importing country. Therefore, similar to an import quota, a VER holds down imports from the perspective of the importing country. VERs are referred to as *voluntary* because exporters are offered a choice between potential barriers imposed by the importing country (such as tariffs and import quotas) and voluntary reductions in exports. Like most trade barriers, the goal is to protect domestic producers from foreign competitors. From the perspective of foreign exporters, a VER may be preferred to government-imposed import restrictions for two main reasons.

a. Producers in the exporting country capture *quota rents–equivalent* revenues: This is so because of the increase in the domestic price of the good in the importing country. Foreign producers who supply the limited amount of the good obtain higher (per unit) revenues.

b. Producers in the exporting country may not want to subject themselves to the whims of politicians in the importing country. Since VERs may be negotiated between producers in two countries, they may allow more flexibility compared to import restrictions imposed by government.

A common example of VERs is the *U.S.-Japan* automobile VER program in the early 1980s. The VER initially restricted Japanese exports of cars to the United States to 1.68 million cars per year. The quota was eventually increased to 2.3 million cars. The program ended in 1994.

By design, VERs are discriminatory. VERs are agreements negotiated between the importing country and producers in a specific exporting country. Therefore, other exporters are not subject to the agreement. For example, when the U.S. auto industry or government negotiates a VER with Japanese automakers, such a VER does not limit imports from Europe. As a result, the demand for third-party (Europe in this case) imports should be expected to increase. In fact, a study conducted by Elias Dinopoulos and Mordechai Kreinin (1988)[5] showed that European producers raised their prices as a result of the U.S.-Japan VER.

Other Effects of Voluntary Export Restraints

1. VERs restrict imports and total domestic supply of the good in the importing country.
2. The domestic price of the good increases due to limited supply.
3. Domestic quantity demanded falls, while domestic production (quantity supplied) of the good increases.
4. Domestic consumer surplus falls, while domestic producer surplus increases.
5. Loss in welfare in the importing country (deadweight/efficiency loss).

Export Subsidies

An **export subsidy** is a subsidy granted by government to producers who ship their products to foreign markets. In general, a subsidy should be understood as a "negative tax." As in the case of tariffs, an export subsidy is either a *specific subsidy* (amount of money per unit) or an *ad valorem subsidy* (a percentage of the monetary value of goods exported). It is important to note that an export subsidy is different from a general production subsidy. A typical production subsidy is provided to producers of a product regardless of where they sell the

---

[5] Elias Dinopoulos and Mordechai E. Kreinin, "Effects of the U.S.–Japan Auto VER on European Prices and on U.S. Welfare." *The Review of Economics and Statistics*, 70 (3) (August 1988): 484–491.

product. On the other hand, an export subsidy is only provided on qualifying products that are exported to foreign markets. An export subsidy does not apply to output sold in the domestic market.

Export subsidies are often used to stabilize a country's domestic price of the subsidized good. Imagine a case where producers of a particular good X produce way more than the domestic market can absorb. This could happen in cases of a bumper harvest in agricultural production that may result from unusually favorable weather conditions. In such instances, the domestic price of the good would drop dramatically. To stabilize the domestic market price in favor of domestic producers, the government may consider providing an export subsidy to encourage producers to ship their produce abroad.

Effects of an Export Subsidy: An export subsidy reduces the supply of the good on the domestic market (exporting country) and therefore raises the domestic price of the good. In contrast, assuming the case of a large country, world prices of the good would fall as a result of increased supply of the good in the world market.

Therefore:

1. Domestic consumers (consumers in the country providing the export subsidy) are worse off (their consumer surplus is reduced).
2. Foreign consumers, on the other hand, benefit (their consumer surplus increases) from lower world prices resulting from the export subsidy.

The export subsidy also causes loss in welfare resulting from the distortionary (both consumption and production) effects of the export subsidy. This is what we referred to as deadweight loss or efficiency loss. Moreover, overall national welfare in the domestic country (the one providing the subsidy) falls because of both the efficiency loss as well as the opportunity costs of funds used to run the government's export subsidy program.

Local Content Requirements

Local content requirements are a type of government regulation that requires domestic producers of a good to use a specified percentage of domestic inputs in their production process. In other words, a specified proportion of the total value of the good has to be produced domestically. This limits importation of intermediate products (inputs or raw materials). The specific forms that local content requirements take vary from country to country, industry to industry, and often within industries. For example, foreign companies may be subjected to different requirements than domestic companies. A requirement that foreign companies partner with a local company in the production or distribution of a good or specific requirements on the composition of the company's workforce (local versus international workers) are examples of local content requirements.

Local content requirements benefit domestic producers of inputs (raw materials) at the expense of domestic producers of the final product, and ultimately, the consumers of the final good (in the form of a higher price). Domestic consumer surplus falls while domestic producer surplus would only be affected to the extent that the producer (seller) is unable to shift the entire increase in the cost of inputs to consumers (buyers).

The goal of restrictions on imports of intermediate products is primarily to boost the local industries that produce these inputs by guaranteeing a portion of the market for their products. This is associated with more local jobs and perhaps more corporate responsibility. Local content requirements, unlike import quotas, do not explicitly limit importation of the goods. Rather, a domestic producer is free to import (and use) as much foreign inputs as long as it also continues to use domestic inputs in the required proportions.

Other Government Bureaucratic Regulations

Governments have a number of other policy tools at their disposal to regulate international trade. These include **government procurement regulations** that require government departments and agencies to purchase only locally (domestic) made products. This directly limits the amount of imports. In addition, bureaucratic regulations related to *product safety and quality standards* may limit the volume of trade. This is especially true when coupled with customs requirements to certify that imported goods meet the specified safety and quality standards. The inconvenience, time, and other resources required to meet such regulatory requirements could be a major impediment to international trade.

SUMMARY

- Although trade is generally proven to provide benefits to trading countries, in practice governments impose a wide range of restriction on the flow of goods and services across nations.
- An import tariff, which is a tax on imported goods, is one of the most widely used policy tools to restrict the amount of goods imported into a country from other nations. Import tariffs are either levied as a fixed fee per unit of the good imported (*specific* tariff) or as a percentage of the value of goods imported (*ad valorem* tariff).
- Import tariffs increase the price of the traded good, limits the amount of the good imported, and increases the domestic production of the good. Therefore, tariffs benefit domestic producers at the expense of domestic consumers.
- A tariff imposed by a small country has no impact on the world price of the taxed good. In this case, the domestic price of the good increases by the full amount of the tariff. This means that domestic consumers (consumers in the importing country that imposed the tariff) pay the entire amount of the tariff.
- A tariff imposed by a large country causes the world price of the good to fall. In this case, the domestic price of the good increases, but does so by a portion of the tariff amount (as opposed to increasing by the entire amount of the tariff as is the case in a small country tariff). In this case, the burden of the tariff is shared between domestic consumers and foreign producers.
- Since import tariffs increase the domestic price of the imported good, domestic consumer surplus falls while domestic producer surplus rises. The government of the importing country receives revenue equal to the product of the tariff per unit and the quantity of imports.

- The tariff-driven increase in the domestic price of the imported good also creates distortions in the economy. Because of the higher price, domestic quantity supplied of the good rises while domestic quantity demanded of the good falls. As a result, consumers lose value on the units of the good not consumed (net value lost = consumers' willingness to pay – the world price of the good). On the other hand, domestic producers are supplying more units of the good than they would without the tariff. The loss in efficiency here results from the difference between the (higher) cost of producing the additional domestic output and the (lower) world price of the good. These losses in efficiency and/or welfare are referred to as *deadweight* loss.

- Besides tariffs, governments use nontariff barriers to limit trade. These include import quotas (a quantitative limit on imports), voluntary export restraints, export subsidies, and other bureaucratic procedures.

- Import quotas are of two types—absolute quotas that set a specified amount of a good that can be imported into the country in a given period of time, and tariff-rate quotas that allow a set amount of the good (quota amount) to be imported into the country at a lower tariff rate (could even be zero) and imposes a higher tariff rate on imports exceeding the quota amount.

- The effects of an import quota on price, domestic consumers, and domestic producers are similar to those of an import tariff—the domestic price of the good increases, domestic consumers are worse as a result of the import restriction, domestic producers of the imported good are better off, and overall national welfare is likely to fall.

- Since an import quota is not a tax, government receives no revenue. Instead, the tax-equivalent revenues go to holders of import licenses (those who are permitted to import the restricted amount or the quota amount). These additional revenues to import license holders are called *quota rents*.

- Voluntary export restraints (VERs) are trade quotas imposed by the exporting country at the request of the importing country. The effects of a VER on the domestic (importing) country are very similar to those of an import quota. However, in the case of a VER, the quota rents–equivalent revenues are received by producers in the exporting country.

- An export subsidy is a subsidy granted to producers who ship their products abroad as opposed to selling them in the domestic market. Such a policy creates a strong incentive for domestic producers of the exported good to sell abroad rather than at home. As a result, the domestic price increases, consumer surplus falls, domestic producer surplus rises, and government revenue falls. Moreover, export subsidies, as is the case for all trade regulations, creates efficiency loss in the form of production distortion and consumption distortion.

- Local content requirements oblige domestic producers to use a specified percentage of local inputs in their production processes. Such regulations require a predetermined proportion of a good to be domestic.

- Other trade regulations include bureaucratic requirements on government agencies to purchase domestically produced goods as well as product safety and quality standards.

KEY TERMS

Tariff
Import tariff
Consumption distortion
Ad valorem tariff
Terms of trade gain
Specific tariff
Import quota
Combination (compound) tariff
Absolute quota
Small country
Forward-shifted tax
Backward-shifted tax

Tariff-rate quota
Large country
Quota rents
Consumer surplus
Voluntary export restraints
Producer surplus
Export subsidy
Deadweight loss; efficiency loss; welfare loss
Local content requirements
Production distortion
Government procurement regulations

PROBLEMS

1. Chapter 5 of this book demonstrates gains from trade. If trade is good for participating nations, why do governments regulate the amount and scope of international trade?
2. Briefly explain why the effects of an import tariff imposed by a *small* country differ from those of an import tariff imposed by a *large* country.
3. In the cell phone market, Liberia is a small country. If Liberia imposes a 15% tariff on all imported cell phones, how is the price of cell phones in the United States affected by this tariff?

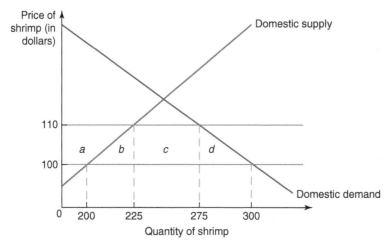

A Small Country Tariff

4. Using the above graph, answer the following questions.
   a. How much is the tariff?
   b. How much is the government revenue from the tariff?

c. How much are imports before the tariff?

d. How much are imports after the tariff?

e. What areas on the graph represent the gain in producer surplus after the tariff?

f. What areas on the graph represent the loss in consumer surplus after the tariff?

g. After the tariff is imposed what areas on the graph represent the loss to the economy as a whole?

5. In January 2013, the price tag on a t-shirt in Trina's T-Shop was $10. In February 2013, the government imposed a new tax of $1.00 on each t-shirt sold. A customer buys a t-shirt in February and pays a total of $10.65.

a. How much of the tax is forward-shifted (to the buyer)?

b. How much of the tax is backward-shifted (to the seller)?

6. What is the main difference between an import tariff and an absolute import quota?

7. If you were a foreign producer exporting goods to the United States, would you prefer that the U.S. government imposes an import tariff or an import quota? Why? (Note: neither is NOT an option.)

8. The graph below shows supply and demand for widgets in a small country. The price of widgets with no quota is $20, as shown. When the government imposes an absolute quota on widgets imported into the country, the price of widgets in the country increases to $30.

a. How many widgets were imported before the quota? _____

b. How many widgets are imported with the quota? _____

c. What is the amount of the imposed quota? _____

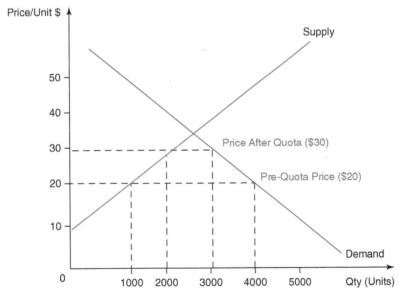

Domestic Supply and Demand for Widgets in a Small Country

9. Define a voluntary export restraint (VER).

10. Discuss two reasons why a foreign exporter may prefer a VER over an import quota imposed by the importing country government.
11. Briefly explain how the effects of a VER on the importing country may differ from those of a government-imposed import quota.
12. State the effect of an export subsidy on the following:
    a. Price of the good in the exporting country
    b. Price of the good in the importing country
    c. Consumer surplus in the exporting country
    d. Consumer surplus in the importing country
    e. National welfare in the exporting country
    f. National welfare in the importing country
13. Define, explain, and compare/contrast the following terms:
    a. Import tariff versus import quota
    b. Specific tariff versus ad valorem tariff
    c. Small country versus large country
    d. Production distortion versus consumption distortion
    e. Absolute quota versus tariff-rate quota
    f. Voluntary export restraints (VERs) versus quota rents
    g. Export subsidy versus local content requirements

10

Trade Agreements and Economic Integration

n Chapter 7, we discussed the substantial role of multilateral negotiations under the GATT and later the World Trade Organization (WTO) in reducing average tariffs on goods. Countries, especially developed countries, have not only reduced their average duty rates on imported goods, but have also agreed not to raise them again. This commitment not to raise tariffs is referred to as **binding** the tariff. According to the WTO, since it began operations in early 1995, developed countries' customs duties (tariffs) on industrial products have dropped by about 40% from an average of 6.3% to 3.8%.

Much as the role of multilateral approaches to global trade liberalization is irrefutable, regional trade and/or bilateral trade agreements have also played an important role in reducing average customs duties on imports. Ironically, the establishment of a majority of preferential trade agreements coincided with the conception and eventual establishment of the WTO.

In this chapter, we describe the various forms of trade agreements and extend the discussion to forms of agreements that go beyond trade in goods and services. The chapter will also discuss the economic effects of preferential trade agreements. A few case studies of regional trading blocs will be examined. Finally, the potential effect of regional trading arrangements on the multilateral trading system is discussed.

LEARNING GOALS

➤ Understand the nature and scope of preferential trade agreements.
➤ Define and describe the different forms of economic integration.
➤ Understand and illustrate the effects of free trade agreements.

➤ Describe the effects of the North American Free Trade Agreement (NAFTA) on the economies of the United States, Canada, and Mexico.

➤ Understand the history of the European Union (EU) and the EU institutions.

➤ Describe the significance of the EU in global trade.

➤ Understand the scope and significance of economic integration in developing countries.

➤ Understand the relationship between preferential trade agreements and the "equal treatment" multilateral trading system.

PREFERENTIAL TRADE ARRANGEMENTS AND FREE TRADE AGREEMENTS

Trade agreements establish preferential treatment in trade between or among countries participating in the agreement. In other words, countries agree to further reduce or remove barriers to trade among participating nations. The degree of free trade and economic integration is determined by the depth and scope of the particular agreement reached. Trade agreements lead to either *preferential trade arrangements* or *free trade areas*. Further integration among countries is achieved through a common market and ultimately an economic union. In the next subsection, we describe these different forms of trade agreements, followed by a subsection on deeper forms of economic integration—*common markets* and *economic unions*.

Forms of Trade Agreements

Trade agreements are generally divided into two categories—preferential trade arrangements (PTAs) and free trade agreements (FTAs).

Preferential trade arrangements (**PTAs**) are agreements that involve partial non-reciprocal preferences offered by a country to another country or group of countries. An important point to note here is that PTAs are mostly unilateral preferences (offered by one country), and the country on the receiving end of the deal does not have to offer the same preferences to the first country (nonreciprocal). Examples of PTAs include the Generalized System of Preferences (GSP) that allows developed countries to offer preferential customs duties on imports from developing countries, the Andean Trade Preference Act (provider: United States; beneficiaries: Columbia and Ecuador), and the African Growth and Opportunity Act (AGOA) (provider: United States; beneficiaries: 40 sub-Saharan African countries). Although about 40 Sub-Saharan African countries have benefited from AGOA, the number of beneficiaries changes from time to time. Beneficiaries change either because a country (or countries) has graduated from AGOA or has been declared ineligible by the United States because it is not meeting the illegibility conditions in the agreement.

PTAs represent the shallowest form of economic integration relative to other forms of agreements discussed in this chapter. There are 29 PTAs currently in force as reported to the WTO. Although the number of agreements is relatively small, the list of beneficiaries is virtually all developing countries.

Free trade agreements (**FTAs**) remove all (or most) barriers to trade among participating nations. FTAs are *reciprocal* agreements in the sense that each participating nation is obliged to offer the same preferences it receives from other participating nations. Often FTAs are (inaccurately) referred to as regional trade agreements (RTAs) because they are commonly established between or among countries in close geographical proximity or in the same region. This is, however, not a requirement for an FTA to be established. The WTO reports 278 FTAs in force as of February 2016. Most of these have been established in the last 20 years. FTAs establish two types of trading arrangements—*free trade areas* and *customs unions*.

A **free trade area** is formed when a trade agreement removes all (or most) trade barriers (such as import tariffs and import quotas) among participating nations (parties to the trade agreement) but allows participating nations to maintain separate trade policies with non-participating nations. An example of a Free Trade Area is the **North American Free Trade Agreement** (NAFTA). NAFTA established a free trade area that includes three countries—Canada, Mexico, and the United States. The three member countries enjoy free trade among themselves, but each of them maintains a separate trade policy with non-NAFTA countries.

In a **customs union**, participating nations under a FTA agree to free movement of goods and services (no trade barriers) among themselves and a common trade policy with nonparticipating countries. Note that the difference between a *free trade area* and a *customs union*

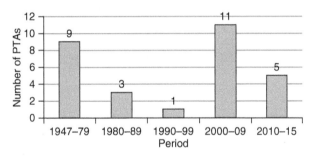

Figure 10.1   Preferential Trade Arrangements in Force as of February 2016
Source: By authors using the WTO's *PTA database*

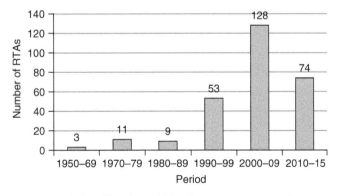

Figure 10.2   Regional Trade Agreements in force as of February 2016
Source: By authors using data from the WTO's *RTA database*

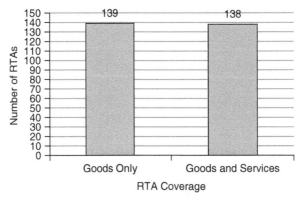

Figure 10.3 **Regional Trade Agreements by Category as of February 2016**
Source: By authors using data from the WTO's *RTA Database*

is the common or uniform trade policy with nonmember countries in a customs union. A free trade area allows member nations to design their own external trade policies. Therefore, a customs union represents a deeper degree of economic integration relative to a free trade area. A common example of a customs union is the **European Union** (EU).

COMMON MARKETS AND ECONOMIC UNIONS

A **common market** is a form of economic integration that goes beyond a customs union. In a common market, countries allow free movement of goods and services, maintain a common external trade policy, and remove all or most restriction on the movement of labor and capital across member nations. A common market represents a stronger degree of economic integration than exists under a free trade area or a customs union. Today's EU (formerly the European Economic Community) is an example of a common market. The EU allows free trade in goods and services as well as free movement of labor and capital among its member countries.[1] This suggests that citizens of EU member countries can move freely for work, school, or any other reason throughout the EU territory.

An **economic union** is the deepest form of economic integration among sovereign nations. An economic union entails all features of a common market—free movement of goods and services, common external trade policy, and unhindered movement of labor and capital—but also comprises a closer coordination and harmonization of participating nations' major economic policies. Such major economic policies may range from harmonized fiscal and monetary policies, environmental protection and economic sustainability

---

[1] You may have noticed the use of the European Union as an example of a customs union and a common market. We certainly do not intend to confuse the reader. However, as discussed in this chapter, every common market should have all elements of a customs union. Simply put, add "free movement of labor and capital" to a customs union and you have a common market. Moreover, examples of actually functioning common markets are hard to come by. Common markets are not common!

policies to agriculture, industrial, and transportation/aviation policies. Although countries in an economic union could opt to adopt a common currency, an economic union does not require its members to have a common official currency. Again, the EU is a good example of an economic union. Advancing from a *common market* to an *economic union* is perhaps in recognition of the fact that a common market without close economic surveillance of individual member nations' economic policies puts the entire union at risk due to the strong economic interdependence under a common market. An economic union provides for a better chance of identifying early warning signs of potential systemic economic risks that can be addressed before turning into full-blown economic crises.

THE EFFECTS OF FREE TRADE AGREEMENTS

When countries agree to offer preferential treatment in trade to one another, there is bound to be changes in how much they trade and whom they trade with. It is reasonable to assume that one of the goals of establishing a free trade area or a customs union is to increase trade among participating nations. In this section of the chapter, we discuss two important concepts regarding the effects of free trade areas and/or customs unions. These concepts are *trade creation* and *trade diversion*.

Trade creation occurs when a country replaces high-cost domestic production with low-cost imports from a member country of a shared FTA. For example, as a result of establishing the North American Free Trade Area (NAFTA), some of the goods and services produced and consumed in the United States prior to NAFTA may have been replaced with cheaper imports from Mexico. Therefore, trade creation unambiguously improves the welfare of the importing country because it replaces expensive domestic products with cheaper imports.

Trade diversion occurs when low-cost imports from a nonmember country are replaced with high-cost imports from a member country to a shared FTA. For example, assume that Brazil is a lower-cost producer of footwear relative to Mexico. This would suggest that with nondiscriminatory treatment (say each country's imports are subjected to a 20% U.S.-imposed tariff) of the two countries, U.S. consumers would choose to import footwear from Brazil rather than from Mexico. However, NAFTA gives preferential treatment (zero percent tariff) to Mexico (a NAFTA member) and not to Brazil (a non-NAFTA member). In this case, it is likely that U.S. consumers will now choose to import footwear from Mexico and not Brazil. This is trade diversion—the creation of NAFTA has diverted some of U.S. trade from Brazil to Mexico. This reduces national welfare in the importing country since it substitutes cheaper imports from a non-NAFTA member with expensive imports from a NAFTA member.

Illustration of Trade Creation and Trade Diversion

In Figure 10.4, we illustrate the concepts of trade creation and trade diversion and their effects on national welfare. Imagine three countries—Country 1, Country 2, and Country 3. Further assume that Country 1 is an importer of widgets (the country does not produce enough of its own widgets, and therefore has to import some), while Countries 2 and 3

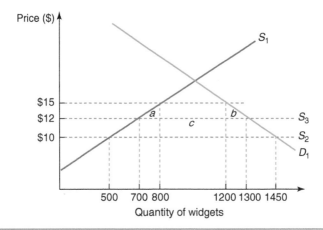

Figure 10.4   **Trade Diversion and Trade Creation**

> This graph illustrates the market for widgets in Country 1. Country 1 is an importer of widgets, and has two potential trade partners (Country 2 and Country 3). The perfectly elastic supply curve denoted by S_2 is Country 2's supply of widgets to Country 1. Similarly, S_3 denotes Country 3's supply of widgets to Country 1. If Country 1 were to impose a nondiscriminatory import tariff of 50% on widgets, it is obvious that Country 2 would be the preferred supplier of widgets to Country 1. However, this changes if Countries 1 and 3 form a free trade area or a customs union.

are exporters of widgets. Obviously, buyers of widgets in Country 1 would prefer a cheaper source for their imports of widgets.

In Figure 10.4, S_1 and D_1 denote Country 1's supply of and demand for widgets, respectively. S_2 and S_3 represent the supply of widgets to country 1 from Country 2 and Country 3, respectively under free trade. Notice that S_2 and S_3 are perfectly elastic supply curves. This suggests that Country 1 takes the free market price of a widget as given.

From Figure 10.4, we know that Country 1 can import widgets at a price of $10 each from Country 2. This should be preferred to imports from Country 3 at a price of $12 per widget. At $10 per widget, Country 1 consumes 1,450 widgets (500 widgets are produced domestically and 950 widgets are imported).

Now let's assume that Country 1 imposes a nondiscriminatory tariff of 50% on imports of widgets. This would increase the price of a widget imported from Country 2 to $15 [$10 + (0.5 × $10)]. At this new price of $15 per widget, Country 1 consumes 1,200 widgets (800 widgets are produced domestically; 400 widgets are imported from Country 2).

What happens when Country 1 and Country 3 form a free trade area or a customs union? The Customs Union provides preferential treatment for imports from Country 3 while maintaining the 50% tariff on widgets imported from Country 2. In this case, Country 3 is a cheaper source of widgets for Country 1. Country 3's free trade price of $12 per widget is lower than the tariff-inclusive price ($15) of a widget imported from Country 2. As a result of the customs union (and a lower price of $12 per widget), Country 1's total quantity demand of widgets increases from 1,200 to 1,300 widgets (700 widgets are produced domestically; 600 widgets are imported from Country 3). The increase in imports from 400 widgets (imports at the pre-customs union price of $15) to 600 widgets (at a post-customs union price of $12) is called *trade creation*. In Figure 10.4, trade creation is associated with welfare gains to Country 1 equal to the sum of areas labeled *a* and *b*. This is equal to $300 [(0.5 × 3 × 100) + (0.5 × 3 × 100)].

However, going by their free trade prices, Country 2 is a more efficient (less costly) producer of widgets. Therefore, a customs union between Country 1 and Country 3 gives a competitive advantage to a less efficient producer of widgets (Country 3) because of the discriminatory tariff. Trade between Country 1 and Country 3 takes place at the expense of Country 1's trade with a more efficient producer of widgets—Country 2. This describes the concept of *trade diversion*.

Without the discriminatory tariff on Country 2's (the nonmember to the customs union) widgets, the original 400 widgets imported from Country 2 would cost $10 (compared to Country 3's free trade price of $12). By no longer importing the 400 widgets from Country 2, Country 1 experiences a welfare loss equal to the area of the rectangle labeled *c* in Figure 10.4. This welfare loss to Country 1 resulting from diverting trade from a more efficient producer of widgets (Country 2) to a less efficient producer (Country 3) is equal to $800 ($2 × 400 widgets).

We conclude this subsection by observing that establishment of free trade areas and/or customs unions leads to both trade creation and trade diversion. Since these two effects have opposite effects on national welfare, the overall welfare effect of free trade areas or customs unions depends on the relative magnitudes of trade creation and trade diversion. In our example, the negative welfare effect of trade diversion exceeds the welfare gain from trade creation (i.e., $c > (a + b)$). In this hypothetical example, the FTA reduces national welfare.

In the case of a *free trade area* (and not *customs union*), external trade policies (e.g., tariffs on goods from nonmember countries) are not harmonized. As such, there is a potential for nonmember countries to circumvent the unfavorable treatment by shipping their goods to one of the member nations in a free trade area in order to gain access the entire free trade area. This is called **trade deflection**.

Let us use our previous example to illustrate how this would work. As assumed, Country 1 and Country 3 are members of a free trade area. Under the free trade area, Country 1 and Country 3 have separate trade policies with Country 2 (the nonmember to the free trade area). If Country 2 were able reach a separate agreement with Country 3 (that does not involve Country 1) that allows some sort of preferential treatment, it might be advantageous for Country 2 to ship widgets to Country 1 through Country 3. If this happened, Country 2 would be engaging in *trade deflection*.

For obvious reasons, the importing member country to a FTA will have interest in preventing or at least reducing trade deflection. One way this is achieved is through provisions in trade agreements know as rules of origin. The **rules of origin** are legal provisions in preferential trade agreements specifying which goods will be eligible for preferential treatment under the FTA. Given the rules of origin, goods shipped from a nonmember country to a member country to a FTA and then shipped to yet another member country within the free trade zone may not be granted preferential treatment under the FTA.

THE NORTH AMERICAN FREE TRADE AREA (NAFTA)

The North American Free Trade Area (NATFA) is a free trade zone created by an agreement signed in 1992 by the governments of Canada, Mexico, and the United States. NAFTA took effect on January 1, 1994. NAFTA eliminated tariffs on goods and services traded among the three signatory nations. Further, the FTA provided for a gradual phase-out of all nontariff barriers to trade among the three member nations. As noted earlier in the definition of a free trade area, NAFTA member countries maintain separate external trade policies. In other words, member countries trade policies with non-NAFTA countries are not harmonized as would be required in a customs union. More than two decades after its establishment, what impact has it had on the economies of member countries? This section seeks to highlight some of what is believed to be NAFTA's impact.

The Effect of NAFTA on the U.S. Economy

The approval of the North American Free Trade Agreement (NAFTA) by the U.S. Congress was preceded by a heated political debate on potential effects of the free trade bloc on the U.S. economy. Opponents of NAFTA argued that the FTA would benefit the Mexican economy at the expense of the United States. They suggested that increased imports from Mexico and relocation of American manufacturing firms to low-wage Mexico would devastate the U.S. job market. Ross Perot, a U.S. presidential candidate in 1992, famously warned of the "Giant Sucking Sound" in reference of U.S. jobs lost to Mexico if the free-trade agreement were approved.

Although a number of NAFTA provisions were to be phased-in over a period of 15 years, researchers have been examining the impact of NAFTA on the U.S. economy and the region at large. This section of the chapter presents a basic description of U.S. trade with the two other NAFTA members—Canada and Mexico—as well as U.S. employment before and after NAFTA.

NAFTA and U.S. Trade with Canada: Canada is the top trade partner of the United States. In 2015, U.S. exports to Canada amounted to about US$338,397 millions (or to about 15.2% of total U.S. exports). U.S. imports from Canada amounted to about US$332,949 millions (or about 12% of total U.S. imports). The question here is how much of this trade between the United States and Canada is attributed to NAFTA. Although we are not providing a definite answer to this question, Figure 10.5 suggests that the establishment of NAFTA did not have a significant effect of U.S.-Canada trade.[2]

In Figure 10.5, the height of the bars represent Canada's share in U.S. imports and exports. For example, during the pre-NAFTA period (1987–1993), about 18.5% of U.S. imports came from Canada and about 21.4% of U.S. exports were shipped out to Canada. NAFTA went into effect on January 1, 1994. We do not observe any significant changes in Canada's share of U.S. trade following the establishment of NAFTA.

---

[2] In the real world, trade flows, just like many other macroeconomic variables are influenced by a number of different factors. Therefore, it is difficult to pin any observed changes to a specific factor.

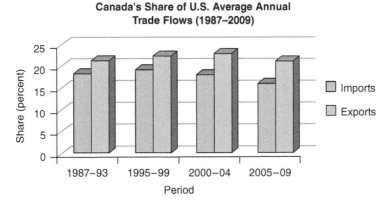

Figure 10.5   The Effect of NAFTA on U.S.-Canada Trade

Source: By authors using data from the *United Nations Conference on Trade and Development* (UNCTAD) and *Statistics Canada*.

If NAFTA was intended to increase trade among the signatory nations, why are we not seeing substantial changes in U.S.-Canada trade? The answer to this question has to do with the U.S.-Canada trade relations prior to NAFTA. Five years before NAFTA took effect, the United States and Canada agreed to a bilateral FTA. The agreement was reached in 1987 between governments of the two countries. The legislatures in the two countries approved the agreement in 1988, and the free trade area (FTA) took effect at the beginning of 1989.

Given this pre-existing FTA, NAFTA essentially added Mexico to the agreement and expanded the size of the regional trade bloc. Therefore, it's not surprising that NAFTA did not substantially affect U.S.-Canada trade flows. Moreover, the United States is, by far, the largest economy in the region (and in the world). As such, it is unlikely that Canada would divert much of its trade with the United States to Mexico as a result of establishing NAFTA.

NAFTA and U.S. Trade with Mexico: Mexico's economy is much smaller than that of the United States as measured by gross domestic product (GDP). In 2015, the U.S. economy was about 15 times larger than the Mexican economy (Mexico's GDP estimated at US$1.144 trillion; U.S. GDP estimated at US$ 17.947 trillion). With a total estimated population of about 127 million in 2015, Mexico's per capita GDP was about US$10,000 (about one-fifth of U.S. per capita GDP). In terms of global trade, Mexico accounts for about 2% to 3% of total global trade.

These statistics notwithstanding, Mexico is one of the top trading partners of the United States. In Chapter 8, we speculated that the volume of trade between the United States and Mexico can be explained by two major factors—proximity and NAFTA. Obviously, the distance between the two countries has not changed. If we observe any changes in trade flows between the two countries coinciding with the establishment of NAFTA, we can reasonably attribute the changes to the formation of the free trade area.

Figure 10.6 shows a substantial change in Mexico's share of U.S. trade. Mexico's share of U.S. imports is the percentage of annual U.S. imports that come from Mexico. Similarly,

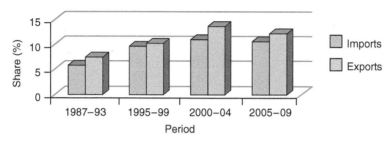

Figure 10.6   **The Effect of NAFTA on U.S.-Mexico Trade**
Source: By authors using data from the *United Nations Conference on Trade and Development* (UNCTAD)

Mexico's share of U.S. exports is the percentage of U.S. annual exports that go to Mexico. Mexico's share of U.S. imports increased from 6% in the pre-NAFTA period (1987–1993) to an average of 9.8% in the years following the formation of NAFTA (1995–1999) and to 11% in the 2000–2004 period. This is a significant change that could be attributed to NAFTA.

NAFTA and U.S. Jobs: As we noted at the beginning of this section, the contentious public debate in the years preceding the approval of NAFTA by the U.S. Congress was, at least in part, on NAFTA's potential implications for U.S. employment. Opponents argued that U.S. workers would have a hard time competing with low-wage Mexican workers. Since the goal of NAFTA was to eliminate barriers to trade, opponents worried that increased cheaper imports from Mexico would cost U.S. jobs. This would be especially true in labor-intensive industries (industries where production requires relatively more labor input that capital). Ultimately, NAFTA opponents argue, American companies would have to move to Mexico to stay competitive.

It is true that free trade would create winners and losers. It is conceivable that a section of the American labor force (those employed in import-competing industries) would lose jobs and consequently, their incomes would fall. However, it is also true that free trade benefits export industries. As a result of FTAs, export industries expand production to supply the larger market and therefore hire more workers. This would increase total employment.

So, what exactly is the impact of a FTA such as NAFTA on wages and employment? This question is an empirical one. In other words, we need to look at data *ex-post* (after the implementation of the agreement) to find out if our *ex-ante* expectations agree with reality. We will look at the total U.S. labor force, national unemployment rate, and employment in manufacturing.[3]

In Figure 10.7, we show that total U.S. labor force grew steadily in the years following NAFTA's approval. For example, during the five years after NAFTA approval (1995–1999) the average annual labor force grew by about 7.8 million (or about 6%) over the immediate

---

[3] The U.S. labor force is the total number of working age people who are either working or actively seeking employment.

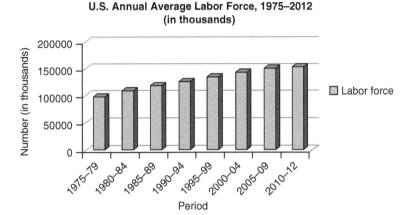

Figure 10.7   NAFTA and the U.S. Labor Market
Source: By authors using data from the Bureau of Labor Statistics.

pre-NAFTA period. In 2012, the annual average labor force was about 154.9 million compared to about 129.2 million in 1993.

Clearly, NAFTA has not reduced the U.S. labor force. However, this observation is not enough for us to conclude that NAFTA has had no effect on U.S. labor markets. Since the labor force includes individuals who are employed and the unemployed, we should attempt to find out what effect, if any, NAFTA has had on unemployment rates in the United States. This is shown in Figure 10.8. The chart in Figure 10.8 shows average annual national unemployment rates for the United States during the period 1985–2015. This period includes 9 years (1985–1993) before NAFTA and 20 years (1994–2015) after NAFTA.

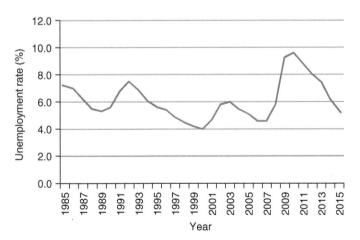

Figure 10.8   NAFTA and U.S. National Unemployment Rate
Source: By authors using data from the Bureau of Labor Statistics.

In Figure 10.8, we can see that NAFTA was approved during a period of falling unemployment. The approval and implementation of NAFTA, however, did not halt the decline in unemployment. U.S. unemployment rate continued to fall in the years following NAFTA. Although, the rate of unemployment is determined by a number of factors (such as the general performance of the economy), we do not find any evidence in Figure 10.8 that NAFTA had an adverse effect on employment in the United States.

However, none of this information excludes the very likely possibility that some U.S. workers lost their jobs because of NAFTA. To explore this possibility further, we look at what happened with U.S. employment in manufacturing. We chose manufacturing because it is mostly labor-intensive and relatively less-skill intensive. With NAFTA, such a sector should be vulnerable to competition from a relatively low-wage country such as Mexico.

As demonstrated in Figure 10.9, there has been a steady decline in U.S. manufacturing employment both in absolute terms and as a share of total employment. In 1990, about 17.7 million people were employed in U.S. manufacturing. This was about 20% of total private sector employment. By 2000, manufacturing employment had only dropped slightly to about 17.3 million (15.3% of private sector employment). By 2015, U.S. manufacturing employment had dropped to only about 12.3 million. This represents a 28% drop from the pre-NAFTA employment. The question is: How much of this change is attributable to NAFTA? Given our basic analysis in this chapter, we cannot give a precise answer to this question. However, we can speculate that some of this change in manufacturing employment is attributable to NAFTA.

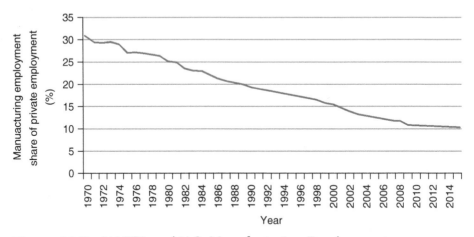

Figure 10.9   NAFTA and U.S. Manufacturing Employment
Source: By authors using data from the Bureau of Labor Statistics.

NAFTA and Canada's Trade Flows

U.S. Share of Canada's Trade: In the preceding section, we noted that Canada's trade with the United States was not affected by NAFTA because of the bilateral FTA between the two countries that existed before NAFTA was established. As such, we should not expect the U.S. share of Canada's trade to have changed substantially following the implementation of

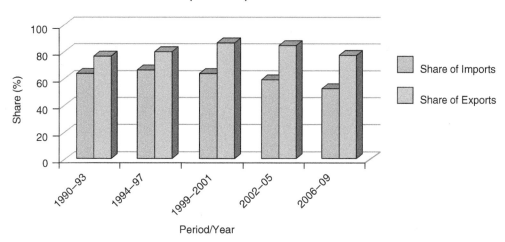

Figure 10.10   **The Effect of NAFTA on the U.S. Share of Canada's Trade**
Source: By authors using data from the *United Nations Conference on Trade and Development* (UNCTAD).

NAFTA. Figure 10.10 shows the U.S. share in Canada's imports and exports. As expected, we do not observe any significant changes following NAFTA's implementation.

Mexico's Share of Canadian Trade: NAFTA is believed to have had an effect on trade flows between Canada and Mexico.

In Figure 10.11, we show the Mexican share of Canada's imports and exports. These shares represent the percentage of total Canada's imports that came from Mexico and the

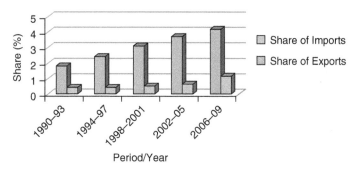

Figure 10.11   **The Effect of NAFTA on Mexico's Share of Canada's Trade**
Source: By authors using data from the *United Nations Conference on Trade and Development* (UNCTAD).

percentage of Canada's exports that was shipped to Mexico. Although Mexico's share of Canada's trade is quite small, there is a noticeable increase in this share following the implementation of NAFTA. In 1990, Mexico's share of Canada's imports was about 1.3%. By 1997, Mexico's share of Canada's imports had doubled to about 2.6%.

THE EUROPEAN UNION (EU)

The 1957 **Treaty of Rome** established a customs union known as the **European Economic Community (EEC)**.[4] The six founding member states include Belgium, Germany, France, Italy, Luxembourg, and the Netherlands. The treaty eliminated trade barriers among member states and introduced a common trade policy within the EEC.

The Treaty of Rome also envisioned a more integrated Europe that included free movement of goods and services, as well as factors of production such as labor and capital. In other words, the customs union was intended to progressively grow into a *common market* and eventually an economic union.

In fact, in Article 8, the treaty is explicit about the intention of forming a common market: "The common market will be progressively established during a transitional period of 12 years, divided into three stages of four years each." Further, some sections of the treaty explicitly outline and provide a framework for eventual common European policies such as the common agricultural policies (CAP) and common transport policy. This would be the ultimate goal of an *economic union* and perhaps a future political union.

Over the years, the membership of the EEC increased as well as the depth of integration among the member countries. In 1973, the United Kingdom, Ireland, and Denmark joined the EEC and raised the membership to nine. Greece was next to join in 1981, Portugal and Spain followed in 1986. In the same year (1986), major amendments were made to the Treaties of Rome. The Single European Act (SEA) of 1986 revised and clarified the powers of key decision-making institutions such as the European Commission, the European Council, and the European Parliament. The key objective of the Act was to ensure smooth progress toward a **single European Market**—an area with unhindered movement of goods, services, and factors of production. This goal of a single European market was achieved by 1993. The Act also emphasizes the establishment of common policies such as social policy, environmental protection policy, and a joint European foreign policy.

In 1995, three more countries—Austria, Finland, and Sweden—joined the Union, increasing the membership to 15. However, the year 2004 saw the largest expansion of the EU with the addition of 10 new members. Nine of the 10 new members were either former Soviet States or former Soviet satellite states (see Table 10.1). Bulgaria and Romania joined

---

[4] Along with the Treaty that established the EEC, a second treaty of Rome (1957) established the European Atomic Energy Community (EURATOM). So, more accurately, we should talk of the "Treaties of Rome" rather than the "Treaty of Rome." However, since our focus is on economic integration, it suffices to focus on the first Treaty (the one that established the EEC). After all, the EEC and the EURATOM (together with the European Coal and Steel Community established in 1952) were later administratively merged by the Treaty of Brussels (the *Merger Treaty*) in 1965.

Table 10.1   **The EU Members**

Year of Entry	Country
1958	Belgium, Germany, France, Italy, Luxembourg, The Netherlands
1973	Denmark, Ireland, United Kingdom
1981	Greece
1986	Spain, Portugal
1995	Austria, Finland, Sweden
2004	Czech Republic, Cyprus, Estonia, Hungary, Latvia, Lithuania, Malta, Poland, Slovakia, Slovenia
2007	Bulgaria, Romania
2013	Croatia

Source: Compiled by authors; information obtained from the official website of the EU (http://europa.eu).

the EU in 2007. The latest addition is Croatia, which joined in 2013. This brings the membership of the EU to its current number of 28.[5]

Institutions of the European Union

The Treaties that established the EU and the subsequent amendments provide for a number of decision-making institutions. In this subsection, we briefly describe a few of the major EU bodies.

The European Commission: Headquartered in Brussels, Belgium, the European Commission is the main executive body of the EU. The Commission is made up of the 28 commissioners (i.e., one commissioner from each of the 28 member countries) including the Commission President and seven Vice-Presidents. The Commission President is nominated by the **European Council** and is subject to confirmation by the **European Parliament**.

The work of the European Commission includes:

- Producing policy proposals and legislation for the European Council and the European parliament.
- Represent the EU in its relationships with countries outside of the EU—for example, negotiating the EU commercial (or trade) policy with nonmember nations of the EU.
- Monitoring compliance with EU policies and laws.
- Implementation of joint EU policies such as the common agricultural policy (CAP) and managing the EU budget.

The European Council: Created in 1974, The European Council provides general political and policy direction on matters concerning the EU, but does not engage in any legislative

---

[5] In a referendum held on June 23, 2016, the United Kingdom voted to leave the EU. Dubbed BREXIT, U.K. voters voted 52% to 48% in favor of leaving the EU. However, the actual exit is yet to be effected.

activity.[6] The Council consists of heads of state of the 28 member countries and the Council President. The Council president is elected by the Council itself. The European Council can be viewed as representing the views of member country governments.

The European Parliament: The European Parliament is the main legislative body of the EU. Parliament is charged with making laws for the Union. The European Parliament is directly elected by citizens of EU member countries. The European Parliament can be seen as representing the interests of EU citizens. Other responsibilities of parliament are to provide oversight on other institutions of the EU (especially the Commission) and adopting the EU budget.

The Court of Justice of the European Union: Working with courts of law in individual member states, the **Court of Justice of the European Union** ensures adherence and uniform application of the European law in member states. The court also ensures the legality of the actions of other EU institutions based on the interpretation of the EU treaties. Therefore, the Court of Justice of the EU is the judicial arm of the EU.

The Economy of the European Union

With the growth of the EU membership to 27 in 2007 and 28 in 2013, the EU's economy has surpassed the United States as the world's largest economy as measured by Gross Domestic Product (GDP)—the total value of goods and services produced. In 2014, the EU GDP was about $18,514.2 billion. With a population of about 508 million in 2014, the EU28's GDP per capita was about $36,400. Figure 10.12 shows changes in total EU GDP in recent decades.

The effect of the recent (2007–2009) financial crises on the EU is clearly visible on the graph. GDP growth stalled in 2007 and dipped at the height of the financial crisis in

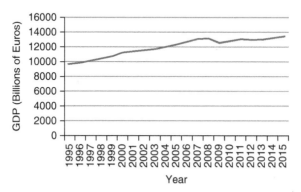

Figure 10.12   **The EU28 GDP at Market Prices**
Source: By authors using data from Eurostat.

---

[6] The Council was initially created as an informal forum for heads of state and government to discuss issues pertaining to the European Union. It formally became one of the EU institutions in 2009 following the implementation of the Treaty of Lisbon.

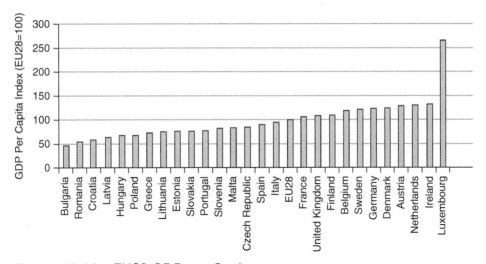

Figure 10.13   EU28 GDP per Capita
Source: By authors using data from Eurostat.

2008–2009. There is also substantial variation in levels of income and standards of living across the EU28 countries. Figure 10.13 illustrates this variation.

The GDP per capita index in Figure 10.13 represents each country's GDP per capita relative to the GDP per capita of the EU. For example, Luxembourg has the highest per capita GDP in the region with a GDP per capita more than 2.5 times that of the EU28. In general, all countries in Figure 10.13 to the right of "EU28" have a GDP per capita higher than the EU28 GDP per capita (their GDP per capita index is higher than 100). In contrast, countries to the left (in Figure 10.13) of the "EU28" have a GDP per capita lower than the EU28 (their GDP per capita index is lower than 100).

The European Union and Global Trade

With its large economy, it should not be surprising that the EU is the largest market for goods and services in the global economy. According to the 2015 edition of the World Trade Organization (WTO) *International Trade Statistics*, the EU28 accounted for 15.0% of global merchandise exports in 2014. This is only second to China at 16.5%. The United States was third at 10.7%, and Japan followed at 4.5%.[7] Extra-EU28 imports of merchandise in 2014 were 14.7% of global merchandise imports. This is only second to the United States at 15.9%.

The EU28 also dominates global trade in commercial services. The EU28 accounted for 26.2% of global exports of commercial services (excluding intra-EU trade) in 2014. The same WTO (2015) statistics show the United States in second position at 18.3%, followed by China at 6.2%, and Japan in fourth place at 4.2%. Extra-EU imports of commercial services

---

[7] Source: www.wto.org/english/res_e/statis_e/its2015_e/its15_charts_e.htm (WTO Statistics, International Trade Statistics 2015). Accessed on May 26, 2016.

in 2014 were 20.1% of global imports of commercial services. The United States follows at 12.2%. China was third at 10.3%, and Japan was fourth at 5.1%.

Although the EU as a whole is a dominant force in global trade, the contribution of individual member countries to EU global trade varies from country to country. The reasons for such variation are discussed in Chapter 8 of this book. These reasons include the economic size of the countries, the geographical location of the countries within Europe, the countries' historical and/or cultural ties with major trading partners such as the United States, and the location of major multinational corporations in Europe.

Table 10.2 shows each EU country's contribution to total EU trade. Not surprisingly, the largest European economies—Germany, France, United Kingdom, Italy, and Spain—account for larger shares of total EU trade.

Table 10.2   EU-28 Member Countries' Share of Extra-EU Trade (2015)

Country	Imports (%)	Exports (%)
Belgium	7.3	5.6
Bulgaria	0.5	0.5
Czech Republic	1.7	1.3
Denmark	1.4	1.9
Germany	18.8	28.2
Estonia	0.1	0.2
Ireland	1.3	2.9
Greece	1.2	0.7
Spain	6.4	5.0
France	9.5	10.5
Croatia	0.2	0.2
Italy	8.9	10.4
Cyprus	0.1	0.0
Latvia	0.2	0.2
Lithuania	0.5	0.5
Luxembourg	0.3	0.1
Hungary	1.1	0.9
Malta	0.1	0.1
Netherlands	14.4	7.0
Austria	1.9	2.3
Poland	3.0	2.1

Table 10.2   EU-28 Member Countries' Share of
Extra-EU Trade (2015) *(continued)*

Country	Imports (%)	Exports (%)
Portugal	0.8	0.8
Romania	0.8	0.8
Slovenia	0.5	0.4
Slovakia	0.8	0.6
Finland	0.9	1.2
Sweden	2.2	2.9
United Kingdom	15.2	12.9

Source: data from Eurostat.

However, there are a couple of small EU economies that also account for a substantial share of EU trade. These include Belgium and the Netherlands. As we noted in Chapter 8, these two small European countries have two of the largest ports in Europe. This makes them a convenient point of entry and exit into and from Europe. The port of Rotterdam, located in the Netherlands, is the largest port in Europe. A short distance south of Rotterdam is Europe's second largest port—Antwerp, located in Belgium. This might explain the substantial role in EU trade of these two relatively small countries.

ECONOMIC INTEGRATION IN DEVELOPING COUNTRIES

The growth of regional trade groups is as noticeable in the developing regions of the world as it is in the developed world. This section provides a brief overview of three best known regional trade blocs in the developing world—the **Association of South East Asian Nations (ASEAN) Free Trade Area (AFTA)**, the **Southern Common Market (MERCOSUR)**, and the **Common Market of Eastern and Southern Africa (COMESA)**.

Table 10.3 provides basic information on a few selected regional trade agreements in developing regions. We note that most of these regional trade groups among developing countries account for relatively small shares of global merchandise trade. This should not be surprising given the domination of global trade by a handful of players including the European Union, NAFTA, China, and Japan. Below we provide a little more detail on three of the eight regional groups in Table 10.3.

The Association of South East Asian Nations (ASEAN) Free Trade Area (AFTA): The ASEAN was established in 1967 to work toward regional political stability during the Vietnam War and ultimately to establish stronger economic cooperation. The founding members of the ASEAN include Indonesia, Malaysia, Philippines, Singapore, and Thailand (ASEAN-6). Five more countries later joined the group—Brunei (1984), Vietnam (1995), Laos PDR (1997), Myanmar (1997), and Cambodia (1999). This makes the total ASEAN membership of 10 countries (ASEAN-10).

Table 10.3   Selected Regional Trading Blocs in the Developing World

RTA Name	Region	Members	Share of Global Merchandise Exports (%)[a]	Year of Entry into Force
ASEAN Free Trade Area (AFTA)	Asia	Brunei Darussalam; Cambodia, Indonesia; Lao People's Democratic Republic; Malaysia; Myanmar; Philippines; Singapore; Thailand; Vietnam	7.1	1992
Common Market for East and Southern Africa (COMESA)	Africa	Burundi; Comoros; DR Congo; Djibouti; Egypt; Eritrea; Ethiopia; Kenya; Libyan Arab Jamahiriya; Kenya; Madagascar; Malawi; Mauritius; Rwanda; Seychelles; Sudan; Swaziland; Uganda; Zambia; Zimbabwe	0.4	1994
Southern Common Market (MERCOSUR)	South America	Argentina; Brazil; Paraguay; Uruguay; Venezuela	1.8	1991
Andean Community (ANCOM)	South America	Bolivia; Columbia; Ecuador; Peru; Venezuela	0.1	1988
South Asian Free Trade Agreement (SAFTA)	Asia	Bangladesh; Bhutan; India; Maldives; Nepal; Pakistan; Sri Lanka	2	2006
Southern African Development Community (SADC)	Africa	Angola; Botswana; DR Congo; Lesotho; Madagascar; Malawi; Mauritius; Mozambique; Namibia; Seychelles; South Africa; Swaziland, Tanzania; Zambia, Zimbabwe	1.0	2000
Economic Community of West African States (ECOWAS)	Africa	Benin; Burkina Faso; Cape Verde; Ivory Coast; Sierra-Leon; Gambia; Ghana; Guinea Bissau; Guinea; Liberia; Mali; Niger; Nigeria; Senegal; Togo	0.5	1993

RTA Name	Region	Members	Share of Global Merchandise Exports (%)[a]	Year of Entry into Force
Caribbean Community (CARICOM)	Caribbean	Antigua and Barbuda; The Bahamas; Barbados; Belize; Dominica; Grenada; Guyana; Haiti; Jamaica; Montserrat; St. Lucia; St. Kitts and Nevis; St. Vincent and the Grenadines; Suriname; Trinidad and Tobago	0.1	1973

Source: Compiled by the authors from various sources including the WTO, UNCTAD, and official websites of the individual regional blocs.
[a] Merchandize trade data are for 2015

In 1992, the member countries of the ASEAN at the time decided to establish a Free Trade Area (AFTA) to strengthen economic integration and cooperation among the member countries. This would, in turn, attract foreign direct investment (FDI) from outside the region. The AFTA required eventual elimination of nontariff barriers and a substantial reduction in tariff barriers (not to exceed 5%) on a list of products (the so-called *Inclusion List* or IL).

The gradual reduction of tariff barriers within the AFTA is done through the *Common Effective Preferential Tariff* (CEPT) scheme introduced at the establishment of the AFTA. Although substantial progress has been made toward a full implementation of the CEPT AFTA scheme among the ASEAN-6, the newer members of the AFTA still lag behind on the reduction of tariffs on intra-AFTA trade. The other challenge that remains is the elimination of nontariff barriers as envisioned by the founding members of the AFTA.

Total ASEAN merchandize trade in 2015 amounted to a little over US$2.5 trillion. This represented about 7.1% of global trade. In Table 10.4, we show that three-quarters of the ASEAN-10 trade is with countries outside the group (extra-ASEAN trade) and only one-quarter is intra-ASEAN trade. This fact is not surprising given that most of the world's major trading countries are not part of ASEAN-10.

The Common Market for East and Southern Africa (COMESA): The predecessor to the COMESA, the Preferential Area for Eastern and Southern Africa (PTA), was conceived at the 1978 meeting of regional Ministers of Trade and Finance in the Zambian capital of Lusaka. The vision was for the PTA to gradually transform into a common market and ultimately an economic community. In December 1981, the treaty establishing the PTA was signed by the regional heads of state and government. In November 1993, the treaty establishing the Common Market for Eastern and Southern Africa (COMESA) was signed in the Ugandan capital of Kampala.

In general, the objectives of COMESA are not that distinct from those of other regional trade blocs—taking advantage of a larger market to attract foreign direct investment to serve

Table 10.4   Intra- and extra-ASEAN trade, 2014

Country	Exports		Imports		Total Trade	
	Intra-ASEAN	Extra-ASEAN	Intra-ASEAN	Extra-ASEAN	Intra-ASEAN	Extra-ASEAN
	Share of total (%)	Share of total (%)	Share of total (%)	Share of total (%)	Share of total (%)	Share of total (%)
Brunei	19.8	80.2	49.1	50.9	27.2	72.8
Cambodia	19.1	80.9	29.4	70.6	25.7	74.3
Indonesia	22.6	77.4	28.6	71.4	25.6	74.4
Lao PDR	55.0	45.0	74.4	25.6	64.9	35.1
Malaysia	27.9	72.1	25.7	74.3	26.9	73.1
Myanmar	39.5	60.5	43.7	56.3	42.0	58.0
Philippines	14.9	85.1	23.8	76.2	19.6	80.4
Singapore	31.2	68.8	20.6	79.4	26.2	73.8
Thailand	26.1	73.9	19.0	81.0	22.6	77.4
Vietnam	12.3	87.7	15.5	84.5	13.9	86.1
ASEAN	**25.5**	**74.5**	**22.5**	**77.5**	**24.1**	**75.9**

Adapted from: ASEANstats website (www.aseansec.org). Accessed on March 26, 2016.

the expanded market. Although, social, cultural, and political cooperation often play a role in establishing regional groups, economic considerations are the primary driver of the choice of countries to be a part of regional trade groups.

Most sub-Saharan African countries attained independence in the 1960s. For the region as a whole, the decade following independence was characterized by political turmoil and declining economic performance. It has been suggested that the desire for economic cooperation and integration in the 1980s and 1990s was a revival of the immediate post-independence spirit of optimism and togetherness.

As noted in Table 10.3, COMESA members (which are a subset of countries reflected in Figure 10.14) account for only 0.4% of global merchandise trade. According to trade statistics obtained from COMESA secretariat web data tool (COMSTAT Data Portal), only about 15% of total COMESA trade is intra-region trade (i.e., trade among COMESA member countries). The remainder 85% is extra-COMESA trade (i.e., trade between COMESA members and non-COMESA members). The relatively small volume of intra-COMESA trade is expected given that most members of COMESA have relatively low per capita income. In 2014, per capita income for sub-Saharan Africa was estimated at US$1,638 (current dollars).[8]

---

[8] World Bank (2015), World Development Indicators Database.

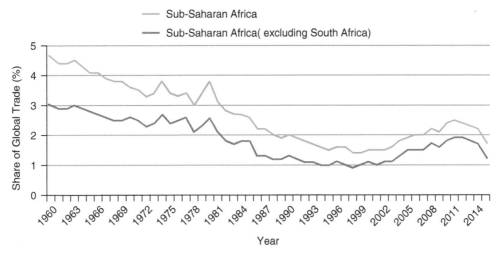

Figure 10.14   Sub-Saharan Africa Trade (1960–2015)
Source: By authors using data from UNCTAD (UNCTADstat).

This compares unfavorably with other developing regions such as Latin America and the Caribbean countries at about $9,000; developing areas of East Asia and the Pacific at about $6,100; and the developing areas in the Middle East and North Africa at about $4,750.

Southern Common Market (MERCOSUR): The Southern Common Market (MERCOSUR) was established by the 1991 Treaty of Asunción.[9] The founding members include Argentina, Brazil, Paraguay, and Uruguay. Later, a number of countries joined as associate members of MERCOSUR. These include Bolivia and Chile in 1996, Peru in 2003, Columbia and Ecuador in 2004. Venezuela was admitted as a MERCOSUR member in 2006 and officially welcomed into the regional trade bloc in 2012. Therefore, MERCOSUR is made up of five full members (the four founding members plus Venezuela) and five associate members (Bolivia, Chile, Columbia, Ecuador, and Peru).

In 2014, MERCOSUR member countries had a combined GDP of about US$1.77 trillion (constant 2005 dollars). This was about 12% of U.S. GDP in the same year (also measured in 2005 dollars) and about 3.1% of total world GDP in 2014 (also in constant 2005 dollars).

With a total population of about 290 million and a per capita GDP (in constant 2005 dollars) of close to $6,100, MERCOSUR is one of the largest regional trading blocs in the world. In 2014, the share of MERCOSUR in global merchandise exports and imports was about 2.1% and 2%, respectively. As shown in Table 10.5, Brazil, the largest economy in South America dominates MERCOSUR's trade followed by Argentina, Venezuela, Uruguay, and Paraguay.

---

[9] Named after the capital city of Paraguay, Asunción; MERCOSUR is an acronym for "*Mercado Comun del Cono Sur*" (Southern Cone Common Market).

Table 10.5   The Southettrn Common Market (MERCOSUR) Members

Country Name	GDP (Constant 2000 US$, millions)	Population (Millions)	GDP per Capita (Constant 2000 US$)	Exports (Constant 2000 US$, million)	Imports (Constant 2000 US$, millions)
Argentina	472,935.36	40.76	11,601.63	56,453.29	66,041.36
Brazil	944,612.35	196.66	4,803.40	125,683.66	184,863.63
Paraguay	10,887.49	6.57	1,657.58	5,227.12	7,537.54
Uruguay	32,274.70	3.37	9,581.06	6,992.99	8,166.59
Venezuela, RB	166,062.25	29.28	5,671.91	23,844.79	49,992.61
Total	1,626,772.14	276.63	5,880.58	218,201.85	316,601.73
		Share of Total (%)			
Argentina	29.07	14.74		25.87	20.86
Brazil	58.07	71.09		57.60	58.39
Paraguay	0.67	2.37		2.40	2.38
Uruguay	1.98	1.22		3.20	2.58
Venezuela, RB	10.21	10.58		10.93	15.79

Source: By Authors using data from the World Bank, *World Development Indicators* (2015) and WTO's International Trade Statistics (2015).

REGIONALISM VERSUS MULTILATERALISM

The proliferation of preferential trade agreements has raised concerns among many observers regarding compatibility with the World Trade Organization's **multilateral** trading system. As we noted in Chapter 7, the WTO multilateral trading system is based on the principle of "equal treatment" embodied in the Most Favored Nation Principle (MFN). Do preferential trade agreements (such as free trade areas and customs unions) help or hurt this cause? This is, no doubt, a debatable policy question.

Technically, preferential trade agreements do not violate WTO rules. Article 24 of the General Agreement on Trade and Tariffs (GATT) permits preferential trading agreements as a special exception to the Most Favored Principle. These nongeneralized preferences are exempted from WTO rules on condition that the formation of these arrangements does not restrict members' trade with nonmember countries.

However, some experts in the field of international economics believe that the growth of preferential trade agreements is out of control and is a threat to the multilateral trading system. Prominent among the proponents of this view is renowned economist, Jagdish Bhagwati. On the other hand, there are those that argue that preferential trade agreements help to achieve the WTO main objective of lower trade barriers. Who is right? Studies conducted to answer this question provide mixed results.

We should emphasize that the core of the *regionalism* versus *multilateralism* debate is the choice between a discriminatory trading system versus a nondiscriminatory (MFN) trading system. In other words, how does the formation of a free trade area or a customs union affect the countries' MFN tariff rates (i.e., the tariff rates applied to all countries without discrimination)? FTAs aim to eliminate trade barriers (including tariffs and nontariff) on the flow of goods and services among participating nations. Therefore, it is conceivable that countries in a preferential trading bloc may compensate for lost tariff revenue by raising their MFN tariff rates. If this is the case, then the discriminatory tariff reduction under a FTA impedes the WTO efforts toward freer global trade.

Some worry about the complex overlapping membership in preferential trade agreements. This increases administrative costs and complicates the "rules of origin" provisions. It is also more costly for private firms to comply with the more complex rules of origin because of overlapping preferential trade agreements. This has been termed as the **spaghetti bowl** phenomenon of trade agreements.

The alternative view (in support of preferential trade agreements) is grounded in the political nature of international trade. Proponents of this view suggest that preferential trade agreements lower tariff barriers, which is in agreement with the WTO's multilateral trading system. Further, preferential trade agreements go much deeper in reducing barriers to trade and expanding the scope of goods and services eligible for lower barriers than has been achieved multilaterally. Moreover, trade agreements among a small group of countries are much easier to reach than ones among 162 members of the WTO. The answer to whether *regionalism* helps or hurts *multilateralism* is more of an empirical one than a theoretical one. As noted above, the results have been mixed. A full discussion of empirical findings on this topic is beyond the scope of this book.

Could the WTO's Multilateralism Lead to More Regionalism?

The WTO's multilateral trading system emphasizes "equal treatment." If a WTO member country wishes to reduce tariff rates on imports from its major trading partners, under the MFN principle, the country is obliged to offer the same tariff reduction to all members of the WTO. A preferential trade agreement may offer such a country a convenient exception to the MFN principle and therefore avoid the "blanket" tariff reduction. In this case, countries' obligations under the WTO multilateral trading system provide an incentive for preferential trading arrangements.

SUMMARY

- Trade agreements establish preferential treatment in trade among participating nations.
- Trade agreements are broadly divided between preferential trade arrangements (PTAs) and free trade agreements (FTAs).
- Preferential trade arrangements involve partial (mostly nonreciprocal) preferential treatment offered by one country to another or to a group of countries. This is the shallowest form of economic integration.
- Free trade agreements eliminate all (or most) trade barriers among participating nations. There are two types of FTAs—free trade areas and customs unions. Free trade areas eliminate trade barriers among participating nations but allow member countries to maintain separate external trade policies. On the other hand, a customs union offers free trade among participating nations but also commits member countries to a common external trade policy.
- Deeper forms of economic integration entail freedom of movement of factors of production such as labor and capital (common market) as well as closer coordination of major economic and social policies (economic union).
- A common market is a form of economic integration that allows free flow of goods and services, a common external trade policy (as in a customs union), as well as unhindered movement of factors of production within participating nations.
- An economic union entails everything in a common market, but also requires a closer coordination of major economic policies such fiscal policy (government spending and taxation), environmental policies, and in some cases, may entail coordinated monetary policies (money supply and interest rates) among participating nations. An economic union is the deepest form of economic integration.
- Free trade agreements may lead to both trade creation and trade diversion. *Trade creation* results from replacing high-cost domestic products with low-cost imports from member countries. *Trade diversion* results from replacing low-cost imports from nonmember countries with high-cost imports from member countries.
- Under a free trade area, the likely adverse effects of trade diversion on producers in nonmember countries encourages *trade deflection*—the act of shipping partially finished products from a nonmember country to a FTA to a member country so as to access preferential treatment under a FTA. *Rules of origin* are provisions in trade agreements specifying which goods are eligible for preferential treatment under the FTA. This is intended to prevent trade deflection.
- The North American Free Trade Agreement (NAFTA) had a substantial impact on U.S.-Mexico trade and Canada-Mexico trade. However, NAFTA had hardly any impact on U.S.-Canada trade. This is because of the FTA between the United States and Canada that preceded NAFTA.
- The *European Union (EU)* was established as the *European Economic Community* by the 1957 *Treaty of Rome*. The EU gradually grew into the world largest and strongest trade bloc. Key institutions of the EU include the *European Commission*, the *European Council*, the *European Parliament*, and the *Court of Justice of the EU*.

- Regional trade blocs in the developing world account for a relatively small share of global trade. Prominent among regional trade blocs in developing regions of the world include the *Association of East Asian Nations (ASEAN) Free Trade Area (AFTA)*; the *Southern Common Market (MERCOSUR)*, the *Common Market for East and Southern Africa (COMESA)*; the *Andean Community (ANCOM)*; the *Caribbean Community (CARICOM)*; the *Economic Community of West African Nations (ECOWAS)*; and the *Southern African Development Community (SADC)*.

- The relationship between *regionalism* (regional trade agreements) and *multilateralism* (equal treatment) is theoretically ambiguous. On one hand, the nongeneralized (discriminatory) preferential treatment may tempt member countries to an agreement to raise tariff rates on goods from nonmembers to make up for lost tariff revenues. This exacerbates trade diversion. On the other hand, preferential trade agreements may be the most politically convenient way to reduce trade barriers. Further, there remains a question of whether regionalism impedes multilateralism or the multilateral trading system encourages regionalism.

KEY TERMS

Trade agreements
Preferential trade arrangements (PTAs)
Free trade agreements (FTAs)
Free trade areas
North American Free Trade Area (NAFTA)
Customs union
European Union
Common market
Economic union
Trade creation
Trade diversion
Trade deflection
Rules of origin
Treaty of Rome
European Economic Community
Single European Market
European Council
European Parliament

Court of Justice of the European Union
Association of South East Asian Nations (ASEAN)
ASEAN Free Trade Area (AFTA)
Southern Common Market (MERCOSUR)
Common Market for East and Southern Africa (COMESA)
Andean Community (ANCOM)
South Asian Free Trade Agreement (SAFTA)
South African Development Community (SADC)
Economic Community of West African States (ECOWAS)
Caribbean Community (CARICOM)
Multilateralism
Regionalism
Spaghetti bowl

PROBLEMS

1. Discuss the benefits of a free trade agreement to participating nations.
2. Why would a group of countries under a common market want to form an economic union? (i.e., What benefits does an economic union offer to member countries beyond those obtained under a common market?)

3. What determines whether a free trade area or a customs union improves the welfare of a member nation?

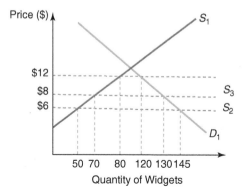

The graph above shows the market for widgets in country 1. Both Countries 2 and 3 are potential trade partners of Country 1. S_2 and S_3 represent Country 2's supply of widgets to Country 1 and Country 3's supply of widgets to Country 1, respectively. Use the information provided on the graph to answer the following questions.

4. First, assume free trade among the three countries,

    a. How many widgets will Country 1 consumer under free trade (no tariffs or any other barriers to trade)?
    b. How many of the consumed widgets will be produced domestically and how many will be imported?
    c. Under free trade (no tariffs or any other trade barriers), from which country should Country 1 import widgets?

5. Second, let's assume that Country 1 imposes a nondiscriminatory tariff of 100% on imports of widgets. Also assume that the economy of Country 1 is not large enough to influence global prices of widgets.

    a. What is the new price per widget in Country 1?
    b. How many widgets does Country 1 consume with the 100% tariff?
    c. How many of the consumed widgets in Country 1 are produced locally and how many are imported?
    d. With the tariff from which country should Country 1 import widgets?

6. Finally, let's assume that Country 1 and Country 3 form a free trade area. This means no tariffs (and nontariff barriers) on Country 3's widgets while the 100% tariff is maintained on Country 2's widgets. Given this new information,

    a. What is the new price per widget in Country 1?
    b. How many widgets will Country 1 consumer at this price?
    c. How many of the widgets consumed are produced domestically and how many are imported?
    d. How much is the welfare gain to Country 1 due to new trade created by the free trade agreement?

   e. How much is the welfare loss to Country 1 due to trade diversion?
   f. What is the net welfare effect of the free trade agreement on Country 1?

7. What has been the impact of NAFTA on the following? Provide a plausible explanation for each of your answers.

   a. U.S. trade with Canada
   b. Canadian trade with Mexico
   c. U.S. trade with Mexico
   d. U.S. employment

8. Describe the key institutions of the European Union and the EU's significance in global trade.

9. For each of the following regional trade blocs, briefly describe the history, membership, and significance in global trade.

   a. The European Union
   b. The ASEAN Free Trade Area (AFTA)
   c. The Common Market for East and Southern Africa (COMESA)
   d. The Southern Common Market
   e. The North American Free Trade Area (NAFTA)

10. Does regionalism help or hurt the WTO's multilateral system whose primary goal is to lower trade barriers through "equal treatment" in trade?

11. How is it possible that the WTO's most favored nation (MFN) could have encouraged the proliferation of regional trading blocs?

12. Define, explain, and compare/contrast the following terms:

   a. Preferential trade arrangements (PTA) versus free trade agreements (FTAs)
   b. Free trade area (FTA) versus customs union
   c. Common market versus economic union
   d. Trade creation versus trade diversion
   e. Trade deflection versus rules of origin

PART 4

GLOBALIZATION: INTRODUCTION TO INTERNATIONAL FINANCE

11

The Balance of Payments and the International Investment Position

n Chapter 6, we described the global economy as comprising two broad sectors—the real sector and the financial sector. Our focus until this point has been on the real sector of the economy. This chapter should be viewed as an introduction to the financial sector of the global economy. After all, transactions in the real sector of the economy are backed by corresponding transactions in the financial sector. When we buy goods and services from other countries, a monetary payment is made by the buyer to the seller. Because sellers and buyers may live in countries with different currencies, the financial sector (foreign exchange market, in particular) plays an important role in facilitating trade in goods and services. As the world has become more globalized, information on each country's dealings with other countries has become increasingly important. Such information is obtained from a country's international transactions records. A summary record of transactions between residents of a country and residents of other countries is known as the **balance of payments**.

A country's balance of payments accounts records a wide range of transactions including exports and imports of goods and services, gift exchanges across national borders, as well as capital flows (investments). As demonstrated in Chapter 6 of this book, data on these transactions allows us to measure the extent of economic interdependence among countries. Most important, though, data on international transactions plays a crucial role in economic policymaking. For example, central banks (such as the U.S. Federal Reserve) use information on international transactions in the formulation of monetary policy (changes in money supply and interest rates). International transactions data also provide valuable information on activities of multinational corporations. Such information gives insight into a country's international competitiveness. Moreover, policymakers are better equipped to assess the performance of the overall global economy and compare economic performance across countries with information on international transactions.

➤ Understand and describe the concept of balance of payments.

➤ Understand the classification of transactions in the balance of payments accounts.

➤ Understand the various accounting balances in the balance of payments accounts.

➤ Understand the meaning of balance of payments deficits and surpluses.

➤ Understand the relationship between the current account balance, a country's international indebtedness, and net international wealth position.

➤ Understand the concept of international investment position (aka balance of international indebtedness).

INTRODUCTION TO THE BALANCE OF PAYMENTS ACCOUNTS

The **balance of payments** is a system consisting of several accounts. Each account within the balance of payments system records a distinct category (or categories) of international transactions. Broadly, there are two main types of transactions: (1) those involving production and sale of goods, services, and income transfers; and (2) those involving financial assets and liabilities (such as trades in securities or claims and liabilities of financial institutions and governments). The third and relatively small category of transactions includes transactions involving *nonproduced nonfinancial assets*. We will come back to this later in the chapter. The first category of international transactions, involving production and sale of goods and services, income, and unilateral transfers, are recorded in the **current account** of the balance of payments. The second and third categories of international transactions, involving financial assets and liabilities, are recorded in the **capital/financial account** of the balance of payments.[1]

The Double-Entry System of Accounting

The balance of payments accounting applies a common accounting system called the **double-entry bookkeeping system**. The double-entry system recognizes the fact that there are two sides to every transaction—the "giving" and the "receiving." For example, when you buy a Toshiba laptop computer from a Japanese company, you part with an amount of money equal to the price of the computer. On the other hand, you receive your new laptop computer. Therefore, for any transaction recorded in the balance of payments accounts, two entries are made. In the balance of payments accounts, each entry is identified as either a *credit* or *debit* entry.

A **credit entry** in the U.S. balance of payments accounts is made when a transaction leads to a payment to a U.S. resident, company, or government by a foreign resident(s).

---

[1] In this book and this chapter in particular, we use *balance of payments accounts* and *international transactions accounts* interchangeably.

Table 11.1   **An Example of Double-Entry Accounting System**

	Credit	Debit
Purchase of a laptop computer by a U.S. resident		−$1,500
Deposit at a U.S.-owned bank in the United States	$1,500	

In other words, credit entries reflect a flow of money into the country. Credit entries are recorded as positive entries with a "+" sign or no sign on the amount of money involved in the transaction.

On the other hand, a **debit entry** in the balance of payments accounts is made when a transaction involves a payment to a foreign resident(s) by a U.S. resident(s), business, or government. Thus, a debit entry reflects a flow of money out of the country. Debit entries are recorded as negative entries with a "−"sign on the amount involved in the transaction.

To demonstrate the double-entry system, we return to our earlier example of a U.S. resident purchasing a laptop computer from a Japanese company. Let's assume that the purchaser of the computer writes a $1,500 check on a U.S. bank as payment for the laptop. Let's also assume that the company's agent in the U.S. deposits the check on the company's account in another U.S. bank. Two offsetting entries are made in the balance of payments accounts. First, the purchase (import) of a computer is recorded as a *debit* entry (reflecting a payment to a foreign company by a U.S. resident). The offsetting *credit* entry would be the deposit of the $1,500 check on a U.S. bank (an increase in foreign-owned assets in the United States). This example is further illustrated in Table 11.1 above.

The Balance of Payments Identity

Because every international transaction recorded in the balance of payments accounts has two offsetting entries, a credit entry (a positive entry) and a debit entry (a negative entry), the sum of all the credit entries and debit entries in the balance of payments accounts should be equal to zero. In other words, the sum of the balances on the current account and the capital/financial account should be equal to zero. This is the fundamental **balance of payments identity**. The credit entries (+) should exactly offset debit (−) entries and vice versa.

CLASSIFICATION OF INTERNATIONAL TRANSACTIONS

Now that we know *how* transactions are recorded in the balance of payments system of accounts, we are ready to talk about *where* in the balance of payments different transactions are recorded. To aid our discussion of the classification of transactions and the various accounts in the balance of payments system, we will use a summary of the U.S. statement of international transactions for calendar year 2015. This is shown in Table 11.2.

Table 11.2   Summary of U.S. International Transactions for 2015 (millions of dollars)

	Credits	Debits
Current Account Transactions		
1 **Exports of goods, services, and income receipts**	**3,006,695**	
2 Goods (merchandise) exports	1,513,453	
3 Services exports	710,165	
4 Income Receipts	783,077	
5 **Imports of goods, services, and income payments**		**−3,355,126**
6 Goods (merchandise) imports		−2,272,760
7 Services Imports		−490,613
8 Income Payments		−591,753
9 **Unilateral Current Transfers, net**		**−135,646**
10 Current transfers to the United States	132,001	
11 Current transfers from the United States		−267,647
12		
Capital/Financial Accounts Transactions[2]		
13 **U.S.-owned Assets abroad, excluding financial Derivatives (increase/financial outflow (−))**		**−242,234**
14 U.S. Official reserve assets	6,292	
15 U.S. government assets, other than official reserve assets	282,933	
16 U.S. private assets		−531,459
17 **Foreign-owned assets in the United States, excluding financial derivatives (increase/financial inflow (+))**	**426,036**	
18 Foreign (official and nonofficial) assets in the United States		−247,197

---

[2] A slight modification is made to help simplify the presentation and discussion of the various transactions. In several recent textbooks as well as official documents, line 20 (Other capital account transactions) is shown as a separate account (labeled the "Capital Account"). Since these transactions are reported as a net balance (a single line) in official reports, we have opted to include them under what we labeled "Capital/Financial Accounts Transactions." A full description of these transactions can be found in the text of this chapter.

	Credits	Debits
19 Other foreign (private) assets in the United States	673,232	
20 Other capital account transactions, net		**−45**
21 Financial Derivatives, net	**25,401**	
22 Statistical discrepancy	**274,919**	
Memoranda		
23 Balance on goods (sum of lines 2 and 6)		−759,307
24 Balance on Services (sum of lines 3 and 7)	219,552	
25 Balance on goods and services (sum of lines 2, 3, 6, and 7)		−539,755
26 Balance on income (sum of lines 4 and 8)	191,324	
27 Unilateral current transfers, net (line 9)		−135,646
28 Balance on current account (sum of lines 1, 5, and 9)		−484,077
30 Net financial flows (sum of lines 13, 17, and 21)	209,203	

Source: Data obtained from the U.S. Bureau of Economic Analysis

The Current Account

The **current account** records international transactions in goods, services, income, and unilateral transfers. Let's briefly describe each of these categories in turn.

Transactions in Goods: International transactions in goods comprise goods exports (goods shipped from the United States for sale abroad) and goods imports (goods shipped into the United States from abroad). In practice, the value of goods transactions may include goods given away (i.e., not sold) to residents of foreign countries. Data on the value of goods transactions can be obtained from the U.S. Census Bureau of the U.S. Department of Commerce. These data are recorded by U.S. Customs as goods cross U.S. boundaries. In Table 11.2, the value of goods exports is recorded in line (2) as a credit (positive) entry. In line (6), we have the value of goods imports, a debit (negative) entry in the balance of payment to indicate a payment by U.S. residents to residents of other countries.

Transactions in Services: International transactions in services comprise services exports as well as services imports. The total U.S. services exports for calendar year 2015 is shown as a credit (positive) entry in line (3) of Table 11.2. Line (7) in the same Table shows total U.S. services imports for the same time period. As expected, services imports are recorded as a debit entry in the balance of payments. The services category comprise a wide range of intangible output such as travel and transportation services, financial services (such as investment, banking, and insurance), legal services and several other services.

Transactions in Income: International income transfers recorded in the current account mainly comprise of returns for the use of capital. Income receipts or payments include interest from holdings of financial assets such as bonds, dividends from holdings of stocks in private firms, as well as reinvested profits of multinational companies.

Income receipts also include wages paid to American residents employed by foreign employers abroad. Income received by U.S. residents from foreign residents or entities leads to a credit entry in the current account of the U.S. balance of payments. This is shown in line (4) of Table 11.2. *Income payments* to foreign residents by American residents, businesses, or government leads to a debit entry in the current account of the U.S. balance of payments. The value of income payments for the year 2015 is shown in line (8) of Table 11.2.

Unilateral Transfers: Unilateral current transfers are essentially gifts or donations of goods and services. These include government donations of goods and services to countries experiencing natural and/or man-made disasters (e.g., earthquakes, floods, famine, and armed conflicts). These transfers are referred to as unilateral transfers because they are *non-quid pro quo* transfers—the recipient of the transfer does not make or promise to make any payment for the goods or services received. Unilateral transfers also include private transfers. Private transfers may include transfers by American charities to countries in need, as well as individual remittances to families and friends. In Table 11.2, current transfers to the United States from foreign countries are recorded in line (10), while transfers from the United States are recorded in line (11). The balance in line (9) shows that, in 2015, the United States recorded a net unilateral transfer of (−) $135,646 million to foreign countries.

The Capital/Financial Account

The financial account records international transactions involving capital flows—sales and purchases of financial assets. Examples of financial assets include shares of stocks, bonds, bills, and certificates of deposit. Entries in the financial accounts of the balance of payments are organized into a number of distinct subcategories.

Official Reserve Assets and Other Official (non-reserve) Assets: Entries in this subcategory of the balance of payments comprise transactions involving governments or agencies of governments like central banks (e.g., the U.S. Federal Reserve or the U.S. Treasury). U.S. reserve assets include monetary gold, special drawing rights (SDRs), the country's reserve position at the International Monetary Fund, and foreign currencies.

Transactions involving monetary gold comprise sales and/or purchases of monetary gold by the country's monetary authorities (e.g., the U.S. Treasury department). *Special drawing rights* are international reserves created by the International Monetary Fund and allocated to IMF member countries based on each country's contribution to the IMF. Essentially, an SDR is a unit of accounting (or a virtual currency) used by the IMF and is convertible to most major currencies. *Special drawing rights* are only held by national monetary authorities and some international organizations. Transactions recorded in line (14) of Table 11.2 may include IMF allocation of SDRs to the United States, cancellation of previously allocated SDRs to the United States or exchange of U.S.-held SDRs for foreign currencies or the U.S. dollar.

Official transactions also include changes in *the U.S. reserve position at the International Monetary Fund*. This relates to changes in the International Monetary Fund's holdings of

U.S. dollars due to IMF transactions with other countries. Finally, official reserve assets include *foreign currencies*. During typical foreign exchange market interventions, the Federal Reserve buys or sells foreign currencies. For example, if the Federal Reserve wants to reduce the value of the U.S. dollar, it would intervene in the foreign exchange market by selling U.S. dollars in exchange for foreign currencies. On the other hand, if the Federal Reserve intended to raise the value of the U.S. dollar, a foreign exchange market intervention would involve a purchase of U.S. dollars using foreign currency reserves. Such transactions change the monetary authority's holdings of foreign currency reserves. These changes are included in line (14) of Table 11.2.

The financial account also records transactions involving *nonreserve government assets*. Included in this subcategory are transactions related to transfer of resources to foreign entities under programs established by the U.S. congress. These are U.S. government credits (often in form of loans) extended to foreign entities and repaid with interest over a relatively long period of time. Non-reserve assets of the U.S. government also include U.S. government contributions and/or subscription to international organizations such as regional development banks that offer development assistance to other countries. Finally, this subsection includes collections of principal on long term credits (loans) and recoveries of U.S. investments abroad. The credit (positive) entries in lines (14) and (15) of Table 11.2 indicate a decrease in the United States holding of the corresponding assets.

Private Assets. Private assets include changes in privately owned assets during the period under consideration. For example, U.S. owned private assets abroad (line 16 in Table 11.2) are foreign assets acquired by U.S. residents. These include direct investment and holdings of foreign securities (shares of stock, bonds, bills, etc.).[3] These are private capital outflows— investments in foreign countries by U.S. residents—and therefore constitute a debit entry in the balance of payments accounts. On the other hand, private capital inflows (line 19 in Table 11.2) are investments in the United States by residents of other countries and therefore lead to a credit (positive) entry in the U.S. balance of payments accounts. The foreign assets in the United States recorded in line (18) include currency and deposits, loans, trade credits, etc. The negative figure reflects a net reduction of these foreign assets in 2015.

Other Capital Account Transactions

These are transactions in *nonproduced, nonfinancial assets* of an economy. Examples include acquisition or disposal of right to tangible assets like right to mineral deposits and offshore drilling rights. Entries in the capital account of the balance of payments also include transactions involving sales and purchases of intangible assets such as trademarks and copyrights. Also included here are capital transfers related to payments for insured losses and debt forgiveness. For example, a credit entry is made in the capital/financial account of the United States balance of payment when a foreign insurance company makes a payment for

---

[3] See Chapter 6 for a discussion of the difference between direct investment and portfolio investment.

an insured catastrophic loss in the United States. On the other hand, a debit entry is made in the capital account when the United States government forgives debt owed by a developing country in sub-Saharan Africa. Debt forgiveness is essentially a transfer from the United States to the beneficiary country and therefore constitutes a debit entry in the U.S. balance of payment. Line (20) in Table 11.2 shows a net debit balance (deficit) of (−) $45 million for 2015. This means that, in 2015, the Unites States paid out a *net* capital transfer of the same amount (−$45 million).

The Statistical Discrepancy

Recall that balance of payments accounting uses the double entry bookkeeping system. Therefore, every credit entry made in the balance of payments accounts should have an offsetting debit entry and vice versa. As such, the overall balance of payments (the sum of all the debit entries and credit entries) should be equal to zero. However, due to errors and omissions, the overall balance of payments is often different than zero. In particular, when only one side (either the debit or credit entry) of the transaction is accurately recorded in the balance of payments while the offsetting entry is either omitted or inaccurately recorded, the overall balance of payments will not equal to zero. On the other hand, when both entries (credit and debit) to a transaction are omitted, such an omission will not affect the overall balance of payments.

The **statistical discrepancy** is simply a balancing item in the balance of payments. It is inserted to ensure a perfect balance between credits and debits. Simply put, the statistical discrepancy is the value required to account for errors in the balance of payments accounts and get the overall balance of payments to equal to zero. In Table 11.2, the sum of all debit and credit entries in the current account and the capital/financial account is equal to −$274,919 million (a debit balance). To get the overall balance of payments of zero, we introduce a credit entry of the same amount. Therefore, the statistical discrepancy is equal to (+) $274,919, million.[4] In practice, the statistical discrepancy is often accounted for by unrecorded short-term capital flows.

ACCOUNTING BALANCES IN THE BALANCE OF PAYMENTS

Lines 23 through 30 in Table 11.2 present several accounting balances in the balance of payments accounts. The **balance on goods** is obtained from the sum of line (2) and line (6). This balance is (−) $759,307 million. A debit (negative) balance on goods means that in 2015, the United States spent more money on foreign-made goods (imports) than foreigners spent on U.S.-made goods (exports). The balance on goods is also referred to as the **balance of trade** (or trade balance). A country is said to have a **trade deficit** if it has a negative trade balance. On the other hand, a country is said to have a **trade surplus** if it has a positive trade balance. As we saw in Chapter 8, the United States has had persistent trade deficits for decades.

---

[4] The statistical discrepancy is the sum of lines 1, 5, 9, 13, 17, 20, and 21, with the sign reversed.

The **balance on services** is obtained from the sum of line (3) and line (7). This balance is $219,552 million. A credit (positive) balance on services suggests that in 2015, foreigners' spending on U.S.-provided services (exports) exceeded spending by U.S. residents on foreign-provided services (imports). The **balance on goods and services** is the sum of the *balance on goods* and the *balance on services*. Equivalently, the balance on goods and services is obtained as a sum of lines (2), (3), (6), and (7). In 2015, this balance was equal to (−) $539,775 million. The debit (negative) balance on goods and services implies that U.S. residents spent more on foreign-made goods and services than foreign residents spent on U.S.-made goods and services. Figure 8.3 (in Chapter 8) shows the three balances described above for the U.S.-balance on goods, balance on services, and balance on goods and services for the period 1992–2015.

Balance on income is the difference between income receipts and income payments. This is obtained by adding entries in line (4) and line (8). This balance is equal to $191,324 million. A credit (positive) balance on income means that U.S. residents' earnings on their asset holdings abroad exceeded earnings by foreign residents on their asset holdings in the United States.

Unilateral transfers (net) is the difference between donations and/or gifts received by residents of a country (including those received by governments and nongovernmental organizations) and donations/gifts given by residents of a country (including government grants). In Table 11.2, the net unilateral transfer is shown in line (9) and is equal to (−) $135,646 million. A net debit (negative) balance indicates that outflows of gifts and donations exceeded inflows of gifts/donations.

The **balance on current account** is the sum of the balance on goods and services, the balance on income, and the net unilateral transfers. This represents the sum of all credit and debit entries in the current account. In Table 11.2, this is easily obtained by summing entries in lines (1), (5) and (9). The U.S. balance on current account in 2015 was equal to (−) $484,077 million. The negative (deficit) balance on current account indicates more payments to foreign residents for goods, services, and income relative to foreign payments for goods, services, and income to U.S. residents.

As we have seen throughout most of this chapter, besides the current account, another big part of the balance of payments comprise transactions in the capital/financial account. International financial transactions are broadly divided into official transactions and private transactions. This distinction is clear in lines (14), (15), and (16) in Table 11.2. Overall **net financial flows** are obtained by summing entries in lines (13), (17), and (21). Line (13) represents the change in U.S.-owned assets abroad during the year 2015. On the other hand, the entry in line (17) represents the change in foreign-own assets in the United States during the same period. Finally, line (21) presents the net value of transactions in financial derivatives. The sum of all these financial transactions (keeping in mind the negative values for debit entries) leads us to the net financial flows during the year under consideration. In Table 11.2, U.S. net financial flows for 2015 were equal to $209,203 million.[5] The positive net financial flows imply that, in 2015, financial inflows into the United States exceeded financial outflows from the United States to the rest of the world.

---

[5] Note that this balance includes official (government), nonofficial (government), and well as private flows.

DEFICITS AND SURPLUSES IN THE BALANCE OF PAYMENTS

From the discussion above, we know that some of the transactions recorded in the balance of payments are official transactions. This means they are conducted by governments or agencies of governments such as central banks. Clearly, such transactions are not market-driven. Instead, they result from policy decisions. Therefore, for purposes of assessing a country's balance of payments position, we exclude official transactions and focus attention on primarily market-driven transactions in the current account, and the capital/financial account (excluding official transactions).

A country has a **balance of payments deficit** if the sum of credit (+) and debit (−) entries in the current, capital/financial (excluding official transactions) accounts, and the statistical discrepancy is negative (a net debit balance). You may wonder why the statistical discrepancy (which we described as a balancing item) is included in this balance of payments measurement. We noted that the statistical discrepancy is mostly accounted for by unrecorded short-term capital flows. Therefore, the statistical discrepancy represents nonofficial financial transactions. A balance of payments deficit implies that the country's nonofficial outflows exceed the country's non-official inflows for the period under consideration. Put differently, the country spent more abroad than it earned from abroad. Since the overall balance of payments (including both official and nonofficial transactions) should equal to zero (because of the double-entry system), a balance of payments deficit also implies a net *credit* (positive) balance on official transactions. A net credit (positive) balance on official transactions implies a decrease in U.S. official reserves.

On the other hand, a country has a **balance of payments surplus** if the sum of credit and debit entries in the current account, the capital/financial account, and the statistical discrepancy is positive (a net credit balance). This would imply that the country's spending abroad was less than its earnings from abroad. The balance of payments surplus has to be offset with a net *debit* on the official transactions. Recall that a net debit (negative) on the official reserve account means an increase in the country's holdings of official reserves.

Finally, **balance of payments equilibrium** means that the sum of credit and debit entries in the current account, the capital/financial account (excluding official reserve transactions), and the statistical discrepancy is equal to zero. This essentially means that the country spent just as much as it earned abroad. In this case the net official reserve transactions balance should be zero as well.

THE CURRENT ACCOUNT BALANCE AND INTERNATIONAL INDEBTEDNESS

When a country has a current account deficit, it implies that the country spent more than it earned. But how is the extra spending (above and beyond the country's earnings) financed? The answer is: through borrowing or sale of assets. Just like an individual or household has to borrow (or sell assets) to spend beyond its income, a country too has to borrow or sell assets in order to spend beyond its earnings.

One way to understand the true meaning of the current account balance is to use national income accounting concepts introduced in Chapter 3 of this book. Two of the most important national income accounting concepts are **gross domestic product (GDP)** and **gross national product (GNP)**. Gross domestic product measures the value of final goods and services produced within a country in a year. The task of determining the value of goods and services produced in a country such as the United States may indeed seem overwhelming. However, as we learned in Chapter 3, it helps to know that the value of goods and services is approximately equal to the country's spending. As such,

$$GDP = C + I + G + (X - M) \qquad [11.1]$$

where C is household spending, I is investment spending by businesses, G is government spending, X is the value of exports of goods and services, and M is the value of imports of goods and services.

Gross domestic product does not measure the total income of a country's citizens and their resources. *GDP* measures production generated within the country and leaves out production of a country's citizens and firms outside of the country. At the same time, *GDP* includes production of foreign-owned resources within the country. A more complete measure of production of a nation's resources is Gross National Product (GNP). *GNP* is the value of final goods and services produced by a nation's citizens and their resources. Therefore *GNP* is equal to *GDP* plus **net factor payments** (NFP). *NFP* represents wages and other factor payments received by nationals of a country from foreigners minus wages and other factor payments made by a country to foreign nationals. Therefore,

$$Y = C + I + G + (X - M) + NFP; \text{ where } \mathbf{Y} \text{ denotes } GNP. \qquad [11.2]$$

From Table 11.2 we should recognize that $(X - M)$ is approximately equal to the balance on goods and services (line 25). Further, *NFP* is equal to the balance on income shown in line (26) in Table 11.2. The current account balance (CAB) is approximately equal to the sum of the balance on goods and services and the balance on income (the sum of lines 1 and 5), which is approximately equal to $[(X - M) + NFP]$. This implies that:

$$Y = C + I + G + CAB \qquad [11.3]$$

or

$$CAB = Y - (C + I + G) \qquad [11.4]$$

Now, Y represents the nation's income while $(C + I + G)$ represent the nation's total spending by households, businesses and government. This suggests that a country with a current account deficit (a negative balance) has to be spending more than its income. To be able to afford this, the nation borrows from other countries or sells assets to foreigners. It should also be clear that borrowing and/or selling assets increases the countries capital inflows and would lead to a net credit (surplus) balance on the country's capital/financial account. As shown in Table 11.2, this was the case for the United States in 2015—a debit (negative) current account balance (line 28) paid for by net financial inflows (net positive/credit balance) on the capital/financial accounts (line 30). Both borrowing and sale of assets to foreigners in order to finance a current account deficit reduces the country's net wealth position. The country is either reducing its asset holdings (by selling off assets) or increasing its liabilities to other nations (through borrowing).

THE INTERNATIONAL INVESTMENT POSITION

The **international investment position** is a measure of total and distribution of a nation's assets abroad as well as total and distribution of foreign-owned assets within the nation at yearend. The international investment position is also referred to as the **balance of international indebtedness**.

Table 11.3 presents a summary of the U.S. international investment position at yearend, 2014 and 2015. The U.S. net international investments position changed from (−) $7,019.7 billion at yearend 2014 to (−) $7,356.8 billion at yearend 2015. This is a slight deterioration in the U.S. international investment position of about (−) $337.1 billion. A few reasons may explain changes in a country's international investment position.

1. **Changes in prices/valuation of assets**. According to the Bureau of Economic Analysis (BEA), U.S. liabilities increased in value due to increases in U.S. stock prices. When U.S. asset prices increase, the value of foreign-owned assets in the United States increases as well. This, in turn, increases U.S. liabilities. However, the BEA also notes that the value of U.S. assets abroad also increased owing to increased foreign equity prices. These two dynamics have offsetting effects on the U.S. international investment position. Moreover, as indicated in Table 11.3, direct investments are valued at current (i.e., replacement) cost. Changes in prices would obviously change the value of such investments.

2. **Changes in currency values**. A change in relative currency values not only affects capital flows, but also affects the valuation of assets. For example, an appreciation of the U.S. dollar relative to other major world currencies increases the relative value of U.S. dollar-denominated investments. Therefore, the value of foreign-owned investments in the United States increases relative to U.S.-owned assets abroad. For example, in 2015 major world currencies depreciated against the U.S dollar. This reduced the dollar value of U.S. assets abroad.

3. **Financial flows**. A more obvious reason for changes in a country's international investment position is international financial flows. A nation that experiences more financial inflows (outflows) relative to outflows (inflows) in a given year will see its international investment position deteriorate (improve). Financial inflows suggest an increase in foreign-owned assets in a country. On the other hand, financial outflows suggest an increase in a country's assets abroad. In other words, an increase in financial inflows, other things constant, reduces a country's net international investment position. In contrast, an increase in financial outflows, other things constant, improves the country's net international investment position.

An April 2016 Bureau of Economic Analysis (BEA) publication indicates that about 38% of the change in the U.S. net international investment position (−$127.9 billion) between

Table 11.3   International Investment Position of the United States at Year-end 2014 and 2015

	2014	2015
1 **Net International Investment Position of the United States (line 2 minus line 9)**	**−7,019,699**	**−7,356,784**
2 **U.S.-owned assets abroad**	**24,595,547**	**23,208,278**
3 U.S. Official Reserve assets	434,251	383,601
4 U.S.-owned private Assets abroad (includes direct investment at market value and portfolio investment)	16,696,573	16,442,344
5 Other investments	4,240,188	3,984,685
6 Financial derivatives (gross positive fair value)	3,224,535	2,397,648
7 **Foreign-owned assets in the United States**	**31,615,246**	**30,565,062**
8 Foreign-owned private assets in the United States (includes direct investment at market value and portfolio investment)	23,145,941	23,179,271
9 Other foreign-owned assets in the United States	5,318,617	5,045,245
10 Financial derivative (gross negative fair value)	3,150,688	2,340,546

yearend 2014 and yearend 2015 is attributed to price changes, currency exchange rate changes, and changes in asset valuation. Net financial transactions account for about 62% (−$209.2 billion) of the change in U.S. international investment position between 2014 and 2015. This suggests that, in 2015, foreign acquisition of U.S. assets (this includes U.S. government securities (foreign-held federal government debt)) exceeded U.S. acquisition of foreign assets.

Figure 11.1 shows that the United States has had a negative net international investment position since mid-1980s. In other words, since mid-1980s, foreign-owned assets in the United States have exceeded U.S.-owned assets abroad. Does this have anything to do with the current account balance discussed earlier in the chapter? The answer is yes. Recall our discussion of the current account balance in the preceding section. A current account deficit implies that a country's spending exceeds its income (equation 11.4). This is only affordable if a country borrows from abroad or sells assets to foreigners, both of which cause an increase in foreign-owned assets in the country. As a result, the country's net international investment position deteriorates. It is therefore not a coincidence that the United States has had both chronic current account deficits and a deteriorating net international investment position.

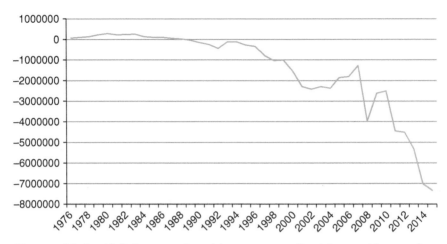

Figure 11.1 U.S. International Investment Position at Yearend, 1976–2015 (millions of dollars)

Source: By authors using data from the U.S. Bureau of Economic Analysis.

SUMMARY

- The *balance of payments* is a system of accounts with records of a country's transactions with the rest of the world during a given year.
- The balance of payments system uses the *double-entry bookkeeping system*. This means that each transaction recorded in the balance of payments has two entries—a *credit* entry and a *debit* entry. A credit entry is made in the balance of payments when a transaction leads to a payment *to* a resident, business or government of a country by a foreign resident or entity. In contrast, a debit entry is made in the balance of payments when a transaction leads to a payment *by* a resident (or entity) of a country to a foreign resident or entity. Credit entries are recorded as *positive* entries, while debit entries are recorded as *negative* entries.
- Because of the double-entry system, the sum of all credit (positive) entries and all debit (negative) entries in the balance of payments should sum to zero. This is a fundamental *balance of payments identity*.
- The balance of payments system is made up of the *current account*, and the *capital/financial* accounts.
- The current account records transactions involving the exchange of goods and services (exports and imports of goods and services) across countries, income receipts, income payments, and unilateral transfers. Income receipts are incomes received by residents of a country from abroad as a return on their asset holdings abroad. On the other hand, income payments are payments to foreign residents as a return on their asset holdings within the country. Unilateral transfers are grants/donations or gifts received or given by a country's residents, businesses, or government.

- Capital/financial accounts record transactions involving sale or purchase of financial assets. Transactions in the capital/financial account are either official (conducted by government) or private (market-driven transactions).
- Due to errors and omissions, often the credits and debits in the balance of payments do not offset (as they should). In practice, errors and omissions in the balance of payments are principally due to unrecorded short-term capital flows. The *statistical discrepancy* is the balancing item introduced in the balance of payments accounts to offset all the errors and omissions.
- The *balance on goods* is the difference between the value of goods (merchandise) exports and goods (merchandise) imports. The balance on goods, also known as *balance of trade* or *trade balance*, is one of the most commonly cited statistics in trade policy discussions. A *trade deficit* (negative balance) means that the value of goods exports exceeds the value of goods imports. A *trade surplus* (positive balance), on the other hand, suggests that the value of merchandise exports exceeds the value of merchandise imports.
- The *balance on services* (less cited in policy debates) is the difference between the value of services exports and the value of services imports. The sum of the balance on goods and balance on services is known the *balance on goods and services.*
- The *balance on income* is the difference between income receipts and income payments. The sum of the balance on goods, the balance on services, the balance on income, and the net unilateral transfers is the balance on *current account.*
- A balance of payments deficit refers to a situation where the sum of credit and debit entries in a country's current account, capital/financial accounts, and the statistical discrepancy is negative.
- A balance of payments surplus refers to a situation where the sum of credit and debit entries in a country's current account, capital/financial accounts, and the statistical discrepancy is positive.
- Balance of payments equilibrium refers to a situation where the sum of credit and debit entries in a country's current account, capital/financial accounts, and the statistical discrepancy is zero.
- A current account deficit (negative balance) suggests that a country is spending more abroad than its earnings from abroad. This is made possible by borrowing from and/or selling assets to foreigners. Therefore a current account deficit has the effect of reducing the country's net international wealth position or increasing its indebtedness to other countries.
- The international investment position, also known as the balance of international indebtedness, is a measure of a country's assets abroad and foreign-owned assets within the country at yearend. This means that the international investment position is a *stock variable* (measured *at* a point in time). In contrast, the balance of payments is a *flow variable* (measure *over* a period of time).
- A negative net international investment position suggests that the value of foreign-owned assets in the country exceed the value of a country's assets abroad. The reverse is true for a positive net international investment position.
- Changes over time of a country's international investment position are due to a number of factors. These include changes in net prices of assets, relative changes in currency values, as well as changes in capital flows.

KEY TERMS

Balance of payments
Current account
Capital/financial account
Double-entry bookkeeping system
Credit entry
Debit entry
Statistical discrepancy
The balance of payments identity
Balance on goods/balance of trade/trade balance
Trade deficit
Trade surplus
Balance on services
Balance on goods and services
Balance on current account
Official settlement balance
Net capital flows
Balance of payments deficit
Balance of payments surplus
Balance of payments equilibrium
Gross domestic product (GDP)
Gross national product (GNP)
Net factor payments (NFP)
International investment position
Balance of international indebtedness

PROBLEMS

1. Each of the following transactions will affect the balance of payments for the United States. Classify the transactions as either debit or credit entries and indicate which account (capital or current) in the U.S. balance of payments would be affected.

   a. A European businesswoman travels to Washington, DC and spends $2,000 on hotel and food. She pays with a check drawn on a European bank.
   b. Samsung sells $500,000 of its cellular phones to a U.S. phone service provider.
   c. Mr. Kwame in the United States sends his nephew in Africa $200 as a graduation gift.
   d. Ms. Williams in Atlanta buys a Swiss Treasury Bill.
   e. The U.S. government sends $1 billion worth of military assistance to the government of Afghanistan.
   f. Fiat, an Italian company, buys a substantial stake in Chrysler, an American company for $1.7 billion.

2. In a given year, a country's exports of goods and services are equal to $2.8 million. The country's imports are equal to $3.2 million. The country's private capital inflows and outflows are equal to $790,000 and 465,000 respectively. Assuming that these are the only transactions the country engaged in, and that the statistical discrepancy is equal to zero, what is the country's official settlement balance?

3. A country's gross national product (GNP) in 2009 was equal to $1.4 trillion. In the same year, total personal consumption spending was equal to $798 billion; total business investment spending was equal to $266 billion; and government expenditure was equal to $294 billion. What was the country's current account balance in 2009?

4. Describe how a country's current account balance is related to its international indebtedness.

5. The United States has had a persistent current account deficit for decades. Is this a cause for concern? Are there any benefits of persistent current account deficits?

6. What is meant by the *international investment position*? What are the implications of a deteriorating international investment position?

7. Define, explain, and compare/contrast the following terms:

   a. Balance of payments versus current account
   b. Double-entry system versus balance of payments identity
   c. Credit entry versus debit entry
   d. Unilateral transfers versus official settlement balance
   e. Balance of payments deficit versus balance of payments equilibrium
   f. Statistical discrepancy versus balance of payments identity

12

Foreign Exchange Markets and Exchange Rates

S everal chapters in this book noted and/or emphasized the increasing interdependence of national economies. In fact, this is the primary focus of this book and the course for which it is intended to be used. The interdependence of economies is seen in the increasing volumes of trade in the real sector (where we trade goods and services) as well as increasing activity in global financial markets (the financial sector). One part of the financial sector that makes most of this economic interdependence possible is the foreign exchange market. A foreign exchange market is a market where currencies are bought and sold. Because nations around the world use different currencies, a foreign exchange market facilitates international transactions in goods and services as well as other financial transactions such as those involving international capital flows.

Imagine that Best Buy, an American company, wants to buy cellular phones from Samsung Group, a South Korean corporation. Best Buy has, say, U.S. $1 million that it wishes to use to pay for Samsung cellular phones. However, Samsung would like to receive payment in Korean *won* since the company's expenses (including workers' wages and other bills) are paid in Korean *won*. How could this transaction be done? One option is for Best Buy to find Korean businesses (or individuals) that would like to do business in the United States and therefore have Korean *won* they are willing to exchange for U.S. dollars. This, however, raises the same difficulties associated with the *barter system* of exchange—the double coincidence of wants.

The foreign exchange market helps to resolve such currency exchange issues. In our example, Best Buy would exchange dollars for Korean *won* in the foreign exchange market and pay Samsung in Korean *won*. Alternatively, Samsung could accept U.S. dollars from Best Buy and then exchange the dollars for Korean *won*. Either way, the foreign exchange market would have facilitated this transaction between the two companies.

The primary goal of this chapter is to provide an overview of the global foreign exchange market and how prices (exchange rates) are determined in this particular market.

LEARNING GOALS

➤ Understand and describe the structure and importance of the foreign exchange market.

➤ Be able to:

  ▪ Do simple currency conversions using exchange rates.

  ▪ Calculate cross exchange rates.

  ▪ Calculate the forward premium/discount.

➤ Understand how exchange rates are determined and factors associated with demand (for) and supply of currencies.

➤ Be able to relate changes in a currency's exchange rate to a country's exports and imports.

➤ Understand the concept of purchasing power parity (PPP) and relate it to the exchange rate between any two currencies.

➤ Understand and describe past and present foreign exchange systems.

THE FOREIGN EXCHANGE MARKET

The **foreign exchange market** is a market where currencies of different nations are traded. Major foreign exchange market centers are located in cities in industrialized countries such as London in the United Kingdom, New York in the United States, Tokyo in Japan, Singapore in China, Sydney in Australia, and Frankfurt in Germany. Because of different time zones, the global foreign exchange market is open 24 hours a day. We should view the different foreign exchange trading centers as decentralized units of a single global foreign exchange market. Due to advances in communication technology, the different trading centers around the world are virtually interconnected to form a single global foreign exchange market.

The global foreign exchange market is the largest financial market in the world with an average daily turnover of approximately US$5.35 trillion in April 2013 (see Figure 12.1 below). This represents an increase of about 160% over the 2004 average daily turnover (US$2.04 trillion). Note that the rate of growth in foreign exchange turnover slowed down significantly between 2007 and 2010 relative to the three years before 2007. This slowdown is attributed to the global financial crisis of 2007–2009. However, the market recovered in 2010 with a daily turnover growth of about 35% between 2010 and 2013.

Most foreign exchange transactions involve the U.S. dollar, which is the most widely used currency in international transactions. This also reflects the dominant role of the United States in the global economy. The euro (a common currency for 17 European countries), the Japanese yen, and the United Kingdom pound sterling are some of the other major currencies traded in the global foreign exchange market. In 2013, 87% of the average daily foreign exchange market turnover involved the U.S. dollar. Figure 12.2 shows the distribution of average daily foreign exchange market turnover by currency.[1]

---

[1] Due to the bilateral nature of foreign exchange transactions (each foreign exchange transaction involves two currencies); the sum of all currency shares (%) is more than 100%. In fact, currency shares should sum up to 200%.

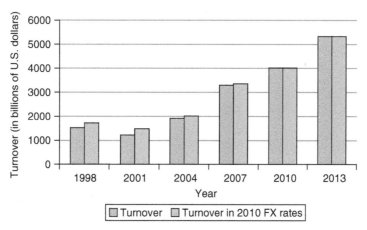

Figure 12.1   Global Foreign Exchange Average Daily Turnover (1998–2013)
Source: By authors using data from the Bank for International Settlements (BIS) 2013 Triennial Central Bank Survey

Although a big part of foreign exchange market turnover involves the U.S. dollar, currency exchange centers in Europe, in general, and the United Kingdom, in particular, dominate currency exchanges. Figure 12.3 shows the dominance of UK banks in global foreign exchange markets. In fact, London is the world's largest currency exchange center. In 2013, banks in the United Kingdom accounted for 41% of the average daily foreign exchange turnover. In the same year, banks in the United States accounted for 19% of the average daily turnover. The United States is followed by Singapore, Japan, Hong Kong SAR, Australia, and Switzerland.

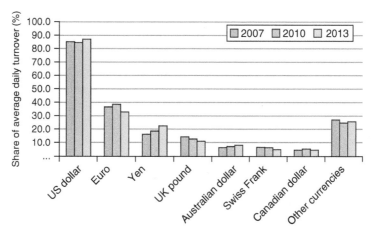

Figure 12.2   Average daily Turnover by currency (% share), 2007–2013
Source: By authors using data from the Bank for International Settlements (BIS) 2013 Triennial Central Bank Survey

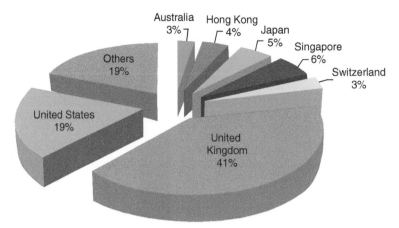

Figure 12.3   **Global Average Daily Foreign Exchange Market Turnover by Geographical Location (% share), 2013.**
Source: By authors using data from the Bank for International Settlements (BIS) 2013 Triennial Central Bank Survey

Major Participants in the Foreign Exchange Market

Participants in the global foreign exchange market range from an American tourist in Paris to multinational corporations engaging in international transactions, to commercial banks and central banks. This subsection highlights the main actors in the foreign exchange market.

Commercial Banks: Commercial banks engage in foreign exchange transactions on behalf of their clients. Let us return to our earlier example where Best Buy intends to purchase US$1 million worth of Samsung cellular phones. Once the two companies have agreed to conduct the transaction, Best Buy will arrange to make the payment. Assume that Best Buy maintains an account at Bank of America. Best Buy would instruct its banker (Bank of America) to debit the company's account with the US$1 million. Bank of America would then pay Samsung the Korean *won* equivalent through its (Samsung) Korean banker. Moreover, a bank may buy and sell currencies to other banks. This is called **interbank trading**. Interbank trading allows banks to buy currencies at more favorable wholesale prices (exchange rates) and sell for a profit at less favorable retail prices.[2] Commercial banks account for a very large share of the global foreign exchange market turnover.

Nonbank Financial Institutions: Besides commercial banks, there is a host of financial institutions that play a substantial role in the foreign exchange market. These include hedge funds, mutual funds, insurance companies, and pension funds. Nonbank financial institutions expect to profit from the difference between the buying price and the selling price—the **bid-ask spread**.

---

[2] We discuss the price of a currency (called an exchange rate) in the next section.

Nonfinancial Businesses: These primarily include corporations that operate in several countries. For example, American multinational companies like General Motors operate assembly plants in Latin American countries such as Brazil, Chile, and Columbia. If GM, with its earnings in U.S. dollars, wants to pay workers in the company's assembly plant in Brazil, it would have to buy the Brazilian *real* using U.S. dollars. This kind of transaction is more efficiently done through the global foreign exchange market.

Central Banks: Central banks often carry out foreign exchange market interventions in order to prevent unwanted fluctuations in the value of the country's currency relative to other currencies. As noted in Chapter 11, the Fed might buy the *euro* (and sell the dollar) if the intended goal is to reduce the value of the dollar relative to the *euro*. The actions of central banks have a significant impact on both the foreign exchange market (since it might be understood as a signal of policy changes to come) as well as a direct impact on trade in the real sector (trade in goods and services) of the global economy.

Other Foreign Exchange market participants: These mainly include households and small nonbank institutions that engage in online currency trades and profit from the bid-ask spread. The "ask" is the buying price, while the "bid" is the selling price. The "spread" is the difference between the two prices, which covers transactions costs and the trader's return. Retail investors are facilitated by financial firms that act as foreign exchange intermediaries.

Exchange Rates

An **exchange rate** is a price of one currency in terms of another currency. For example, the dollar price of a Japanese yen is the *dollar/yen* exchange rate. This simply means the amount of U.S. dollars one would need to obtain one Japanese yen.

At 1:20 PM EST on May 1, 2016, one Japanese yen cost US$0.0094. This can be written as 0.0094$/¥ (i.e., 1¥ = $0.0094). Exchange rates written in terms of U.S. dollars per unit of the other currency are said to be expressed in **direct** or **American** terms.

The dollar/yen exchange rate can also be written in terms of Japanese yen per U.S. dollar. This would be the *yen* price of a dollar and is the reciprocal of the dollar price of a yen. Therefore, the yen price of a dollar for the May 1, 2016 example above is

$$\$1 = \frac{1¥}{0.0094} = 106.3830¥$$

This means that it would take 106.3830 yen to buy US$1 (or simply 106.38¥/$). When exchange rates are written in terms of units of a foreign currency per U.S. dollar, they are said to be expressed in **indirect** or **European** terms.

Foreign exchange rates allow us to denominate goods prices in a common currency. For example, if a Lexus GX costs ¥4,500,000 in Japan and $52,000 in the United States, in which country is the GX cheaper? Using the current dollar/yen exchange rate, we can convert the prices into a common currency (i.e., have both prices denominated in either U.S. dollars or Japanese yen). This should make it possible to compare the two prices.

At the current dollar/yen exchange rate, 1¥ = $0.0094.

This means that ¥4,500,000 = $0.0094 × 4,500,000 = $ 42,300.

Now that we have both prices denominated in U.S. dollars, it is easy to compare price and make informed purchase decisions. Changes in the dollar/yen exchange rate will affect the dollar price of a Lexus GX relative to the yen price of the same car. We will have more discussion on this later in the chapter.

Exchange Rate Determination

Like other markets, exchange rates (prices of currencies) are, in part, determined by demand and supply. **Demand for a currency** comes from residents of other countries who desire to buy a country's goods and services or to invest in a country's assets. For example, when residents of other countries purchase U.S.-made goods or invest in U.S. assets, they exchange their currencies for the U.S. dollar in order to pay for the purchased U.S. goods or investments. Who actually does the exchange is immaterial. What is important is someone somewhere will need to purchase dollars using a foreign currency. This increases the demand for the dollar.

The **supply of a currency** comes from a country's residents' desire to buy goods and services or investments in other countries. For example, when U.S. residents purchase goods from China, they spend U.S. dollars. However, at some point, the U.S. dollars have to be converted into Chinese Yuan so that the companies that produce these goods in China can pay their workers' wages and other expenses of running their business. This increases the supply of U.S. dollars in the foreign exchange market.

These two forces (demand and supply) determine the equilibrium exchange rate for any given currency. Figure 12.4 illustrates this basic market-based exchange rate determination. In Figure 12.4, the market equilibrium yen/dollar exchange rate is ¥95 per U.S. dollar. In other words, the yen price of a dollar is ¥95. As is the case in most markets (and more so in the foreign exchange market), relative prices of currencies (exchange rates) often change. Short-term changes in currency prices are often a result of speculative activities of currency traders. However, medium to long-term changes are often a result of fundamental macroeconomic factors such changes in relative rates of inflation, changes in demand for imports, and changes in rates of return on investment.

Let us consider an *increase in foreign demand for U.S.-made goods*. Recall that demand for U.S.-made goods indirectly means demand for the U.S. dollar. Why is this so? Producers of U.S. goods and services need dollars to run their businesses. Therefore, foreign buyers of U.S. products would need dollars to buy U.S. goods.[3] In Panel (a) of Figure 12.5, increased Japanese demand for U.S. goods (U.S. exports to Japan) increases the demand for the U.S.

---

[3] As explained earlier, in practice, foreign buyers of U.S. products may not have to directly convert their own currencies to U.S. dollars in order to purchase U.S. goods. If the U.S. seller of the goods accepts the foreign currency as payment for goods sold to foreign buyers, then the U.S. seller would have to convert the foreign currency to U.S. dollars. In either case, the demand for the dollar increases

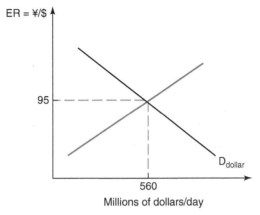

Figure 12.4   **The U.S. dollar/Yen exchange rate**

dollar (shifts the demand curve for the U.S. dollar to the right). This increases both the yen price of the U.S. dollar (exchange rate) as well as the volume of U.S. dollars traded in the foreign exchange market.

In Panel (b) of Figure 12.5, an *increase in U.S. demand for Japanese goods* (U.S. imports from Japan) increases the supply of the dollar in the foreign exchange market. Increased demand for Japanese goods by *U.S. residents* implies that U.S. residents are spending more of their dollars to buy Japanese goods. Since Japanese producers would like payment for their goods in yen, the dollars have to be converted to yen. By doing so, the supply of U.S. dollars in the foreign exchange market increases. As reflected in Figure 12.5 (Panel b), this causes the yen price of the U.S. dollar (the yen/dollar exchange rate) to drop and the volume of dollars traded to increase.

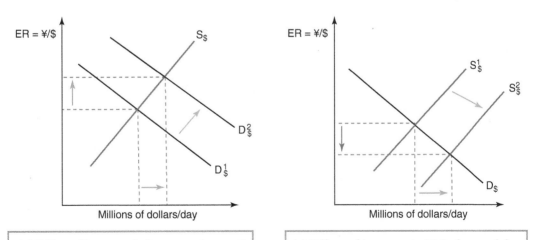

(a) Effect of increase in Japanese demand for U.S.-made goods and/or U.S. assets

b) Effect of increase in U.S. demand for Japanese goods and/or assets

Figure 12.5   **Changes in Market Equilibrium Exchange Rates**

Changes in U.S. domestic demand for imports or Japanese demand for U.S. exports could result from changes in *relative performance of the two economies*. For example, when the U.S. economy is in a downturn (or a recession), U.S. demand for Japanese goods drops and the supply of dollars (or the demand for the Japanese yen) drops as well. The reverse is true when the U.S. economy experiences an expansion (the opposite of a recession).

Changes in *relative price levels* will also affect foreign exchange rates. In this case, a higher rate of inflation (rate of change or increase in prices) in the United States makes it more expensive for Japanese consumers to buy U.S. goods. To sustain U.S. exports to Japan, the yen price of the dollar should fall (i.e., the dollar should cost fewer yen than before). Here is how this would happen. First, Japanese buyers will want to purchase fewer goods and services at the existing market exchange rate. This means a decrease in the demand for the dollar. Second, U.S. consumers will opt to buy more from Japan and less from the United States. This means an increase in the supply of the dollar. The combination of lower demand for the dollar and increased supply of the dollar would inevitably lead to a drop in the yen price of the dollar (the ¥/$ exchange rate).

Figure 12.6 illustrates the effect of an increase in *relative* inflation on exchange rates.[4] In this case, we assumed that U.S. prices are increasing at a faster rate (higher U.S. inflation) relative to Japanese prices. As a result, Japanese demand for U.S. goods falls and so does the demand for the U.S. dollar. At the same time, U.S. consumers would prefer Japanese goods over U.S. goods, which increases the supply of the U.S. dollar in the foreign exchange market. The combination of these two factors causes the Japanese price of the U.S. dollar for drop from ¥95 to ¥92.

When the Japanese Yen price of the U.S. dollar falls, the U.S. dollar is said to have *depreciated*. **Depreciation of a currency** occurs when the amount of another currency

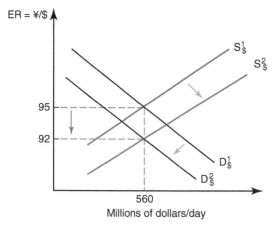

Figure 12.6   **The Effect of U.S. Inflation on dollar/Yen Exchange Rate**

---

[4] Note that what matters for exchange rates is how one country's prices change (inflation) relative to changes in prices in the other country. An increase in U.S. inflation would not affect the dollar/yen exchange rate if Japanese inflation also increased at the same rate as U.S. inflation.

required to purchase one unit of the currency decreases. In Figure 12.6, the amount of Japanese yen required to purchase a dollar dropped by about $(-)3.2\%$ $\{[(92-95)/95] \times 100\}$. Put simply, the dollar depreciation against the yen means that the dollar lost value against the yen. The dollar is cheaper to obtain using the Japanese yen. When this happens as a result of U.S. inflation, Japanese demand for U.S. goods can be sustained because a cheaper dollar compensates Japanese buyers for the higher U.S. inflation.

On the other hand, when the yen price of the U.S. dollar increases, the dollar is said to have *appreciated*. **Appreciation of a currency** occurs when the amount of another currency required to purchase one unit of the currency increases. Panel (a) of Figure 12.5 shows an appreciation of the U.S. dollar against the Japanese yen. This means that the dollar is more expensive to obtain for Japanese residents. Other things constant, this will reduce U.S. exports to Japan and increase U.S. imports from Japan.

To see how this would happen, let us return to our Lexus GX example discussed earlier in this chapter. In that example, at a dollar/yen exchange rate of 106.3830¥/$, a ¥4,500,000 Lexus GX would cost about US$42,300 (4,500,000/106.3830 ≈ 42,300). Now suppose two scenarios:

1. The *dollar depreciates* such that the new exchange rate is ¥100/$. Given the new exchange rate, the same ¥4,500,000 Lexus GX now costs about $45,000 (4,500,000/100 = 45,000). Potential buyers of the Lexus GX in the United States would have to spend more to get it. The increase in the dollar price of the Lexus, other things constant, will reduce the number of Lexus GX imported from Japan. However, note that the dollar depreciation against the yen also means that the yen appreciates against the dollar. Therefore, Japanese consumers would find it less expensive to buy U.S. goods owing to a relatively stronger yen.
2. The *dollar appreciates* against the yen (or the yen depreciates against the dollar) such that the new exchange rate is ¥110/$. In this case the ¥4,500,000 Lexus GX would cost $40,909 (4,500,000/110 ≈ 40,909). The Lexus GX is now less expensive to U.S. buyers, thanks to a stronger U.S. dollar relative to the yen.

This example demonstrates that changes in relative currency prices (exchange rates) play an important role in the real sector of the global economy.

Spot and Forward Exchange Rates

In April 2013, about 37.4% of the daily global foreign exchange market turnover was made up of what are called spot transactions.[5] A **spot transaction** is one where parties agree to an exchange of currencies and delivery of currency is made "immediately." *Immediately* might mean up to two days—the time it takes for parties involved in the transactions (typically banks) to debit and credit the relevant accounts. With the recent advances in communication technology, an increasingly larger share of spot transactions is settled within a day. The exchange rates in spot transactions are called **spot rates**.

---

[5] This excludes foreign *exchange swaps* (also conducted in spot markets). A discussion of foreign exchange swaps is beyond the scope of this book.

However, there are situations where immediate delivery of the currencies is not desirable. An American firm that has to make a payment in UK pounds three months from now may not want (or even afford) to buy UK pounds at the current spot market. On the other hand, the firm faces uncertainty about changes in the dollar/pound market exchange rate between now and three months' time when payment is due. In such a situation, the American firm can buy a **forward contract**. A forward contract specifies a future date for delivery of foreign exchange. The date could be one month, three months, six months, etc. from the date of the contract. The exchange rates that apply to forward contracts are called **forward exchange rates**. Forward exchange rates are different from spot rates and also differ by length of the contract (one month, three months, six months, etc.). A forward contract allows parties to lock in a predetermined exchange rate at which currency will be exchanged at a future date. The future date of foreign exchange delivery is called the **value date**.

Example: An American firm has purchased office premises in London for £10 million. Payment is to be made six months from the day of purchase. The dollar/pound spot rate (the dollar price of a pound) is 1.4603$/£. The American firm has three options to obtain the UK pounds needed to pay for the property in London.

1. **Buy the UK pounds now:** At the current dollar/pound spot exchange rate, the firm will need $14,603,000 ($1.4603 × £10 million) to buy the UK pounds. However, this option may not be available for the American firm. The firm may not have the $14,603,000 on hand to pay for the London property. After all, there is a reason the firm negotiated to defer the payment to six months after the purchase agreement is signed.
2. **The second option is to wait and buy the pound in six months when payment is due.** However, this exposes the firm to a foreign exchange risk. Suppose that within the next six months before payment is made, the dollar price of the UK pound increases to $1.5333 (about a 5% depreciation of the dollar against the pound or a 5% appreciation of the pound). In this case, the American firm needs $15,333,000 ($1.5333 × £10 million). This represents a $730,000 increase in the dollar price of the property.
3. **To avoid this risk, the American firm can buy a forward contract** to "buy pounds forward" and "sell dollars forward." This means agreeing to buy pounds at a future date at a predetermined exchange rate (the forward rate).[6] Let us assume that the six-month forward exchange rate is $1.4676 per UK pound. In this case, the American firm has a guaranteed exchange rate no matter what happens to the spot market exchange rates. The firm would spend $14,676,000 ($1.4676 × £10 million).

Therefore, the forward contract helps the American firm to *hedge* against the foreign exchange risk that results from changes in spot market exchange rates. The **foreign exchange risk** represents the risk that the payment denominated in the buyer's domestic currency (the U.S. dollar) will change due to changes in the dollar price of the UK pound (the dollar/pound exchange rate).

---

[6] Of course, by buying pounds using dollars, the U.S. firm is also selling dollars (selling dollars forward).

Demand and supply for forward contracts primarily determines the forward exchange rates.[7] For any given currency, the forward exchange rate could be the same as spot rate, higher than the spot rate, or even lower than the spot rate. In the dollar/pound example above, the forward exchange rate (1.4676$/£) is higher than the spot rate (1.4603$/£). In this case, the UK pound is said to be at a **forward premium** relative to the U.S. dollar.

When the dollar/pound forward exchange rate is lower than the dollar/pound spot exchange rate, then the pound is said to be at a **forward discount** relative to the dollar. For example, if the dollar/pound spot rate is 1.4603$/£ (i.e., £1 = $1.4603); and the dollar/pound six-month forward rate is 1.4457$/£ (£1 = $1.4457), then the UK pound is said to be at a forward discount relative to the dollar.

The forward premium (P) or discount (D) is equal to the difference between the forward rate and the spot rate expressed as a percentage of the spot rate per year. Therefore, the premium or discount is given by:

$$\text{Forward Premium or Discount} = \frac{FR - SP}{SP} \times \frac{12}{N} \times 100$$

Where *FR* denotes the forward rate; *SP* denotes the spot rate; *N* is the number of months (the length) of the forward contract. For the two examples above—the first example showing the UK pound at a forward premium and the second showing the UK pound at a forward discount—the forward premium or discount can be calculated as follows.

$$\text{Forward Premium} = \frac{\$1.4676 - \$1.4603}{\$1.4603} \times \frac{12}{6} \times 100 \approx 1\%$$

The next example shows the UK pound at a forward discount.

$$\text{Forward Discount} = \frac{\$1.4457 - \$1.4603}{\$1.4603} \times \frac{12}{6} \times 100 \approx -2\%$$

(The minus sign indicates that the UK pound is at a six-month forward discount).

Table 12.1 presents spot rates for various currencies against the U.S. dollar. The spot exchange rates in Table 12.1 relate to wholesale transactions (transactions involving exchange of US$1 million or more). Retail exchanges are made at less favorable rates. Most major daily newspapers around the world report exchange rates at the close of the previous day for a particular trading center. The rates in Table 12.1 are for the New York trading center at closing on April 20, 2016.

Exchange rates are reported in both the *direct* (*American* terms) and *indirect* (*European* terms). The column titled "USD per Currency" is the amount of U.S. dollars needed to purchase one unit of each of the currencies in the first column. This is the direct or *American terms* format. The next column titled "Currency per USD" is the amount of each of the currencies required to purchase one U.S. dollar. This is the indirect or *European terms* format.

---

[7] Forward rates are closely related to spot rates. This chapter omits the discussion of this close relationship.

Table 12.1 USD Exchange Rate Quotations, New York Closing on Wednesday, April 20, 2016

Country/currency (1)	USD Per Currency (2)	Currency Per US (3)	US$ vs. YTD % chg (4)
Americas			
Argentina peso	0.0697	14.349	10.9
Brazil real	0.2833	3.5299	–10.9
Canada dollar	0.7902	1.2656	–8.5
Chile peso	0.001519	658.3	–7.1
Colombia peso	0.000345	2898.22	–8.7
Ecuador US dollar	1	1	unch
Mexico peso	0.0579	17.2769	0.4
Peru new sol	0.3082	3.245	–5
Uruguay peso	0.03138	31.87	6.6
Venezuela bolivar	0.10013669	9.9864	58.4
Asia-Pacific			
Australian dollar	0.7795	1.2829	–6.5
China yuan	0.1546	6.4691	–0.4
Hong Kong dollar	0.1289	7.7559	0.1

Country/currency (1)	USD Per Currency (2)	Currency Per US (3)	US$ vs. YTD % chg (4)
Europe			
Bulgaria lev	0.5774	1.732	–3.8
Croatia kuna	0.1506	6.64	–5.3
Czech Rep. koruna	0.04181	23.919	–3.9
Denmark krone	0.1518	6.5863	–4.2
Euro area euro	1.1298	0.8852	–3.9
Hungary forint	0.003657	273.43	–5.9
Iceland krona	0.008097	123.51	–5.1
Norway krone	0.1232	8.1167	–8.2
Poland zloty	0.2646	3.7798	–3.7
Romania leu	0.2521	3.9661	–4.6
Russia ruble	0.01534	65.173	–9.4
Sweden krona	0.123	8.1293	–3.7
Switzerland franc	1.0284	0.9724	–3
Turkey lira	0.3555	2.8131	–3.6
Ukraine hryvnia	0.0394	25.367	5.7

Currency			
India rupee	0.01511	66.1655	−0.1
Indonesia rupiah	0.0000758	13184	−4.7
Japan yen	0.0091	109.85	−8.7
Kazakhstan tenge	0.00296	337.98	−0.2
Macau pataca	0.1251643	7.99	−0.2
Malaysia ringgit	0.2581	3.8752	−9.9
New Zealand dollar	0.6978	1.4331	−2.1
Pakistan rupee	0.00956	104.65	−0.2
Philippines peso	0.0216	46.278	−1.2
Singapore dollar	0.7438	1.3444	−5.2
South Korea won	0.0008822	1133.59	−3.6
Sri Lanka rupee	0.0068339	146.33	1.5
Taiwan dollar	0.03102	32.24	−2.1
Thailand baht	0.02867	34.88	−3.2
Vietnam dong	0.00004486	22291	0.6
UK pound	1.4333	0.6977	2.8
Middle East/Africa			
Bahrain dinar	2.6539	0.3768	−0.1
Egypt pound	0.1127	8.8769	13.4
Israel shekel	0.2656	3.7649	−3.3
Kuwait dinar	3.3169	0.3015	−0.7
Oman sul rial	2.59737	0.39	unch
Qatar rial	0.2746	3.6415	unch
Saudi Arabia riyal	0.2667	3.7501	−0.1
South Africa rand	0.0704	14.2109	−8.2

Source: Republished with permission of Dow Jones and Company, Inc., from the *Wall Street Journal*, online Market Data Center, April 20, 2016; permission conveyed through Copyright Clearance Center, Inc.

Column (4), labeled "US$ vs. YTD% chg." represents the change in the value of the U.S. dollar relative to each of the other currencies from the beginning of the year to April 20, 2016. For example, the U.S. dollar depreciated by (–) 10.9% against the Brazilian *real* from the beginning of 2016 to April 20, 2016. On the other hand, during the same period, the U.S. dollar appreciated by (+) 2.8% relative to the UK *Pound*.

Cross Exchange Rates

The spot exchange rates in Table 12.1 are all bilateral exchange rates of various currencies against the U.S. dollar. It is not by accident that most major newspapers report U.S. dollar/ currency exchange rates (and not bilateral exchange rates between, say the UK pound and the Japanese yen). We saw in Figure 12.2 that the bulk of foreign exchange transactions involve the U.S. dollar. This is a reflection of the important role the U.S. dollar plays in settlement of international transactions.

Using two U.S. dollar bilateral exchange rates, we can obtain a third bilateral exchange rate between the other two currencies. For example using the pound/dollar and yen/dollar bilateral exchange rates, we can obtain the yen/pound bilateral exchange rate. This third bilateral exchange rate is called a **cross exchange rate**.

Example. In Table 12.1, the pound/dollar spot exchange rate is 0.6977£/$; the yen/dollar spot exchange rate is 109.85¥/$. What is the yen/pound exchange rate?

$$0.6977£/\$ \rightarrow \$1 = £0.6977; \text{ similarly,}$$

$$109.85¥/\$ \rightarrow \$1 = ¥\ 109.85$$

Since the left-hand sides of the two equations are both equal to $1, the right-hand sides must be equal as well. Therefore,

$$0.6977 \text{ pound} = 109.85 \text{ yen; dividing both sides by } 0.6977 \text{ yields:}$$

$$1 \text{pound} \approx 157.4459 \text{ yen (or } 157.4459¥/£ - \text{ the yen price of a UK pound)}$$

This is equivalent to dividing the yen price of the dollar (yen/dollar exchange rate) by the pound price of the dollar (pound/dollar exchange rate). The reciprocal would yield the pound price of a yen (i.e., the cost of ¥1 in terms of UK pounds).

Because currency trading takes place in several major trading centers around the world, any differences in exchange rates across the several trading centers can be exploited for a profit by currency traders. The process of buying a currency at a low exchange rate in one trading center and immediately selling it at a higher exchange rate in another trading center is called **arbitrage**.

For example, suppose the dollar/euro exchange rate is 1.2936$/€ (1€ = $1.2936) at the New York trading center, and 1.3065$/€ (€1 = $1.3065) at the London trading center, a currency trader can buy $100,000 worth of euros in New York (€77,303.65 = $100,000/$1.2936) and sell the euros at the London trading center. The sale of €77,303.65 at the London trading

Table 12.2   The Big Mac Index, January 2016

Country (1)	Big Mac Price in Local Currency (2)	Actual EXR (currency/ dollar) (3)	Big Mac Price in dollars (4)	Implied PPP exchange rate (5)	Local currency under (−) or over (+) valuation against the USD (6)
United States	4.93	1.00	4.93	1.00	0.00
Argentina	33.00	13.81	2.39	6.69	−51.53
Australia	5.30	1.42	3.74	1.08	−24.06
Brazil	13.50	4.02	3.35	2.74	−31.96
Britain	2.89	0.68	4.22	0.59	−14.36
Canada	5.84	1.41	4.14	1.18	−15.94
Chile	2100.00	715.22	2.94	425.96	−40.44
China	17.60	6.56	2.68	3.57	−45.56
Egypt	16.93	7.83	2.16	3.43	−56.14
Euro area	3.72	0.93	4.00	0.75	−18.88
India	127.00	66.80	1.90	25.76	−61.44
Indonesia	30500.00	13947.50	2.19	6186.61	−55.64
Israel	16.90	3.94	4.29	3.43	−13.02
Japan	370.00	118.65	3.12	75.05	−36.74
Malaysia	8.00	4.39	1.82	1.62	−63.06
Mexico	49.00	17.44	2.81	9.94	−43.00
Pakistan	300.00	104.89	2.86	60.85	−41.98
Russia	114.00	74.66	1.53	23.12	−69.03
Saudi Arabia	12.00	3.75	3.20	2.43	−35.17
Singapore	4.70	1.44	3.27	0.95	−33.67
South Africa	28.00	15.81	1.77	5.68	−64.08
South Korea	4300.00	1197.75	3.59	872.21	−27.18
Switzerland	6.50	1.01	6.44	1.32	30.70
UAE	13.00	3.67	3.54	2.64	−28.21

Source: Data obtained from http://www.economist.com/content/big-mac-index; accessed on April 21, 2016.

The Big Mac Index was created by the *Economist* magazine back in 1986. Premised on the PPP theory, the index is a simple test of currency overvaluation or undervaluation. Table 12.2 above presents actual exchange rates and PPP implied exchange rates for selected currencies. The last column shows the "undervalued" currencies (−) as well "overvalued" currencies (+). We should note that the discrepancies between the actual currency/$ exchange rate and the PPP implied exchange rate may result from differences in the cost of the nonfood inputs such as wages, rent, etc. that are reflected in the local currency price of a Big Mac.

center will yield $100,997 ($1.3065 × €77,303.65) for a profit of $997 ($100,997 − $100,000). This might not seem like a lot of money, but it is quite a lot of money for a few minutes work. Moreover, if the amount of dollars invested in the transaction had instead been $100 million; the return (for the same amount of time) would be about $1 million.

However, profits from arbitrage can only last a short period of time. If currency traders realize the opportunity for arbitrage by buying euros in New York and selling euros in London, the demand for euros in New York would go up, and the supply of euros in London would go up as well. An increase in the demand for euros at the New York trading center would increase the dollar price of the euro, and increased supply of euros at the London trading center would cause the dollar price of the euro to go down at the London trading center. Ultimately, as a result of arbitrage, the dollar price of the euro (dollars per euro) would be the same across trading centers and the opportunity for arbitrage would no longer exist.

Purchasing Power Parity (PPP) and Exchange Rates

The theory of **purchasing power parity (PPP)** is based on the idea that, in the presence of free trade and no transportation costs, changes in relative currency values depend on the currency's purchasing power. A currency's purchasing power is determined by the domestic price level (a weighted average price of a basket of goods). The PPP theory derives its intuition from the **law of one price**—the idea that, under free trade, an identical good would sell at the same price regardless of where it is sold.

To understand the law of one price, let us return once again to our Lexus GX example. At a dollar/yen exchange rate of 0.0094$/¥, a ¥4,500,000 Lexus GX in Japan should cost $42,300 ($0.0094 × ¥4,500,000) in the United States. Therefore, the law of one price implies the following:

The U.S. price of the Lexus GX = dollar/yen exchange rate ×
Japanese price of the Lexus GX.

Equivalently,

The dollar/yen exchange rate = U.S. price of the Lexus GX /
Japanese price of the Lexus GX.

= $42,300 / 4,500,000 = $0.0094.

Now let us suppose that the dollar/yen exchange rate were instead 0.00909$/¥ (or 110¥/$). At the existing prices (i.e., $42,300 in the United States and ¥4,500,000 in Japan), the dollar price of a Lexus GX in Japan is $40,909 ($0.00909 × ¥4,500,000). U.S. importers would buy Lexus GX in Japan and ship them to the United States for sale at $42,300. This would ultimately increase the yen price of the Lexus GX in Japan and lower the U.S. price of the Lexus GX until the ratio of the prices is equal to the dollar/yen exchange rate.

The above example demonstrates the *law of one price*. However, the PPP theory is based on the price level as opposed to the price of a specific good. In other words, we can use the same language as in the *law of one price* to describe the PPP theory. That is, with unrestricted trade, a basket of goods should cost the same price regardless of where it is sold. Equivalently, the exchange rate between two currencies is given by the ratio of the currencies purchasing power (price level) in the respective domestic economies. Therefore:

$$\text{ER}_{\$/\yen} = \frac{P_{US}}{P_J},$$

where $\text{ER}_{\$/\yen}$ is the dollar price of a yen; P_{US} denotes the U.S. price level; and P_J denotes the Japanese price level. If the U.S. price level rises (or the Japanese price level falls), the dollar must depreciate (while the yen appreciates) to maintain the purchasing power parity. The reverse is true for a fall in the U.S. price level (or a rise in the Japanese price level). Therefore, price levels (currencies' purchasing power) are predictors of changes in exchange rates between any two currencies. The exchange rate between two currencies should change to one that equalizes prices of a similar basket of goods in the two countries.

Effective Exchange Rates

As shown in Table 12.1, since the beginning of the year, the U.S. dollar has appreciated relative to some currencies and depreciated against others (see column (4) labeled "US$ vs. YTD % chg."). Therefore, it is hard to determine changes in the overall strength of a currency relative to other currencies. Fortunately, there is an alternative form of exchange rate that fixes this problem. It is known as an *effective exchange rate.*

An **effective exchange rate** is a weighted average of a currency's exchange rate against a "basket" of other currencies. The basket of currencies typically includes the world's major currencies (based on countries share of global trade) or simply currencies of a country's major trading partners. In any case, the currencies in the basket can be changed when deemed necessary. Effective exchange rates are conventionally expressed in the form of an index with a currency's effective exchange rate in particular time period (usually an annual average) used as the base. This allows us to examine changes in the strength of a currency over time.

Figure 12.7 presents effective exchange rates for four major currencies—the euro (a common currency for 17 European countries), the Japanese yen, the UK pound, and the U.S. dollar. The data are annual average exchange values for each currency against a basket of currencies with 2010 exchange averages as the base.

The effects of the 2007–2009 subprime mortgage crises on each of these currencies are very visible on the graph. The UK pound depreciated sharply between 2007 and 2009 before leveling out between 2009 and 2011. Between 2012 and 2015, the pound appreciated by a modest 10.6%. The U.S. dollar depreciation, although less dramatic than the British pound, started in 2009 and ended about 2011 followed by a modest appreciation in 2012 through 2015. The euro depreciated slightly from 2009 to 2010, leveled out in 2010–2011, and then depreciated slightly in 2012 through 2015. On the other hand, the Japanese yen appreciated from 2007 through 2010 but dropped by about 28% between 2011 and 2015.

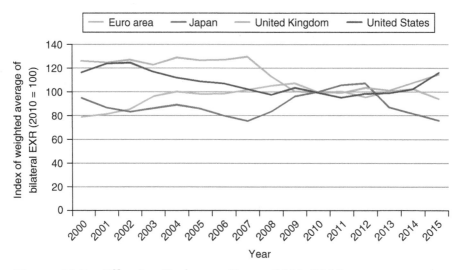

Figure 12.7   **Effective Exchange Rates, 2000–2015**
Source: By authors using data from the Bank for International Settlements (BIS) Effective Exchange Rate, Monthly averages (2010 = 100).

EXCHANGE RATE SYSTEMS

Over the course of history, societies have used different types of money ranging from *commodity money* (such as salt, silver, gold, etc.), *commodity-backed money* (money valued in terms of a commodity such as gold), and *fiat money* (money not backed by any commodity). A **foreign exchange system** defines the rules determining the value of each currency relative to other currencies.

Up until this point, our discussion of exchange rates has assumed that market forces (demand and supply) determine each currency's value relative to other currencies. Although this assumption is generally valid, it is far from absolute. As is the case in most markets, governments intervene in foreign exchange markets in varying degrees. The level of government (or monetary authority) intervention in a foreign exchange market defines the foreign exchange regime for any given currency.

The goal of this section is to provide a brief overview of foreign exchange systems that have defined the overall international monetary system in the past and in the present. Like any other market, society decides the rules of exchange and how prices and quantities are set. Therefore, foreign exchange systems range from those that allow free markets to determine prices and quantities of currencies traded to those where some authority sets prices and quantities. A free market-based foreign exchange system is called a **flexible (or floating) exchange rate system (or regime)**. At the other extreme is a **fixed exchange rate system (or regime)**. In between the two extremes are a number of hybrid systems that combine aspects of flexible exchange rate systems and fixed exchange rate systems.

The Fixed Exchange Rate System

Under a **fixed exchange rate system**, the government sets the value of a country's currency relative to other currencies, and it is not allowed to adjust freely as market forces change. Historically, countries that have implemented a fixed exchange rate have pegged their currencies to a fixed amount of a foreign currency, a fixed weighted average of a "basket of currencies" or to a fixed amount of a commodity such as gold. For this reason, a fixed exchange rate system is also often referred to as a **pegged exchange rate system**. In order for a country to sustain the set exchange rate, the country's monetary authority (usually the central bank) has to constantly buy and/or sell the country's currency at the predetermined fixed exchange rate.

A discussion of exchange rate systems, particularly the fixed exchange rate system, often begins with the *gold standard* era (1870s through the early 1930s). Under the **gold standard**, a country's currency was converted to gold at a fixed exchange rate. For example, an ounce of gold could be worth US$20 or £5. As long as the currency's gold equivalents are fixed, the bilateral exchange rates between currencies themselves are fixed as well.

In the dollar/pound example, the fixed exchange rate between the U.S. dollar and the UK pound is calculated as follows.

$$1 \text{ ounce of gold} = \$20$$

$$1 \text{ ounce of gold} = £5$$

This means that £5 = $20 (since both are equal to 1 ounce of gold)

Therefore, £1 = $20/5 = $4.

For a country to sustain a fixed gold equivalent for a unit of currency, the country's monetary authority must stand ready to buy and sell gold as necessary. The country's currency is backed by gold. The country's monetary authority can only increase money supply by increasing its gold reserves. Since the quantity of monetary gold was expected to be more or less constant over time (owing to the substantial cost of mining gold and the fact that there is a finite amount of gold, at least in the short to medium term), the gold standard was believed to instill discipline in policy makers in order to ensure appropriate levels of money supply and maintain stable prices.

However, the claim that the gold standard (a commodity-backed monetary system) ensured stable prices is widely disputed. In the recent past, the debate about the effectiveness of the Gold Standard seems to have been somewhat revived after a number of prominent U.S. politicians called for its return. As shown in Figure 4.2 (in Chapter 4), prices have been more stable in the past three decades than they were in the pre-World War II period. We should note that the gold standard was practically abandoned by some leading nations (such as the United Kingdom and France) during the interwar period. It seems clear that advocates of the return to the gold standard on the basis of stabilizing prices have a tough argument to sell. The data are not very supportive of the case for the Gold Standard, at least for the case of the United States.

Besides the price stability argument, the gold standard is associated with a few other challenges. Imagine each country deciding on its currency's gold parity rate (how much a unit of gold is worth in terms of a country's currency). If the United States decided that one ounce of gold is equivalent to $20 and the United Kingdom decided that one ounce of gold is equivalent to £4, the dollar price of a pound is equal to $5.

On the other hand, if the United States choses a gold parity rate at $30 per ounce of gold, the dollar price of a pound is now $7.50. Therefore, depending on the chosen gold parity rates, some countries may have **overvalued currencies** (the pound in this example), while others would have **undervalued currencies** (the dollar in this example). Countries with overvalued currencies would experience high interest rates, possibly slow growth rates, and high unemployment. Recall that under the gold standard, monetary authorities, primarily the country's central bank (the Federal Reserve in the United States), cannot do anything to restore stability in the economy since their ability to change money supply is severely limited. Because of these shortcomings, the gold standard was abandoned in the 1930s. The United States abandoned the gold standard in 1933.

After the gold standard, leading nations needed to replace it with another system to facilitate international transactions and payments. The search for a new international payments system, in part, led to the **United Nations Monetary Conference** in July 1944. The conference took place in Bretton Woods, New Hampshire (USA), and, as we discussed in Chapter 7, established the International Monetary Fund (IMF) and the International Bank for Reconstruction and Development (the World Bank).

The Bretton Woods UN conference established the so-called **Bretton Woods exchange rate system**. The new system maintained some aspects of the gold standard, but also differed from the gold standard in profound ways. Under the Bretton Woods system, countries *pegged* their currencies to the U.S. dollar. Therefore, the dollar served as an **anchor currency** to the system and emerged as the major **international reserve currency**. However, the dollar was pegged to gold at a fixed value. Therefore, the dollar was directly tied to gold while all the other currencies were only indirectly tied to gold.

One key feature of the Bretton Woods System was that countries decided their currencies' pegged exchange rate relative to the dollar (aka the *par value* relative to the dollar) and were able to adjust it with approval from the International Monetary Fund. Therefore, this exchange rate regime can be described as an **adjustable peg**. A nation could devalue or revalue the currency. A currency **devalues** when the currency's *par value* relative to the dollar increases (i.e., the amount of the currency per U.S. dollar increases). On the other hand, a currency **revalues** when the currency's *par value* relative to the U.S. dollar decreases (i.e., the amount of the currency per U.S. dollar decreases).[8]

---

[8] The currency devaluation and revaluation are comparable to currency depreciation and appreciation, respectively. The key difference is that devaluation and revaluation are a result of policy decisions while depreciation or appreciation of a currency are caused by free market activity.

Countries' monetary authorities would stand ready to buy and sell the dollar to ensure that the currency's dollar exchange value stayed within 1% of the *par value* relative to the dollar (known as the **parity band**).

Since all currencies were convertible to U.S. dollars and only the U.S. dollar was directly convertible to gold, the system had a major design flaw that exposed the U.S. dollar to a potentially severe speculative attack. Countries would trade their currencies for dollars freely. The U.S. monetary authorities, however, had committed to exchanging gold for the dollar. Both private and public agents could present dollars in exchange for gold. In this case, a *run* on U.S. stock of monetary gold would devalue the dollar and make the system unsustainable for the United States. This threat came true through the second half of the 1960s with increasing outflows of gold. In 1971, the United States, under President Richard Nixon, unilaterally discontinued the convertibility of the U.S. dollar into gold and effectively brought down the Bretton Woods System.

The end of the Bretton Woods system ushered in a free market-based system—the **flexible (or floating exchange rate system)**. Under the flexible exchange rate, the exchange rate between any two currencies is determined by demand (for) and supply of the currencies. A flexible exchange rate system was the *de facto* system upon the collapse of the Bretton Woods System despite the fact that it was not formally recognized as such. The formal endorsement of the system by major countries and the International Monetary Fund came in 1975–1976.

Although a flexible exchange rate system is, by design, subject to fluctuation in currency values, such fluctuations have not been so severe in the case of the world's most dominant currencies. Figure 12.8 shows a fairly stable effective exchange rate for the UK pound, the U.S. dollar, and the Japanese yen.

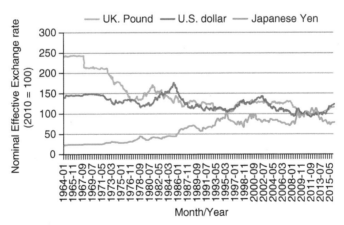

Figure 12.8   **Effective Exchange Rates, 1964–2012 (2010 = 100)**
Source: By authors using data from the Bank for International Settlements (BIS) Effective Exchange Rate, Monthly averages (2010 = 100).

One of the reasons we are not seeing the predicted fluctuations in currency values is because, in practice, most currency values are not determined by market forces alone. We do not have a *pure flexible exchange rate system*. In all major countries (and most countries in general), monetary authorities maintain a degree of intervention in foreign exchange markets. The goal is to avoid drastic fluctuations in exchange rates that are not driven by market fundamentals. Below, we provide a brief description of two of these hybrid systems—a *managed float* (aka *dirty float*) exchange rate system, and a *crawling peg* system.

A **managed float** is a flexible exchange with occasional foreign exchange market interventions by a country's monetary authorities to stabilize the value of the currency. The value of the currency under a managed float is primarily determined by market forces. Interventions by monetary authorities are intended to smooth out short-term fluctuations that are often a result of market speculation.

Under a **crawling peg**, a country pegs its currency to another currency but frequently changes the *par value* by small, but regularly scheduled amounts. Unlike a fixed peg, a crawling peg allows a degree of flexibility in the currency value. The scheduled (and preannounced) changes in the peg allow policymakers to respond to changes in the currency market environment. A *fixed peg* lacks this flexibility.

SUMMARY

- A foreign exchange market is a market where currencies are traded.
- The global foreign exchange market is the largest financial market in the world with average daily turnover of about $5.35 trillion in 2013. The U.S. dollar is the most traded currency in the global foreign exchange market.
- Major participants in the foreign exchange market include commercial banks, nonbank financial institutions, nonfinancial institutions, and central banks.
- An exchange rate is the value of a currency relative to another currency. Exchange rates are currency prices. Exchange rates presented in terms of U.S. dollars per unit of another currency are said to be in *direct* or *American* terms. On the other hand, exchange rates presented in terms of units of a currency per U.S. dollar are said to be in *indirect* or *European* terms.
- Exchange rates are primarily determined by demand (for) and supply of currencies. The demand for a currency is derived from the demand for a nation's goods, services, and investments by residents of other nations. On the other hand, the supply of a currency is derived from the demand for foreign-made goods, services, and investments by a nation's residents.
- The demand for a currency can be affected by such factors as relative inflation rates, relative rates of return on investment, and differences in economic performance between economies.
- A currency is said to have *depreciated* if the amount of another currency required to buy on unit of the currency decreases. Therefore, depreciation means a decrease in the value of the currency relative to other currencies. On the other hand, a currency is said to have *appreciated* if the amount of another currency required to buy one unit of the currency increases. As such, currency appreciation represents a gain in the value of the currency.

- Currency depreciation makes a nation's goods and services cheaper to residents of foreign nations and imports expensive for domestic residents. Therefore, currency depreciation, other things constant, increases a nation's exports while reducing a nation's imports. On the other hand, currency appreciation makes a nation's goods and services expensive for residents of foreign nations and imports cheaper for domestic residents. As such, currency appreciation, other things equal, would increase imports and decrease exports.

- A *spot exchange market* is a part of the foreign exchange market where currencies are traded and delivered immediately (at most within two days). The exchange rates that apply to such transactions are called *spot exchange rates.*

- A *forward exchange market* is a part of the foreign exchange market where currencies are traded for future delivery (one-month, three-months, six-months, etc.). The future date of delivery is known as the *value date.* The rates that apply to forward contracts are called *forward exchange rates.*

- A *forward contract* is a hedge against foreign exchange risk resulting for uncertainty about future spot rates.

- When a currency's forward rate is higher than the spot rate, the currency is said to be at a *forward premium.* On the other hand, if the currency's forward rate is lower than the spot rate, the currency is said to be at a *forward discount.*

- Currency values (exchange rates) at various trading centers are equalized through *arbitrage*—buying currency at a trading center with a low exchange rate and selling the currency at a trading center with a higher exchange rate.

- *Purchasing Power Parity (PPP)* is the idea that the price of a basket of goods should be the same in all countries. Any deviation from this condition would cause a change in the relative currency value and ultimately equalize the price of an identical basket of goods. The PPP theory derives its intuition from the law of one price.

- A *foreign exchange system* is a set of rules that determine how the value a nation's currency relative to other currencies is determined. Exchange rate systems range from purely market driven (flexible or floating exchange rate system) to purely policy-driven ones (fixed exchange rate system). In between the two extremes are a number of hybrid systems.

KEY TERMS

Foreign exchange market	Forward contract
Interbank trading	Forward exchange rates
Bid-ask spread	Value date
Exchange rate	Foreign exchange risk
"direct" or "American" terms	Forward premium
"indirect" or "European" terms	Forward discount
Demand for a currency	Cross exchange rate
Supply of a currency	Arbitrage
Currency depreciation	Purchasing Power Parity (PPP)
Currency appreciation	Law of one price
Spot transaction	Effective exchange rate
Spot rates	Foreign exchange system

Fixed exchange rate

Fixed/pegged exchange rate system

Gold standard

Overvalued currencies

Undervalued currencies

United Nations Monetary Conference

Bretton Woods exchange rate system

Anchor currency

International reserve currency

Adjustable peg

Currency devaluation

Currency revaluation

Parity band

Flexible or floating exchange rate system

Managed float

Crawling peg

PROBLEMS

EXCHANGE RATE TABLE (Currency units per U.S. dollar except where noted)					
COUNTRY	Monetary UNIT	2010	2009	2008	2007
*AUSTRALIA	DOLLAR	0.92	0.7927	0.8537	0.8391
BRAZIL	REAL	1.7601	1.9976	1.8326	1.9461
*EMU MEMBERS	EURO	1.3261	1.3935	1.4726	1.3711
JAPAN	YEN	87.78	93.68	103.39	117.76
MEXICO	PESO	12.623	13.498	11.143	10.928
SOUTH AFRICA	RAND	7.3161	8.4117	8.248	7.0477
SWITZERLAND	FRANC	1.0432	1.086	1.0816	1.1999
*UNITED KINGDOM	POUND	1.5452	1.5661	1.8545	2.002

Source: Federal Reserve Bank

*U.S. dollars per currency unit

Assumption 1: It costs $7,000 a year to attend GSU and this figure hasn't changed since 2007.

Assumption 2: All costs are incurred and paid at the beginning of the academic year. For example, for the 2008–2009 academic year, costs are paid in August 2008.

Assumption 3: 2008–2009, 2009–2010, and 2010–11 is sophomore year, junior year, and senior year, respectively.

Assumption 4: Maria is from Mexico and she attended GSU. She graduated in May 2011 after four years of study.

1. Use the table and the assumptions to answer the following questions.

   a. How much did it cost in pesos for Maria to attend GSU her senior year?

   b. Did the peso appreciate, depreciate, or stay the same between Maria's sophomore and junior year?

   c. Maria returned to school her senior year with 200 pesos. How many dollars was that worth?

d. President Becker brags to a gathering of parents at May's graduation ceremony, claiming that he has maintained constant costs over the past three years. How do Maria's parents respond?

2. Why is the U.S. dollar the most traded currency in the foreign exchange rate market?
3. The following are paraphrased excerpts from a lead article in the December 2nd–8th, 2006 issue of *The Economist* magazine.

"Housing market troubles (in the U.S.) are having a wider impact on the economy. New home sales fell by 3.2% in October, and the stock of unsold new properties continued to rise. Consumer confidence and durable goods orders fell more sharply than expected.

In contrast, German business confidence has risen. There are also concerns that central banks in China and elsewhere may start selling dollars."

a. What is the likely impact of the events described in the passage on the value of the U.S. dollar relative to other major currencies?
b. What (if anything) should the U.S. Federal Reserve do in response to such a situation?

4. Use Table 12.1 to calculate the following cross rates.

a. The Korean *won* price of a Japanese *yen*
b. The Canadian *dollar* price of an Australian *dollar*
c. The Russian *ruble* price of a South African *rand*
d. The Mexican *peso* price of a Brazilian *real*

5. Use the Table below to calculate the forward *premium* or *discount* for the following:

Country/Currency	USD Per Currency	Currency per USD
Australian *dollar* [Spot rate]	1.0379	0.9635
1-mos forward	1.0354	0.9658
3-mos forward	1.0307	0.9702
6-mos forward	1.0235	0.977
Japan *yen* [Spot rate]	0.01042	96.01
1-mos forward	0.01042	95.99
3-mos forward	0.01042	95.95
6-mos forward	0.01043	95.86
Switzerland *franc* [Spot rate]	1.058	0.9452
1-mos forward	1.0584	0.9448
3-mos forward	1.0593	0.944
6-mos forward	1.0609	0.9426
UK *pound* [Spot rate]	1.5098	0.6623
1-mos forward	1.5095	0.6625
3-mos forward	1.5091	0.6627
6-mos forward	1.5087	0.6628

    a. A one-month forward contract for the Australian *dollar*
    b. A three-month forward contract for the Japanese *yen*
    c. A six-month forward contract for the Switzerland *franc*
    d. A three-month forward contract for the UK *pound*

6. Define, explain, and compare/contrast the following terms

    a. Currency depreciation versus currency appreciation
    b. Spot exchange rates versus forward exchange rates
    c. Forward premium versus forward discount
    d. Exchange rates versus arbitrage
    e. Exchange rate versus Purchasing Power Parity (PPP)
    f. Flexible exchange rates versus fixed exchange rates
    g. Fixed exchange rate versus the gold standard
    h. Managed float versus crawling peg

Index